The wisdom of

Thich Nhat Hanh

The wisdom of Thich Nhat Hanh

The Miracle of Mindfulness
Being Peace
The Sun My Heart
Touching Peace

Thich Nhat Hanh

ONE SPIRIT
New York

The Wisdom of Thich Nhat Hanh

CONTENTS

The Miracle of Mindfulness

A Manual on Meditation

Revised Edition

Translated by Mobi Ho

Drawings by Vo-Dinh Mai

Contents

❀

Translator's Preface

The Miracle of Mindfulness was originally written in Vietnamese as a long letter to Brother Quang, a main staff member of the School of Youth for Social Service in South Vietnam in 1974. Its author, the Buddhist monk Thich Nhat Hanh, had founded the School in the 1960s as an outgrowth of "engaged Buddhism." It drew young people deeply committed to acting in a spirit of compassion. Upon graduation, the students used the training they received to respond to the needs of peasants caught in the turmoil of the war. They helped rebuild bombed villages, teach children, set up medical stations, and organize agricultural cooperatives.

The workers' methods of reconciliation were often misunderstood in the atmosphere of fear and mistrust engendered by the war. They persistently refused to support either armed party and believed that both sides were but the reflection of one reality, and the true enemies were not people, but ideology, hatred, and ignorance. Their stance threatened those engaged in the conflict, and in the first years of the School, a series of attacks were carried out against the students. Several were kidnapped and murdered. As the war dragged on, even after the Paris Peace Accords were signed in 1973, it seemed at times impossible not to succumb to exhaustion and bitterness. Continuing to work in a spirit of love and understanding required great courage.

From exile in France, Thich Nhat Hanh wrote to Brother Quang to encourage the workers during this dark time. Thay Nhat Hanh ("Thay," the form of address for Vietnamese monks, means "teacher") wished to remind them of the essential discipline of following one's breath to nourish and maintain calm mindfulness, even in the midst of the most difficult circumstances. Because Brother Quang and the students were his colleagues and friends, the spirit of this long letter that became *The Miracle of Mindfulness* is personal and direct. When Thay speaks here of village paths, he speaks of paths he had actually walked with Brother Quang. When he mentions the bright eyes of a young child, he mentions the name of Brother Quang's own son.

I was living as an American volunteer with the Vietnamese Buddhist Peace Delegation in Paris when Thay was writing the letter. Thay headed the delegation, which served as an overseas liaison office for the peace and reconstruction efforts of the Vietnamese Buddhists, including the School of Youth for Social Service. I remember late evenings over tea, when Thay explained sections of the letter to delegation members and a few close friends. Quite naturally, we began to think of other people in other countries who might also benefit from the practices described in the book.

Thay had recently become acquainted with young Buddhists in Thailand who had been inspired by the witness of engaged Buddhism in Vietnam. They too wished to act in a spirit of awareness and reconciliation to help avert the armed conflict erupting in Thailand, and they wanted to know how to work without being overcome by anger and discouragement. Several of them spoke English, and we discussed translating Brother Quang's letter. The idea of a translation took on a special poignancy when the confiscation of Buddhist publishing houses in Vietnam made the project of printing the letter as a small book in Vietnam impossible.

I happily accepted the task of translating the book into English. For nearly three years, I had been living with the Vietnamese Buddhist Peace Delegation, where day and night I was immersed in the lyrical sound of the Vietnamese language. Thay had been my "formal" Vietnamese teacher; we had slowly read through some of his earlier books, sentence by sentence. I had thus acquired a rather unusual vocabulary of Vietnamese Buddhist terms. Thay, of course, had been teaching me far more than language during those three years. His presence was a constant gentle reminder to return to one's true self, to be awake by being mindful.

As I sat down to translate *The Miracle of Mindfulness,* I remembered the episodes during the past years that had nurtured my own practice of mindfulness. There was the time I was cooking furiously and could not find a spoon I'd set down amid a scattered pile of pans and ingredients. As I searched here and there, Thay entered the kitchen and smiled. He asked, "What is Mobi looking for?" Of course, I answered, "The spoon! I'm looking for a spoon!" Thay answered, again with a smile, "No, Mobi is looking for Mobi."

Thay suggested I do the translation slowly and steadily, in order to maintain mindfulness. I translated only two pages a day. In the evenings, Thay and I went over those pages, changing and correcting words and sentences. Other friends provided editorial assistance. It is difficult to describe the actual experience of translating his words, but my awareness of the feel of pen and paper, awareness of the position of my body and of my breath enabled me to see most clearly the mindfulness with which Thay had written each word. As I watched my breath, I could see Brother Quang and the workers of the School of Youth for Social Service. More than that, I began to see that the words held the same personal and lively directness for any reader because they had been written in mindfulness and lovingly directed to real people. As I continued to translate, I could see an expanding community—the School's workers, the young Thai Buddhists, and many other friends throughout the world.

When the translation was completed we typed it, and Thay printed a hundred copies on the tiny offset machine squeezed into the delegation's bathroom. Mindfully addressing each copy to friends in many countries was a happy task for delegation members.

Since then, like ripples in a pond, *The Miracle of Mindfulness* has traveled far. It has been translated into several other languages and has been printed or distributed on every continent in the world. One of the joys of being the translator has been to hear from many people who have discovered the book. I once met someone in a bookstore who knew a student who had taken a copy to friends in the Soviet Union. And recently, I met a young Iraqi student in danger of being deported to his homeland, where he faces death for his refusal to fight in a war he believes cruel and senseless; he and his mother have both read *The Miracle of Mindfulness* and are practicing awareness of the breath. I have learned, too, that proceeds from the Portuguese edition are being used to assist poor children in Brazil. Prisoners, refugees, health-care workers, educators, and artists are among those whose lives have been touched by this little book. I often think of *The Miracle of Mind-*

fulness as something of a miracle itself, a vehicle that continues to connect lives throughout the world.

American Buddhists have been impressed by the natural and unique blending of Theravada and Mahayana traditions, characteristic of Vietnamese Buddhism, which the book expresses. As a book on the Buddhist path, *The Miracle of Mindfulness* is special because its clear and simple emphasis on basic practice enables any reader to begin a practice of his or her own immediately. Interest in the book, however, is not limited to Buddhists. It has found a home with people of many different religious traditions. One's breath, after all, is hardly attached to any particular creed.

Those who enjoy this book will likely be interested in other books by Thich Nhat Hanh which have been translated into English. His books in Vietnamese, including short stories, novels, essays, historical treatises on Buddhism and poetry, number in the dozens. While several of his earlier books in English are no longer in print, more recent works available in translation include *A Guide to Walking Meditation, Being Peace,* and *The Sun My Heart.*

Denied permission to return to Vietnam, Thich Nhat Hanh spends most of the year living in Plum Village, a community he helped found in France. There, under the guidance of the same Brother Quang to whom *The Miracle of Mindfulness* was originally addressed years ago, community members tend hundreds of plum trees. Profits from the sales of their fruit are used to assist hungry children in Vietnam. In addition, Plum Village is open every summer to visitors from around the world who wish to spend a month of mindfulness and meditation. In recent years, Thich Nhat Hanh has also made annual visits to the United States and Canada to conduct week-long retreats organized by the Buddhist Peace Fellowship.

I would like to express special gratitude to Beacon Press for having the vision to print this new edition of *The Miracle of Mindfulness*. I hope that each new person whom it reaches will sense that the book is addressed as personally to him or her as it was to Brother Quang and the workers of the School of Youth for Social Service.

Mobi Ho
August 1987

The Miracle of
Mindfulness

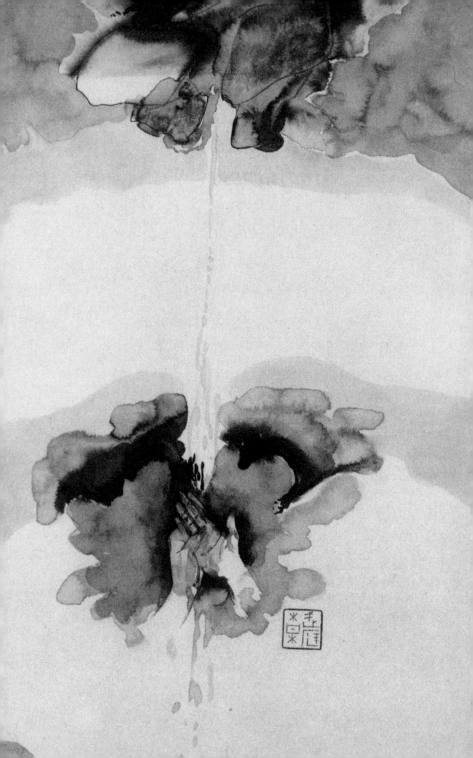

One

The Essential Discipline

Yesterday Allen came over to visit with his son Joey. Joey has grown so quickly! He's already seven years old and is fluent in French and English. He even uses a bit of slang he's picked up on the street. Raising children here is very different from the way we raise children at home. Here parents believe that "freedom is necessary for a child's development." During the two hours that Allen and I were talking, Allen had to keep a constant eye on Joey. Joey played, chattered away, and interrupted us, making it impossible to carry on a real conversation. I gave him several picture books for children but he barely glanced at them before tossing them aside and interrupting our conversation again. He demands the constant attention of grown-ups.

Later, Joey put on his jacket and went outside to play with a neighbor's child. I asked Allen, "Do you find family life easy?" Allen

1

didn't answer directly. He said that during the past few weeks, since the birth of Ana, he had been unable to sleep any length of time. During the night, Sue wakes him up and—because she is too tired herself—asks him to check to make sure Ana is still breathing. "I get up and look at the baby and then come back and fall asleep again. Sometimes the ritual happens two or three times a night."

"Is family life easier than being a bachelor?" I asked. Allen didn't answer directly. But I understood. I asked another question: "A lot of people say that if you have a family you're less lonely and have more security. Is that true?" Allen nodded his head and mumbled something softly. But I understood.

Then Allen said, "I've discovered a way to have a lot more time. In the past, I used to look at my time as if it were divided into several parts. One part I reserved for Joey, another part was for Sue, another part to help with Ana, another part for household work. The time left over I considered my own. I could read, write, do research, go for walks.

"But now I try not to divide time into parts anymore. I consider my time with Joey and Sue as my own time. When I help Joey with his homework, I try to find ways of seeing his time as my own time. I go through his lesson with him, sharing his presence and finding ways to be interested in what we do during that time. The time for him becomes my own time. The same with Sue. The remarkable thing is that now I have unlimited time for myself!"

Allen smiled as he spoke. I was surprised. I knew that Allen hadn't learned this from reading any books. This was something he had discovered for himself in his own daily life.

Washing the dishes to wash the dishes

Thirty years ago, when I was still a novice at Tu Hieu Pagoda, washing the dishes was hardly a pleasant task. During the Season of Retreat when all the monks returned to the monastery, two novices had to do all the cooking and wash the dishes for sometimes well over one hundred monks. There was no soap. We had only ashes, rice husks, and coconut husks, and that was all. Cleaning such a high stack of bowls was a chore, especially during the winter when the water was freezing cold. Then you had to heat up a big pot of water before you could do any scrubbing. Nowadays one stands in a kitchen equipped with liquid soap, special scrubpads, and even running hot water which makes it all the more agreeable. It is easier to enjoy washing the dishes now. Anyone can wash them in a hurry, then sit down and enjoy a cup of tea afterwards. I can see a machine for washing clothes, although I wash my own things out by hand, but a dishwashing machine is going just a little too far!

While washing the dishes one should only be washing the dishes, which means that while washing the dishes one should be completely aware of the fact that one is washing the dishes. At first glance, that might seem a little silly:

why put so much stress on a simple thing? But that's precisely the point. The fact that I am standing there and washing these bowls is a wondrous reality. I'm being completely myself, following my breath, conscious of my presence, and conscious of my thoughts and actions. There's no way I can be tossed around mindlessly like a bottle slapped here and there on the waves.

The cup in your hands

In the United States, I have a close friend named Jim Forest. When I first met him eight years ago, he was working with the Catholic Peace Fellowship. Last winter, Jim came to visit. I usually wash the dishes after we've finished the evening meal, before sitting down and drinking tea with everyone else. One night, Jim asked if he might do the dishes. I said, "Go ahead, but if you wash the dishes you must know the way to wash them." Jim replied, "Come on, you think I don't know how to wash the dishes?" I answered, "There are two ways to wash the dishes. The first is to wash the dishes in order to have clean dishes and the second is to wash the dishes in order to wash the dishes." Jim was delighted and said, "I choose the second way—to wash the dishes to wash the dishes." From then on, Jim knew how to wash the dishes. I transferred the "responsibility" to him for an entire week.

If while washing dishes, we think only of the cup of tea that awaits us, thus hurrying to get the dishes out of the way as if they were a nuisance, then we are not "washing the dishes to wash the dishes." What's more, we are not alive during the time we are washing the dishes. In fact we are completely incapable of realizing the miracle of life while standing at the sink. If we can't wash the dishes, the chances are we won't be able to drink our tea either. While drinking the cup of tea, we will only be thinking of other things, barely aware of the cup in our hands. Thus we are sucked away into the future —and we are incapable of actually living one minute of life.

Eating a tangerine

I remember a number of years ago, when Jim and I were first traveling together in the United States, we sat under a tree and shared a tangerine. He began to talk about what we would be doing in the future. Whenever we thought about a project that seemed attractive or inspiring, Jim became so immersed in it that he literally forgot about what he was doing in the present. He popped a section of tangerine in his mouth and, before he had begun chewing it, had another slice ready to pop into his mouth again. He was hardly aware he was eating a tangerine. All I had to say was, "You ought to eat the tangerine section you've already taken." Jim was startled into realizing what he was doing.

It was as if he hadn't been eating the tangerine at all. If he had been eating anything, he was "eating" his future plans.

A tangerine has sections. If you can eat just one section, you can probably eat the entire tangerine. But if you can't eat a single section, you cannot eat the tangerine. Jim understood. He slowly put his hand down and focused on the presence of the slice already in his mouth. He chewed it thoughtfully before reaching down and taking another section.

Later, when Jim went to prison for activities against the war, I was worried about whether he could endure the four walls of prison and sent him a very short letter: "Do you remember the tangerine we shared when we were together? Your being there is like the tangerine. Eat it and be one with it. Tomorrow it will be no more."

The Essential Discipline

More than thirty years ago, when I first entered the monastery, the monks gave me a small book called "The Essential Discipline for Daily Use," written by the Buddhist monk Doc The from Bao Son pagoda, and they told me to memorize it. It was a thin book. It couldn't have been more than 40 pages, but it contained all the thoughts Doc The used to awaken his mind while doing any task. When he woke up in the morning, his first thought was, "Just awakened, I hope that every person will attain great awareness and see in complete clarity." When he washed his hands, he used this thought to place himself in mindfulness: "Washing my hands, I hope that every person will have pure hands to receive reality." The book is comprised entirely of such sentences. Their goal was to help the beginning practitioner take hold of his own consciousness. The Zen Master Doc The helped all of us young novices to practice, in a relatively easy way, those things which are taught in the Sutra of Mindfulness. Each time you put on your robe, washed the dishes, went to the bathroom, folded your mat, carried buckets of water, or brushed your teeth, you could use one of the thoughts from the book in order to take hold of your own consciousness.

The Sutra of Mindfulness* says, "When walking, the practitioner must be conscious that he is walking. When sitting, the practitioner must be conscious that he is sitting. When lying down, the practitioner must be conscious that he is lying down. . . . No matter what position one's body is in, the practitioner must be conscious of that position. Practicing thus, the practitioner lives in direct and constant mindfulness of the body . . ." The mindfulness of

_____

*In the Sutras, Buddha usually teaches that one should use one's breath in order to achieve Concentration. The Sutra which speaks about the use of your breath to maintain mindfulness is the Anapanasati Sutra. This Sutra was translated and commentated on by a Vietnamese Zen Master of Central Asian origin named Khuong Tang Hoi, around the beginning of the Third Century A.D. Anapana means breath and sati means mindfulness. Tang Hoi translated it as "Guarding the Mind." The Anapanasati Sutra, that is, is the sutra on using one's breath to maintain mindfulness. The Sutra on Breath to Maintain Mindfulness is the 118th Sutra in the Majhima Nikaya collection of sutras and it teaches 16 methods of using one's breath.

the positions of one's body is not enough, however. We must be conscious of each breath, each movement, every thought and feeling, everything which has any relation to ourselves.

But what is the purpose of the Sutra's instruction? Where are we to find the time to practice such mindfulness? If you spend all day practicing mindfulness, how will there ever be enough time to do all the work that needs to be done to change and to build an alternative society? How does Allen manage to work, study Joey's lesson, take Ana's diapers to the laundromat, and practice mindfulness at the same time?

Two

The Miracle Is
to Walk on Earth

Allen said that since he's begun to consider Joey's and Sue's time as his own, he has "unlimited time." But perhaps he has it only in principle. Because there are doubtless times when Allen forgets to consider Joey's time as his own time while going over Joey's homework with him, and thus Allen may lose that time. Allen might hope for the time to pass quickly, or he may grow impatient because that time seems wasted to him, because it isn't his own time. And so, if he really wants "unlimited time," he will have to keep alive the realization that "this is my time" throughout the time he's studying with Joey. But during such times, one's mind is inevitably distracted by other thoughts, and so if one really wants to keep one's consciousness alive (from now on I'll use the term "mindfulness" to refer to keeping one's consciousness alive to the present reality), then one must practice right now in

11

one's daily life, not only during meditation sessions.

When you are walking along a path leading into a village, you can practice mindfulness. Walking along a dirt path, surrounded by patches of green grass, if you practice mindfulness you will experience that path, the path leading into the village. You practice by keeping this one thought alive: "I'm walking along the path leading into the village." Whether it's sunny or rainy, whether the path is dry or wet, you keep that one thought, but not just repeating it like a machine, over and over again. Machine thinking is the opposite of mindfulness. If we're really engaged in mindfulness while walking along the path to the village, then we will consider the act of each step we take as an infinite wonder, and a joy will open our hearts like a flower, enabling us to enter the world of reality.

I like to walk alone on country paths, rice plants and wild grasses on both sides, putting each foot down on the earth in mindfulness, knowing that I walk on the wondrous earth. In such moments, existence is a miraculous and mysterious reality. People usually consider walking on water or in thin air a miracle. But I think the real miracle is not to walk either on water or in thin air, but to walk on earth. Every day we are engaged in a miracle which we don't even recognize: a blue sky, white clouds, green leaves, the black, curious eyes of a child—our own two eyes. All is a miracle.

Sitting

Zen Master Doc The says that when sitting in meditation, one should sit upright, giving birth to this thought, "Sitting here is like sitting on the Bodhi spot." The Bodhi spot is where Lord Buddha sat when he obtained Enlightenment. If any person can become a Buddha, and the Buddhas are all those countless persons who have obtained enlightenment, then many have sat on the very spot I sit on now. Sitting on the same spot as a Buddha gives rise to happiness and sitting in mindfulness means itself to have become a Buddha. The poet Nguyen Cong Tru experienced the same thing when he sat down on a certain spot, and suddenly saw how others had sat on the same spot countless ages ago, and how in ages to come others would also come to sit there:

On the same spot I sit today
Others came, in ages past, to sit.
One thousand years, still others will come.
Who is the singer, and who the listener?

That spot and the minutes he spent there became a link in eternal reality.

But active, concerned people don't have time to spend leisurely, walking along paths of green grass and sitting beneath trees. One must prepare projects, consult with the neighbors, try to resolve a million difficulties; there is hard work to do. One must deal with every kind of hardship, every moment keeping one's attention focused on the work, alert, ready to handle the situation ably and intelligently.

You might well ask: Then how are we to practice mindfulness?

My answer is: keep your attention focused on the work, be alert and ready to handle ably and intelligently any situation which may arise —this is mindfulness. There is no reason why mindfulness should be different from focusing all one's attention on one's work, to be alert and to be using one's best judgment. During the moment one is consulting, resolving, and dealing with whatever arises, a calm heart and self-control are necessary if one is to obtain good results. Anyone can see that. If we are not in control of ourselves but instead let our impatience or anger interfere, then our work is no longer of any value.

Mindfulness is the miracle by which we master and restore ourselves. Consider, for example: a magician who cuts his body into many parts and places each part in a different region—hands in the south, arms in the east, legs in the north, and then by some miraculous power lets forth a cry which reassembles whole every part of his body. Mindfulness is like that —it is the miracle which can call back in a flash our dispersed mind and restore it to wholeness so that we can live each minute of life.

Taking hold of one's breath

Thus mindfulness is at the same time a means and an end, the seed and the fruit. When we practice mindfulness in order to build up concentration, mindfulness is a seed. But mindfulness itself is the life of awareness: the presence of mindfulness means the presence of life, and therefore mindfulness is also the fruit. Mindfulness frees us of forgetfulness and dispersion and makes it possible to live fully each minute of life. Mindfulness enables us to live.

You should know how to breathe to maintain mindfulness, as breathing is a natural and extremely effective tool which can prevent dispersion. Breath is the bridge which connects life to consciousness, which unites your body to your thoughts. Whenever your mind becomes scattered, use your breath as the means to take hold of your mind again.

Breathe in lightly a fairly long breath, conscious of the fact that you are inhaling a deep breath. Now breathe out all the breath in your lungs, remaining conscious the whole time of the exhalation. The Sutra of Mindfulness teaches the method to take hold of one's breath in the following manner: "Be ever mindful you breathe in and mindful you breathe out. Breathing in a long breath, you know, 'I am breathing in a long breath.' Breathing out a long breath, you know, 'I am breathing out a long breath.' Breathing in a short breath, you know, 'I am breathing in a short breath.' Breathing out a short breath, you know, 'I am breathing out a short breath.'"

"Experiencing a whole breath-body, I shall breathe in," thus you train yourself. "Experiencing the whole breath-body, I shall breathe out," thus you train yourself. "Calming the activity of the breath-body, I shall breathe in," thus you train yourself. "Calming the activity of the breath-body, I shall breathe out," thus you train yourself.

In a Buddhist monastery, everyone learns to use breath as a tool to stop mental dispersion and to build up concentration power. Concentration power is the strength which comes from practicing mindfulness. It is the concentration which can help one obtain the Great Awakening. When a worker takes hold of his own breath, he has already become awakened. In order to maintain mindfulness throughout a long period, we must continue to watch our breath.

❀

It is autumn here and the golden leaves falling one by one are truly beautiful. Taking a 10-minute walk in the woods, watching my breath and maintaining mindfulness, I feel refreshed and restored. Like that, I can really enter into a communion with each leaf.

Of course, walking alone on a country path, it is easier to maintain mindfulness. If there's a friend by your side, not talking but also watching his breath, then you can continue to maintain mindfulness without difficulty. But if the friend at your side begins to talk, it becomes a little more difficult.

If, in your mind, you think, "I wish this fellow would quit talking, so I could concentrate," you have already lost your mindfulness. But if you think, instead, "If he wishes to talk, I will answer, but I will continue in mindfulness, aware of the fact that we are walking along this path together, aware of what we say, I can continue to watch my breath as well."

If you can give rise to that thought, you will be continuing in mindfulness. It is harder to practice in such situations than when you are alone, but if you continue to practice nonetheless, you will develop the ability to maintain much greater concentration. There is a line from a Vietnamese folk song that says: "Hardest of all is to practice the Way at home, second in the crowd, and third in the pagoda." It is only in an active and demanding situation that mindfulness really becomes a challenge!

Counting one's breath and following one's breath

In the meditation sessions I recently began for non-Vietnamese, I usually suggest various methods that I myself have tried, methods that are quite simple. I suggest to beginners the method of "Following the length of the breath." The student lies, back down, on the floor. Then I invite all of the participants to gather around so I can show them a few simple points:

1) Although inhaling and exhaling are the work of the lungs, and take place in the chest area, the stomach area also plays a role. The stomach rises with the filling of the lungs. At the beginning of the breath the stomach begins to push out. But after inhaling about two-thirds of the breath, it starts to lower again.

2) Why? Between your chest and stomach there is a muscular membrane, the diaphragm. When you breathe in correctly the air fills the lower part of the lungs first, before the upper lungs fill with air, the diaphragm pushes down on the stomach, causing the stomach to rise. When you have filled your upper lungs with air, the chest pushes out and causes the stomach to lower again.

3) That is why, in former times, people spoke of the breath as originating at the navel and terminating at the nostrils.

For beginners, lying down to practice breathing is very helpful. The important thing is to guard against making too much of an effort: too great an effort can be dangerous for the lungs, especially when the lungs are weak from many years of incorrect breathing. In the beginning, the practitioner should lie on his or her back on a thin mat or blanket, the two arms loosely at the sides. Don't prop your head on a pillow. Focus your attention on your exhalation and watch how long it is. Measure it slowly by counting in your mind: 1, 2, 3. . . After several times, you will know the "length" of your breath: Perhaps it is 5. Now try to extend the exhalation for one more count (or 2) so that the exhalation's length becomes 6 or 7. Begin to exhale counting from 1 to 5. When you reach 5, rather than immediately inhaling as before, try to extend the exhalation to 6 or 7. This way you will empty your lungs of more air. When you have finished exhaling, pause for an instant to let your lungs take in fresh air on their own. Let them take in just as much air as they want without making any effort. The inhalation will normally be "shorter" than the exhalation. Keep a steady count in your mind to measure the length of both. Practice several weeks like this, remaining mindful of all your exhalations and inhalations while lying down. (If you have a clock with a loud tick you can use it to help you keep track of the length of your inhalation and exhalation.)

Continue to measure your breath while walking, sitting, standing, and especially whenever you are outdoors. While walking, you might use your steps to measure your breath. After a month or so, the difference between the length of your exhalation and inhalation will lessen, gradually evening out until they are of equal measure. If the length of your exhalation is 6, the inhalation will also be 6.

If you feel at all tired while practicing, stop at once. But even if you do not feel tired, don't prolong the practice of long, equal breaths beyond short periods of time—10 to 20 breaths are enough. The moment you feel the least fatigue, return your breathing to normal. Fatigue is an excellent mechanism of our bodies and the best advisor as to whether one should rest or continue. In order to measure your breath you can count—or use a rhythmic phrase that you like. (If the length of your breath is

6, you might use instead of numbers, the six words, "My heart is now at peace." If the length is 7 you might use, "I walk on the new green earth." A Buddhist might say, "I take refuge in the Buddha." For a Christian it could be "Our Father who art in heaven." When you are walking, each step should correspond to one word.

Quiet breathing

Your breath should be light, even, and flowing, like a thin stream of water running through the sand. Your breath should be very quiet, so quiet that a person sitting next to you cannot hear it. Your breathing should flow gracefully, like a river, like a watersnake crossing the water, and not like a chain of rugged mountains or the gallop of a horse. To master our breath is to be in control of our bodies and minds. Each time we find ourselves dispersed and find it difficult to gain control of ourselves by different means, the method of watching the breath should always be used.

The instant you sit down to meditate, begin watching your breath. At first breathe normally, gradually letting your breathing slow down until it is quiet, even, and the lengths of the breaths are fairly long. From the moment you sit down to the moment your breathing has become deep and silent, be conscious of everything that is happening in yourself.

As the Buddhist Sutra of Mindfulness says: "Breathing in a long breath, you know, 'I am breathing in a long breath.' Breathing out a long breath, the practitioner knows, 'I am breathing out a long breath.' Breathing in a short breath, you know, 'I am breathing in a short breath.' Breathing out a short breath, you know, 'I am breathing out a short breath.' Experiencing the whole breath-body, I shall breathe in." Thus you train yourself. "Experiencing the whole breath-body, I shall breathe out." Thus you train yourself. "Calming the activity of the breath-body, I shall breathe in." Thus you train yourself. "Calming the activity of the breath-body, I shall breathe out." Thus you train yourself.

After about 10 to 20 minutes, your thoughts will have quieted down like a pond on which not even a ripple stirs.

Counting your breath

Making your breath calm and even is called the method of following one's breath. If it seems hard at first, you can substitute the method of counting your breath. As you breathe in, count 1 in your mind, and as you breathe out, count 1. Breathe in, count 2. Breathe out, count 2. Continue through 10, then return to 1 again. This counting is like a string which attaches your mindfulness to your breath. This exercise is the beginning point in the process of becoming continuously conscious of your breath. Without mindfulness, however, you will quickly lose count. When the count is lost, simply return to 1 and keep trying until you can keep the count correctly. Once you can truly focus your attention on the counts, you have reached the point at which you can begin to abandon the counting method and begin to concentrate solely on the breath itself.

In those moments when you are upset or dispersed and find it difficult to practice mindfulness, return to your breath: Taking hold of your breath is itself mindfulness. Your breath is the wondrous method of taking hold of your consciousness. As one religious community says in its rule, "One should not lose oneself in mind-dispersion or in one's surroundings. Learn to practice breathing in order to regain control of body and mind, to practice mindfulness, and to develop concentration and wisdom."

Every act is a rite

Suppose there is a towering wall from the top of which one can see vast distances—but there is no apparent means to climb it, only a thin piece of thread hanging over the top and coming down both sides. A clever person will tie a thicker string onto one end of the thread, walk over to the other side of the wall, then pull on the thread bringing the string to the other side. Then he will tie the end of the string to a strong rope and pull the rope over. When the rope has reached the bottom of one side and is secured on the other side, the wall can be easily scaled.

Our breath is such a fragile piece of thread. But once we know how to use it, it can become a wondrous tool to help us surmount situations which would otherwise seem hopeless. Our breath is the bridge from our body to our mind, the element which reconciles our body and mind and which makes possible one-ness of body and mind. Breath is aligned to both body and mind and it alone is the tool which can bring them both together, illuminating both and bringing both peace and calm.

Many persons and books discuss the immense benefits that result from correct breathing. They report that a person who knows how to breathe is a person who knows how to build up endless vitality: breath builds up the lungs, strengthens the blood, and revitalizes every organ in the body. They say that proper breathing is more important than food. And all of these statements are correct.

Years ago, I was extremely ill. After several years of taking medicine and undergoing medical treatment, my condition was unimproved. So I turned to the method of breathing and, thanks to that, was able to heal myself.

Breath is a tool. Breath itself is mindfulness. The use of breath as a tool may help one obtain immense benefits, but these cannot be considered as ends in themselves. These benefits are only the by-products of the realization of mindfulness.

In my small class in meditation for non-Vietnamese, there are many young people. I've told them that if each one can meditate an hour each day that's good, but it's nowhere near enough. You've got to practice meditation when you walk, stand, lie down, sit, and work, while washing your hands, washing the dishes, sweeping the floor, drinking tea, talking to friends, or whatever you are doing: "While washing the dishes, you might be thinking about the tea afterwards, and so try to get them out of the way as quickly as possible in order to sit and drink tea. But that means that you are incapable of living during the time you are washing the dishes. When you are washing the dishes, washing the dishes must be the most important thing in your life. Just as when you're drinking tea, drinking tea must be the most important thing in your life. When you're using the toilet, let that be the most important thing in your life." And so on. Chopping wood is meditation. Carrying water is meditation. Be mindful 24 hours a day, not just during the one hour you may allot for formal meditation or reading scripture and reciting prayers. Each act must be carried out in mindfulness. Each act is a rite, a ceremony. Raising your cup of tea to your mouth is a rite. Does the word "rite" seem too solemn? I use that word in order to jolt you into the realization of the life-and-death matter of awareness.

Three ❄

A Day of Mindfulness

Every day and every hour, one should practice mindfulness. That's easy to say, but to carry it out in practice is not. That's why I suggest to those who come to the meditation sessions that each person should try hard to reserve one day out of the week to devote entirely to their practice of mindfulness. In principle, of course every day should be your day, and every hour your hour. But the fact is that very few of us have reached such a point. We have the impression that our family, place of work, and society rob us of all our time. So I urge that everyone set aside one day each week. Saturday, perhaps.

If it is Saturday, then Saturday must be entirely your day, a day during which you are completely the master. Then Saturday will be the lever that will lift you to the habit of practicing mindfulness. Every worker in a peace or service community, no matter how urgent its work, has the right to such a day, for without it we will lose ourselves quickly in a life full of worry and action, and our responses will become increasingly useless. Whatever the day chosen, it can be considered as the day of mindfulness.

To set up a day of mindfulness, figure out a way to remind yourself at the moment of waking that this day is your day of mindfulness. You might hang something on the ceiling or on the wall, a paper with the word "mindfulness" or a pinebranch—anything that will suggest to you as you open your eyes and see it that today is your day of mindfulness. Today is your day. Remembering that, perhaps you can feel a smile which affirms that you are in complete mindfulness, a smile that nourishes that perfect mindfulness.

While still lying in bed, begin slowly to follow your breath—slow, long, and conscious breaths. Then slowly rise from bed (instead of turning out all at once as usual), nourishing mindfulness by every motion. Once up, brush your teeth, wash your face, and do all your morning activities in a calm and relaxing way, each movement done in mindfulness. Follow your breath, take hold of it, and don't let your thoughts scatter. Each movement should be done calmly. Measure your steps with quiet, long breaths. Maintain a half smile.

Spend at least a half hour taking a bath. Bathe slowly and mindfully, so that by the time you have finished, you feel light and refreshed. Afterwards, you might do household work such as washing dishes, dusting and wiping off the tables, scrubbing the kitchen floor, arranging books on their shelves. Whatever the tasks, do them slowly and with ease, in mindfulness. Don't do any task in order to get it over with. Resolve to do each job in a relaxed way, with all your attention. Enjoy and be one with your work. Without this, the day of mindfulness will be of no value at all. The feeling that any task is a nuisance will soon disappear if it is done in mindfulness. Take the example of the Zen Masters. No matter what task or motion they undertake, they do it slowly and evenly, without reluctance.

For those who are just beginning to practice, it is best to maintain a spirit of silence throughout the day. That doesn't mean that on the day of mindfulness, you shouldn't speak at all. You can talk, you can even go ahead and sing, but if you talk or sing, do it in complete mindfulness of what you are saying or singing, and keep talking and singing to a minimum. Naturally, it is possible to sing and practice mindfulness at the same time, just as long as one is conscious of the fact that one is singing and aware of what one is singing. But be warned that it is much easier, when singing or talking, to stray from mindfulness if your meditation strength is still weak.

At lunchtime, prepare a meal for yourself. Cook the meal and wash the dishes in mindfulness. In the morning, after you have cleaned and straightened up your house, and in the afternoon, after you have worked in the garden

30

or watched clouds or gathered flowers, prepare
a pot of tea to sit and drink in mindfulness. Allow
yourself a good length of time to do this. Don't
drink your tea like someone who gulps down
a cup of coffee during a workbreak. Drink your
tea slowly and reverently, as if it is the axis on
which the whole earth revolves—slowly,
evenly, without rushing toward the future.
Live the actual moment. Only this actual moment is life. Don't be attached to the future.
Don't worry about things you have to do. Don't
think about getting up or taking off to do anything. Don't think about "departing."

> Be a bud sitting quietly in the hedge
> Be a smile, one part of wondrous existence
> Stand here. There is no need to depart.
> This homeland is as beautiful as the homeland of
>   our childhood
> Do not harm it, please, and continue to sing . . .
> ("Butterfly Over the Field of Golden Mustard Flowers")

In the evening, you might read scripture
and copy passages, write letters to friends, or
do anything else you enjoy outside of your
normal duties during the week. But whatever
you do, do it in mindfulness. Eat only a little for
the evening meal. Later, around 10 or 11 o'clock,
as you sit in meditation, you will be able to sit
more easily on an empty stomach. Afterwards
you might take a slow walk in the fresh night
air, following your breath in mindfulness and
measuring the length of your breaths by your
steps. Finally, return to your room and sleep
in mindfulness.

Somehow we must find a way to allow each worker a day of mindfulness. Such a day is crucial. Its effect on the other days of the week is immeasurable. Ten years ago, thanks to such a day of mindfulness, Chu Van and our other sisters and brothers in the Tiep Hien Order were able to guide themselves through many difficult times. After only three months of observing such a day of mindfulness once a week, I know that you will see a significant change in your life. The day of mindfulness will begin to penetrate the other days of the week, enabling you to eventually live seven days a week in mindfulness. I'm sure you agree with me on the day of mindfulness's importance!

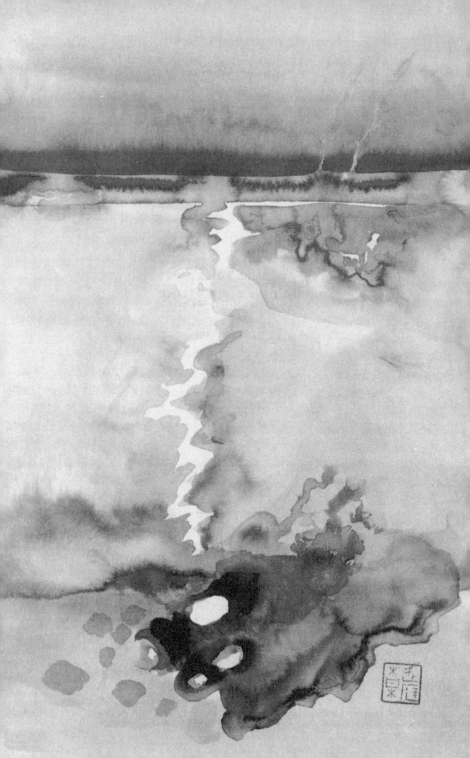

Four

The Pebble

Why should you meditate? First of all, because each of us needs to realize total rest. Even a night of sleep doesn't provide total rest. Twisting and turning, the facial muscles tense, all the while dreaming—hardly rest! Nor is lying down rest when you still feel restless and twist and turn. Lying on your back, with your arms and legs straight but not stiff, your head unsupported by a pillow—this is a good position to practice breathing and to relax all the muscles; but this way it is also easier to fall asleep. You cannot go as far in meditation lying down as by sitting. It is possible to find total rest in a sitting position, and in turn to advance deeper in meditation in order to resolve the worries and troubles that upset and block your consciousness.

Among our workers in Vietnam there are many who can sit in the lotus position, the left foot placed on the right thigh and the right foot placed on the left thigh. Others can sit in the half lotus, the left foot placed on the right thigh, or the right foot placed on the left thigh. In our meditation class in Paris, there are people who do not feel comfortable in either of the above two positions and so I have shown them how to sit in the Japanese manner, the knees bent, resting on their two legs. By placing a pillow beneath one's feet, it is possible to sit that way for more than an hour and a half. Even so, anyone can learn to sit in the half lotus, though at the beginning it may be somewhat painful. But after a few weeks of practice, the position gradually becomes quite comfortable. During the initial period, when the pain can be bothersome, alternate the position of the legs or change to another sitting position. If one sits in the lotus or half-lotus position, it is necessary to use a cushion to sit on so that both knees touch the floor. The three points of bodily contact with the floor created by this position provide an extremely stable position.

Keep your back straight. This is very important. The neck and head should be aligned with the spinal column; they should be straight but not stiff or wood-like. Keep your eyes focused a yard or two in front of you. If you can, maintain a half smile.

Now begin to follow your breath and to relax all of your muscles. Concentrate on keeping your spinal column straight and on following your breath. As for everything else, let it go. Let go of everything. If you want to relax the worry-tightened muscles in your face, let the half smile come to your face. As the half smile appears, all the facial muscles begin to relax. The longer the half smile is maintained, the better. It is the same smile you see on the face of the Buddha.

Place your left hand, palm side up, in your right palm. Let all the muscles in your hands, fingers, arms, and legs relax. Let go of everything. Be like the waterplants which flow with the current, while beneath the surface of the water the riverbed remains motionless. Hold on to nothing but your breath and the half smile.

For beginners, it is better to sit no longer than 20 or 30 minutes. During that time, you can readily obtain total rest. The technique for obtaining this rest lies in two things—watching and letting go: watching your breath, and letting go of everything else. Release every muscle in your body. After about 15 minutes or so, it is possible to reach a deep quiet filled with inner peace and joy. Maintain this quiet and peace.

Some people look on meditation as a toil and want the time to pass quickly in order to rest afterwards. Such persons do not know how to sit yet. If you sit correctly, it is possible to find total relaxation and peace right in the position of sitting. Often it helps to meditate on the image of a pebble thrown into a river.

How is one helped by the image of the pebble? Sit down in whatever position suits you best, the half lotus or lotus, back straight, the half smile on your face. Breathe slowly and deeply, following each breath, becoming one with the breath. Then let go of everything. Imagine yourself as a pebble which has been thrown into a river. The pebble sinks through the water effortlessly. Detached from everything, it falls by the shortest distance possible, finally reaching the bottom, the point of perfect rest. You are like a pebble which has let itself fall into the river, letting go of everything. At the center of your being is your breath. You don't need to know the length of time it takes before reaching the point of complete rest on the bed of fine sand beneath the water. When you feel yourself resting like a pebble which has reached the riverbed, that is the point when you begin to find your own rest. You are no longer pushed or pulled by anything.

If you cannot find joy in peace in these very moments of sitting, then the future itself will only flow by as a river flows by, you will not be able to hold it back, you will be incapable of living the future when it has become the present. Joy and peace are the joy and peace possible in this very hour of sitting. If you cannot find it here, you won't find it anywhere. Don't chase after your thoughts as a shadow follows its object. Don't run after your thoughts. Find joy and peace in this very moment.

❀

This is your own time. This spot where you sit is your own spot. It is on this very spot and in this very moment that you can become enlightened. You don't have to sit beneath a special tree in a distant land. Practice like this for a few months, and you will begin to know a profound and renewing delight.

The ease of sitting depends on whether you practice mindfulness a little or a lot each day. And it depends on whether or not you sit regularly. Whenever possible, join with friends or relatives and organize an hour of sitting each night, say from 10 to 11. Whoever wishes could come to sit for a half hour, or even an entire hour.

Mindfulness of the mind

Someone might well ask: is relaxation then the only goal of meditation? In fact the goal of meditation goes much deeper than that. While relaxation is the necessary point of departure, once one has realized relaxation, it is possible to realize a tranquil heart and clear mind. To realize a tranquil heart and clear mind is to have gone far along the path of meditation.

Of course, to take hold of our minds and calm our thoughts, we must also practice mindfulness of our feelings and perceptions. To take hold of your mind, you must practice mindfulness of the mind. You must know how to observe and recognize the presence of every feeling and thought which arises in you. The Zen Master Thuong Chieu wrote, "If the practitioner knowns his own mind clearly he will obtain results with little effort. But if he does not know anything about his own mind, all of his effort will be wasted." If you want to know your own mind, there is only one way: to observe and recognize everything about it. This must be done at all times, during your day-to-day life no less than during the hour of meditation.

During meditation, various feelings and thoughts may arise. If you don't practice mindfulness of the breath, these thoughts will soon lure you away from mindfulness. But the breath isn't simply a means by which to chase away such thoughts and feelings. Breath remains the vehicle to unite body and mind and to open the gate to wisdom. When a feeling or thought arises, your intention should not be to chase it away, even if by continuing to concentrate on the breath the feeling or thought passes naturally from the mind. The intention isn't to chase it away, hate it, worry about it, or be frightened by it. So what exactly should you be doing concerning such thoughts and feelings? Simply acknowledge their presence. For example, when a feeling of sadness arises, immediately recognize it: "A feeling of sadness has just arisen in me." If the feeling of sadness continues, continue to recognize "A feeling of sadness is still in me." If there is a thought like, "It's late but the neighbors are surely making a lot of noise," recognize that the thought has arisen. If the thought continues to exist, continue to recognize it. If a different feeling or thought arises, recognize it in the same manner. The essential thing is not to let any feeling or thought arise without recognizing it in mindfulness, like a palace guard who is aware of every face that passes through the front corridor.

If there are no feelings or thoughts present, then recognize that there are no feelings or thoughts present. Practicing like this is to become mindful of your feelings and thoughts. You will soon arrive at taking hold of your mind. One can join the method of mindfulness of the breath with the mindfulness of feelings and thoughts.

The guard—or the monkey's shadow?

While practicing mindfulness, don't be dominated by the distinction between good and evil, thus creating a battle within oneself. Whenever a wholesome thought arises, acknowledge it: "A wholesome thought has just arisen." And if an unwholesome thought arises, acknowledge it as well: "An unwholesome thought has just arisen." Don't dwell on it or try to get rid of it, however much you don't like it. To acknowledge it is enough. If you have departed, then you must know that you have departed, and if you are still there, know that you are still there. Once you have reached such an awareness, there will be nothing you need fear anymore.

When I mentioned the guard at the emperor's gate, perhaps you imagined a front corridor with two doors, one entrance and one exit, with your mind as the guard. Whatever feeling or thought enters, you are aware of its entrance, and when it leaves, you are aware of its exit. But the image has a shortcoming: it suggests that those who enter and exit the corridor are different from the guard. In fact our thoughts and feelings are us. They are a part of ourselves. There is a temptation to look upon them, or at least some of them, as an enemy force which is trying to disturb the concentration and understanding of your mind. But, in fact, when we are angry, *we ourselves* are anger. When we are happy, *we ourselves* are happiness. When we have certain thoughts, *we are those thoughts*. We are both the guard and the visitor at the same time. We are both the mind and the observer of the mind. Therefore, chasing away or dwelling on any thought isn't the important thing. The important thing is to be aware of the thought. This observation is not an objectification of the mind: it does not establish distinction between subject and object. Mind does not grab on to mind; mind does not push mind away. Mind can only observe itself. This observation isn't an observation of some object outside and independent of the observer.

Remember the Koan of the Zen Master Bach An who asked, "What is the sound of one hand clapping?" Or take the example of the taste the tongue experiences: what separates taste and tastebud? The mind experiences itself directly within itself. This is of special importance, and so in the Sutra of Mindfulness, Buddha always uses the phrasing "mindfulness of feeling in feeling, mindfulness of mind in mind." Some have said that the Buddha used this phrasing in order to put emphasis on such words as feeling and mind, but I don't think they have fully grasped the Buddha's intention. Mindfulness of feeling in feeling is mindfulness of feeling directly while experiencing feeling, and certainly not contemplation of some *image* of feeling which one creates to give feeling some objective, separate existence of its own outside of oneself. Descriptive words make it sound like a riddle or paradox or tongue twister: mindfulness of feeling in feeling is the mind experiencing mindfulness of the mind in the mind. The objectivity of an outside observer to examine something is the method of science, but it is not the method of meditation. Thus the image of the guard and the visitor fails to illustrate adequately the mindful observation of mind.

The mind is like a monkey swinging from branch to branch through a forest, says the Sutra. In order not to lose sight of the monkey by some sudden movement, we must watch the monkey constantly and even to be one with it. Mind contemplating mind is like an object and its shadow—the object cannot shake the shadow off. The two are one. Wherever the mind goes, it still lies in the harness of the mind. The Sutra sometimes uses the experession "Bind the monkey" to refer to taking hold of the mind. But the monkey image is only a means of expression. Once the mind is directly and continually aware of itself, it is no longer like a monkey. There are not two minds, one which swings from branch to branch and another which follows after to bind it with a piece of rope.

The person who practices meditation usually hopes to see into his or her own nature in order to obtain awakening. But if you are just beginning, don't wait to "see into your own nature." Better yet, don't wait for anything. Especially don't wait to see the Buddha or any version of "ultimate reality" while you're sitting.

In the first six months, try only to build up your power of concentration, to create an inner calmness and serene joy. You will shake off anxiety, enjoy total rest, and quiet your mind. You will be refreshed and gain a broader, clearer view of things, and deepen and strengthen the love in yourself. And you will be able to respond more helpfully to all around you.

Sitting in meditation is nourishment for your spirit and nourishment for your body, as well. Through sitting, our bodies obtain harmony, feel lighter, and are more at peace. The path from the observation of your mind to seeing into your own nature won't be too rough. Once you are able to quiet your mind, once your feelings and thoughts no longer disturb you, at that point your mind will begin to dwell in mind. Your mind will take hold of mind in a direct and wondrous way which no longer differentiates between subject and object. Drinking a cup of tea, the seeming distinction between the one who drinks and the tea being drunk evaporates. Drinking a cup of tea becomes a direct and wondrous experience in which the distinction between subject and object no longer exists.

Dispersed mind is also mind, just as waves rippling in water are also water. When mind has taken hold of mind, deluded mind becomes true mind. True mind is our real self, is the Buddha: the pure one-ness which cannot be cut up by the illusory divisions of separate selves, created by concepts and language. But I don't want to say a lot about this.

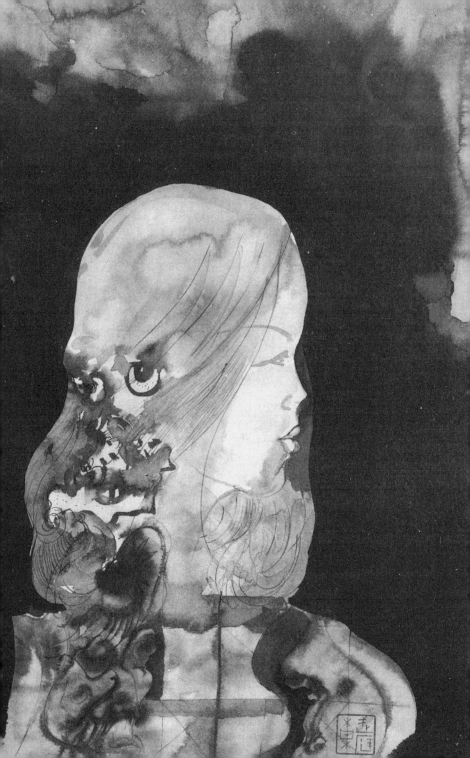

Five ❀

One Is All, All Is One: The Five Aggregates

Let me devote a few lines here to talk about the methods you might use in order to arrive at liberation from narrow views, and to obtain fearlessness and great compassion. These are the contemplations on interdependence, impermanency, and compassion.

While you sit in meditation, after having taken hold of your mind, you can direct your concentration to contemplate on the interdependent nature of certain objects. This meditation is *not* a discursive reflection on a philosophy of interdependence. It is a penetration of mind into mind itself, using one's concentrative power to reveal the real nature of the object being contemplated.

Recall a simple and ancient truth: the subject of knowledge cannot exist independently from the object of knowledge. To see is to see something. To hear is to hear something. To be angry is to be angry over something. Hope is hope for something. Thinking is thinking about something. When the object of knowledge (the something) is not present, there can be no subject of knowledge. The practitioner meditates on mind and, by so doing, is able to see the interdependence of the subject of knowledge and the object of knowledge. When we practice mindfulness of breath, then the knowledge of breath is mind. When we practice mindfulness of the body, then the knowledge of body is mind. When we practice mindfulness of objects outside ourselves, then the knowledge of these objects is also mind. Therefore the contemplation of the nature of interdependence of all objects is also the contemplation of the mind.

Every object of the mind is itself mind. In Buddhism, we call the objects of mind the dharmas. Dharmas are usually grouped into five categories:

1. bodily and physical forms
2. feelings
3. perceptions
4. mental functionings
5. consciousness

These five categories are called *the five aggregates*. The fifth category, consciousness, however, contains all the other categories and is the basis of their existence.

Contemplation on interdependence is a deep looking into all dharmas in order to pierce through to their real nature, in order to see them as part of the great body of reality and in order to see that the great body of reality is indivisible. It cannot be cut into pieces with separate existences of their own.

The first object of contemplation is our own person, the assembly of the five aggregates in ourselves. You contemplate right here and now on the five aggregates which make up yourself.

You are conscious of the presence of bodily form, feeling, perception, mental functionings, and consciousness. You observe these "objects" until you see that each of them has intimate connection with the world outside yourself: if the world did not exist then the assembly of the five aggregates could not exist either.

Consider the example of a table. The table's existence is possible due to the existence of things which we might call "the non-table world": the forest where the wood grew and was cut, the carpenter, the iron ore which became the nails and screws, and countless other things which have relation to the table, the parents and ancestors of the carpenter, the sun and rain which made it possible for the trees to grow.

If you grasp the table's reality then you see that in the table itself are present all those things whch we normally think of as the non-table world. If you took away any of those non-table elements and returned them to their sources—the nails back to the iron ore, the wood to the forest, the carpenter to his parents—the table would no longer exist.

A person who looks at the table and can see the universe is a person who can see the way. You meditate on the assembly of the five aggregates in yourself in the same manner. You meditate on them until you are able to see the presence of the reality of one-ness in your own self, and can see that your own life and the life of the universe are one. If the five aggregates return to their sources, the self no longer exists. Each second, the world nourishes the five aggregates. The self is no different from the assembly of the five aggregates themselves. The assembly of the five aggregates plays, as well, a crucial role in the formation, creation, and destruction of all things in the universe.

Liberation from suffering

People normally cut reality into compartments, and so are unable to see the interdependence of all phenomena. To see one in all and all in one is to break through the great barrier which narrows one's perception of reality, a barrier which Buddhism calls the attachment to the false view of self.

Attachment to the false view of self means belief in the presence of unchanging entities which exist on their own. To break through this false view is to be liberated from every sort of fear, pain, and anxiety. When the Bodhisattva Quan the Am, who has been such a source of inspiration of peace workers in Vietnam, saw into the reality of the five aggregates giving rise to emptiness of Self, she was liberated from every suffering, pain, doubt, and anger. The same would apply to everyone. If we contemplate the five aggregates in a stubborn and diligent way, we, too, will be liberated from suffering, fear, and dread.

We have to strip away all the barriers in order to live as part of the universal life. A person isn't some private entity traveling unaffected through time and space as if sealed off from the rest of the world by a thick shell. Living for 100 or for 100,000 lives sealed off like that not only isn't living, but it isn't possible. In our lives are present a multitude of phenomena, just as we ourselves are present in many different phenomena. We are life, and life is limitless. Perhaps one can say that we are only alive when we live the life of the world, and so live the sufferings and joys of others. The suffering of others is our own suffering, and the happiness of others is our own happiness. If our lives have no limits, the assembly of the five aggregates which makes up our self also has no limits. The impermanent character of the universe, the successes and failures of life can no longer manipulate us. Having seen the reality of interdependence and entered deeply into its reality, nothing can oppress you any longer. You are liberated. Sit in the lotus position, observe your breath, and ask one who has died for others.

Meditation on interdependence is to be practiced constantly, not only while sitting, but as an integral part of our involvement in all ordinary tasks. We must learn to see that the person in front of us is ourself and that we are that person. We must be able to see the process of inter-origination and interdependence of all events, both those which are happening and those which will happen.

A ride on the waves of birth and death

I cannot leave out the problem of life and death. Many young people and others have come out to serve others and to labor for peace, through their love for all who are suffering. They are always mindful of the fact that the most important question is the question of life and death, but often not realizing that life and death are but two faces of one reality. Once we realize that we will have the courage to encounter both of them.

When I was only 19 years old, I was assigned by an older monk to meditate on the image of a corpse in the cemetery. But I found it very hard to take and resisted the meditation. Now I no longer feel that way. Then I thought that such a meditation should be reserved for older monks. But since then, I have seen many young soldiers lying motionless beside one another, some only 13, 14, and 15 years old. They had no preparation or readiness for death. Now I see that if one doesn't know how to die, one can hardly know how to live—because death is a part of life. Just two days ago Mobi told me that she thought at 20 one was old enough to meditate on the corpse. She has only turned 21 herself.

We must look death in the face, recognize and accept it, just as we look at and accept life.

The Buddhist Sutra on Mindfulness speaks about the meditation on the corpse: meditate on the decomposition of the body, how the body bloats and turns violet, how it is eaten by worms until only bits of blood and flesh still cling to the bones, meditate up to the point where only white bones remain, which in turn are slowly worn away and turn into dust. Meditate like that, knowing that your own body will undergo the same process. Meditate on the corpse until you are calm and at peace, until your mind and heart are light and tranquil and a smile appears on your face. Thus, by overcoming revulsion and fear, life will be seen as infinitely precious, every second of it worth living. And it is not just our own lives that are recognized as precious, but the lives of every other person, every other person, every other being, every other reality. We can no longer be deluded by the notion that the destruction of others' lives is necessary for our own survival. We see that life and death are but two faces of Life and that without both, Life is not possible, just as two sides of a coin are needed for the coin to exist. Only now is it possible to rise above birth and death, and to know how to live and how to die. The Sutra says that the Bodhisattvas who have seen into the reality of interdependence have broken through all narrow views, and have been able to enter birth and death as a person takes a ride in a small boat without being submerged or drowned by the waves of birth and death.

Some people have said that if you look at reality with the eyes of a Buddhist, you become pessimistic. But to think in terms of either pessimism or optimism oversimplifies the truth. The problem is to see reality as it is. A pessimistic attitude can never create the calm and serene smile which blossoms on the lips of the Bodhisattvas and all others who obtain the Way.

Six ❧

The Almond Tree
in Your Front Yard

I've spoken about the contemplation on interdependence. Of course all the methods in the search for truth should be looked on as means rather than as ends in themselves or as absolute truth. The meditation on interdependence is intended to remove the false barriers of discrimination so that one can enter into the universal harmony of life. It is not intended to produce a philosophical system, a philosophy of interdependence. Herman Hesse, in his novel *Siddartha*, did not yet see this and so his Siddhartha speaks about the philosophy of interdependence in words which strike us as somewhat naive. The author offers us a picture of interdependence in which everything is interrelated, a system in which no fault can be found: everything must fit into the foolproof system of mutual dependence, a system in which one cannot consider the problem of liberation in this world.

According to an insight of our tradition, reality has three natures: imagination, interdependence, and the nature of ultimate perfection. One first considers interdependence. Because of forgetfulness and prejudices, we generally cloak reality with a veil of false views and opinions. This is seeing reality through imagination. Imagination is an illusion of reality which conceives of reality as an assembly of small pieces of separate entities and selves. In order to break through, the practitioner meditates on the nature of interdependence or the interrelatedness of phenomena in the processes of creation and destruction. The consideration is a way of contemplation, not the basis of a philosophic doctrine. If one clings merely to a system of concepts, one only becomes stuck. The meditation on interdependence is to help one penetrate reality in order to be one with it, not to become caught up in philosophical opinion or meditation methods. The raft is used to cross the river. It isn't to be carried around on your shoulders. The finger which points at the moon isn't the moon itself.

Finally one proceeds to the nature of ultimate perfection—reality freed from all false views produced by the imagination. Reality is reality. It transcends every concept. There is no concept which can adequately describe it, not even the concept of interdependence. To assure that one doesn't become attached to a philosophical concept, our teaching speaks of the three *non*-natures to prevent the individual from becoming caught up in the doctrine of the three natures. The essence of Mahayana Buddhist teaching lies in this.

When reality is perceived in its nature of ultimate perfection, the practitioner has reached a level of wisdom called non-discrimination mind—a wondrous communion in which there is no longer any distinction made between subject and object. This isn't some far-off, unattainable state. Any one of us—by persisting in practicing even a little—can at least taste of it. I have a pile of orphan applications for sponsorship on my desk.* I translate a few each day. Before I begin to translate a sheet, I look into the eyes of the child in the photograph, and look at the child's expression and features closely. I feel a deep link between myself and each child, which allows me to enter a special communion with them. While writing this to you, I see that during those moments and hours, the communion I have experienced while translating the simple lines in the applications has been a kind of non-discrimination mind. I no longer see an "I" who translates the sheets to help each child, I no longer see a child who received love and help. The child and I are one: no one pities; no one asks for help; no one helps. There is no task, no social work to be done, no compassion, no special wisdom. These are moments of non-discrimination mind.

---

*The Vietnamese Buddhist Peace Delegation has carried on a program of raising financial support for families within Vietnam who took in orphans. In the United States the sponsor contributed $6 a month for the family of the orphan he or she was helping.

When reality is experienced in its nature of ultimate perfection, an almond tree that may be in your front yard reveals its nature in perfect wholeness. The almond tree is itself truth, reality, your own self. Of all the people who have passed by your yard, how many have really seen the almond tree? The heart of an artist may be more sensitive; hopefully he or she will be able to see the tree in a deeper way than many others. Because of a more open heart, a certain communion already exists between the artist and the tree. What counts is your own heart. If your heart is not clouded by false views, you will be able to enter into a natural communion with the tree. The almond tree will be ready to reveal itself to you in complete wholeness. To see the almond tree is to see the way. One Zen Master, when asked to explain the wonder of reality, pointed to a cypress tree and said, "Look at the cypress tree over there."

The voice of the rising tide

When your mind is liberated your heart floods with compassion: compassion for yourself, for having undergone countless sufferings because you were not yet able to relieve yourself of false views, hatred, ignorance, and anger; and compassion for others because they do not yet see and so are still imprisoned by false views, hatred, and ignorance and continue to create suffering for themselves and for others. Now you look at yourself and at others with the eyes

of compassion, like a saint who hears the cry of
every creature in the universe and whose voice
is the voice of every person who has seen reality
in perfect wholeness. As a Buddhist Sutra hears
the voice of the Bodhisattva of compassion:

> The wondrous voice, the voice of the one
>   who attends to the cries of the world
> The noble voice, the voice of the rising
>   tide surpassing all the sounds of the
>   world
> Let our mind be attuned to that voice.

> Put aside all doubt and meditate on the
>   pure and holy nature of the regarder
>   of the cries of the world
> Because that is our reliance in situations
>   of pain, distress, calamity, death.

> Perfect in all merits, beholding all sentient
>   beings with compassionate eyes, mak-
>   ing the ocean of blessings limitless,
> Before this one, we should incline.

Practice looking at all beings with the eyes
of compassion: this is the meditation called
"the meditation on compassion."

The meditation on compassion must be
realized during the hours you sit and during
every moment you carry out service for others.
No matter where you go or where you sit, remember the sacred call: "Look at all beings
with the eyes of compassion."

There are many subjects and methods for

meditation, so many that I could never hope to write them all down for our friends. I've only mentioned a few, simple but basic methods here. A peace worker is like any one else. She or he must live her own life. Work is only a part of life. But work is life only when done in mindfulness. Otherwise, one becomes like the person "who lives as though dead." We need to light our own torch in order to carry on. But the life of each one of us is connected with the life of those around us. If we know how to live in mindfulness, if we know how to preserve and care for our own mind and heart, then thanks to that, our brothers and sisters will also know how to live in mindfulness.

Meditation reveals and heals

Sitting in mindfulness, both our bodies and minds can be at peace and totally relaxed. But this state of peace and relaxation differs fundamentally from the lazy, semi-conscious state of mind that one gets while resting and dozing. Sitting in such lazy semi-consciousness, far from being mindfulness, is like sitting in a dark cave. In mindfulness one is not only restful and happy, but alert and awake. Meditation is not evasion; it is a serene encounter with reality. The person who practices mindfulness should be no less awake than the driver of a car; if the practitioner isn't awake he will be possessed by dispersion and forgetfulness, just as the drowsy driver is likely to cause a grave accident. Be as awake as a person walking on high stilts—any mis-step could cause the walker to fall. Be like a medieval knight walking weaponless in a forest of swords. Be like a lion, going forward with slow, gentle, and firm steps. Only with this kind of vigilance can you realize total awakening.

For beginners, I recommend the method of pure recognition: recognition without judgment. Feelings, whether of compassion or irritation, should be welcomed, recognized, and treated on an absolutely equal basis; because both are ourselves. The tangerine I am eating is me. The mustard greens I am planting are me. I plant with all my heart and mind. I clean this teapot with the kind of attention I would have were I giving the baby Buddha or Jesus a bath. Nothing should be treated more carefully than anything else. In mindfulness, compassion, irritation, mustard green plant, and teapot are all sacred.

When possessed by a sadness, an anxiety, a hatred, or a passion or whatever, the method of pure observation and recognition may seem difficult to practice. If so, turn to meditation on a fixed object, using your own state of mind as meditation's subject. Such meditation reveals and heals. The sadness or anxiety, hatred or passion, under the gaze of concentration and meditation reveals its own nature—a revelation that leads naturally to healing and emancipation. The sadness (or whatever has caused the pain) can be used as a means of liberation from torment and suffering, like using a thorn to remove a thorn. We should treat our anxiety,

our pain, our hatred and passion gently, respectfully, not resisting it, but living with it, making
peace with it, penetrating into its nature by
meditation on interdependence. One quickly
learns how to select subjects of meditation that
fit the situation. Subjects of meditation—like
interdependence, compassion, self, emptiness,
non-attachment—all these belong to the categories of meditation which have the power to
reveal and to heal.

Meditation on these subjects, however,
can only be successful if we have built up a
certain power of concentration, a power
achieved by the practice of mindfulness in
everyday life, in the observation and recognition of all that is going on. But the objects of
meditation must be realities that have real
roots in yourselves—not just subjects of philosophical speculation. Each should be like a kind
of food that must be cooked for a long time
over a hot fire. We put it in a pot, cover it, and
light the fire. The pot is ourselves and the heat
used to cook is the power of concentration.
The fuel comes from the continuous practice
of mindfulness. Without enough heat the food
will never be cooked. But once cooked, the
food reveals its true nature and helps lead us
to liberation.

The water clearer, the grass greener

The Buddha once said that the problem
of life and death is itself the problem of mindfulness. Whether or not one is alive depends

on whether one is mindful. In the Samyutta Nikaya Sutra, the Buddha tells a story which took place in a small village:

A famous dancer had just come to the village and the people were swarming the streets to catch a glimpse of her. At that same moment, a condemned criminal was obliged to cross the village carrying a bowl of oil filled to the very brim. He had to concentrate with all his might on keeping the bowl steady, for even if one drop of oil were to spill from the bowl to the ground, the soldier directly behind him had orders to take out his sword and cut off the man's head. Having reached this point in the story, Gautama Buddha asked: "Now, do you think our prisoner was able to keep all his attention so focused on the bowl of oil that his mind did not stray to steal a glimpse of the famous dancer in town, or to look up at the throngs of villagers making such a commotion in the streets, any of whom could bump into him at any moment?"

Another time the Buddha recounted a story which made me suddenly see the supreme importance of practicing mindfulness of one's own self—that is, to protect and care for one's self, not being preoccupied about the way others look after themselves, a habit of mind which gives rise to resentment and anxiety. The Buddha said, "There once were a couple of acrobats. The teacher was a poor widower and the student was a small girl named Meda. The two of them performed in the streets to earn enough to eat. They used a tall bamboo pole which the teacher balanced on the top of his head while the little girl slowly climbed to the top. There she remained while the teacher continued to walk along the ground.

"Both of them had to devote all their attention to maintain perfect balance and to prevent any accident from occurring. One day the teacher instructed the pupil: 'Listen, Meda, I will watch you and you watch me, so that we can help each other maintain concentration and balance and prevent an accident. Then we'll be sure to earn enough to eat.' But the little girl was wise and answered, 'Dear master, I think it would be better for each of us to watch ourself. To look after oneself means to look after both of us. That way I am sure we will avoid any accidents and will earn enough to eat.'" The Buddha said: "The child spoke correctly."

In a family, if there is one person who practices mindfulness, the entire family will be more mindful. Because of the presence of one member who lives in mindfulness, the entire family is reminded to live in mindfulness. If in one class, one student lives in mindfulness, the entire class is influenced.

In peace-serving communities, we must follow the same principle. Don't worry if those around you aren't doing their best. Just worry about how to make yourself worthy. Doing your best is the surest way to remind those around you to do their best. But to be worthy requires the continuing practice of mindfulness. That is a certainty. Only by practicing mindfulness will we not lose ourselves but acquire a bright joy and peace. Only by practicing mindfulness will we be able to look at everyone else with the open mind and eyes of love.

I was just invited downstairs for a cup of tea, into an apartment where a friend who helps us has a piano. As Kirsten—who is from Holland —poured tea for me, I looked at her pile of work and said, "Why don't you stop translating orphan applications for a minute and play the piano for me?" Kirsten was glad to put down her work for a moment and sat down at the piano to play a selection of Chopin she has known since she was a child. The piece has several measures which are soft and melodic but others which are loud and quick. Her dog was lying beneath the tea table, and when the music became excited, it began to bark and whine. I knew that it felt uneasy and wanted the music to stop. Kirsten's dog is treated with the kindness one gives to a small child, and perhaps is more sensitive to music than most children. Or perhaps it responded this way because its ears pick up certain vibrations that human ears do not. Kirsten continued to play while trying to console the dog at the same time, but to no avail. She finished and began to play another piece by Mozart which was light and harmonious. Now the dog lay quietly and appeared to be at peace. When Kirsten had finished she came over and sat down beside me and said, "Often when I play a piece of Chopin that is the least bit loud, the dog comes and grabs hold of my pantsleg, trying to force me to leave the piano. Sometimes I have to put her outside before I can continued playing. But whenever I play Bach or Mozart, she is peaceful."

Kirsten mentioned a report that in Canada people tried playing Mozart for their plants during the night. The plants grew more quickly than normal, and the flowers inclined toward the direction of the music. Others played Mozart every day in wheat and rye fields and were able to measure that the wheat and rye in these fields grew more quickly than the wheat and rye in other fields.

As Kirsten spoke, I thought about conference rooms where people argue and debate, where angry and reproachful words are hurled back and forth. If one placed flowers and plants in such rooms, chances are they would cease to grow.

I thought about the garden tended by a monk living in mindfulness. His flowers are always fresh and green, nourished by the peace and joy which flow from his mindfulness. One of the ancients said,

> When a great Master is born, the water in the rivers turns clearer and the plants grow greener.

We ought to listen to music or sit and practice breathing at the beginning of every meeting or discussion.

Seven ❧

Three Wondrous Answers

To end, let me retell a short story of Tolstoy's, the story of the Emperor's three questions. Tolstoy did not know the emperor's name . . .

One day it occurred to a certain emperor that if he only knew the answers to three questions, he would never stray in any matter.

What is the best time to do each thing?
Who are the most important people to work with?
What is the most important thing to do at all times?

The emperor issued a decree throughout his kingdom announcing that whoever could answer the questions would receive a great reward. Many who read the decree made their way to the palace at once, each person with a different answer.

In reply to the first question, one person

advised that the emperor make up a thorough time schedule, consecràting every hour, day, month, and year for certain tasks and then follow the schedule to the letter. Only then could he hope to do every task at the right time.

Another person replied that it was impossible to plan in advance and that the emperor should put all vain amusements aside and remain attentive to everything in order to know what to do at what time.

Someone else insisted that, by himself, the emperor could never hope to have all the foresight and competence necessary to decide when to do each and every task and what he really needed was to set up a Council of the Wise and then to act according to their advice.

Someone else said that certain matters required immediate decision and could not wait for consultation, but if he wanted to know in advance what was going to happen he should consult magicians and soothsayers.

The responses to the second question also lacked accord.

One person said that the emperor needed to place all his trust in administrators, another urged reliance on priests and monks, while others recommended physicians. Still others put their faith in warriors.

The third question drew a similar variety of answers.

Some said science was the most important pursuit. Others insisted on religion. Yet others claimed the most important thing was military skill.

The emperor was not pleased with any of the answers, and no reward was given.

After several nights of reflection, the emperor resolved to visit a hermit who lived up on the mountain and was said to be an enlightened man. The emperor wished to find the hermit to ask him the three questions, though he knew the hermit never left the mountains and was known to receive only the poor, refusing to have anything to do with persons of wealth or power. So the emperor disguised himself as a simple peasant and ordered his attendants to wait for him at the foot of the mountain while he climbed the slope alone to seek the hermit.

Reaching the holy man's dwelling place, the emperor found the hermit digging a garden in front of his hut. When the hermit saw the stranger, he nodded his head in greeting and continued to dig. The labor was obviously hard on him. He was an old man, and each time he thrust his spade into the ground to turn the earth, he heaved heavily.

The emperor approached him and said, "I have come here to ask your help with three questions: When is the best time to do each thing? Who are the most important people to work with? What is the most important thing to do at all times?"

The hermit listened attentively but only patted the emperor on the shoulder and continued digging. The emperor said, "You must be tired. Here, let me give you a hand with that." The hermit thanked him, handed the emperor the spade, and then sat down on the ground to rest.

After he had dug two rows, the emperor stopped and turned to the hermit and repeated his three questions. The hermit still did not answer, but instead stood up and pointed to the spade and said, "Why don't you rest now? I can take over again." But the emperor continued to dig. One hour passed, then two. Finally the sun began to set behind the mountain. The emperor put down the spade and said to the hermit, "I came here to ask if you could answer my three questions. But if you can't give me any answer, please let me know so that I can get on my way home."

The hermit lifted his head and asked the emperor, "Do you hear someone running over there?" The emperor turned his head. They both saw a man with a long white beard emerge from the woods. He ran wildly, pressing his hands against a bloody wound in his stomach. The man ran toward the emperor before falling unconscious to the ground, where he lay groaning. Opening the man's clothing, the emperor and hermit saw that the man had received a deep gash. The emperor cleaned the wound thoroughly and then used his own shirt to bandage it, but the blood completely soaked it within minutes. He rinsed the shirt out and bandaged the wound a second time and continued to do so until the flow of blood had stopped.

At last the wounded man regained consciousness and asked for a drink of water. The emperor ran down to the stream and brought back a jug of fresh water. Meanwhile, the sun had disappeared and the night air had begun to turn cold. The hermit gave the emperor a hand in carrying the man into the hut where they laid him down on the hermit's bed. The man closed his eyes and lay quietly. The emperor was worn out from a long day of climbing the mountain and digging the garden. Leaning against the doorway, he fell asleep. When he rose, the sun had already risen over the mountain. For a moment he forgot where he was and what he had come here for. He looked over to the bed and saw the wounded man also looking around him in confusion. When he saw the emperor, he stared at him intently and then said in a faint whisper, "Please forgive me."

"But what have you done that I should forgive you?" the emperor asked.

"You do not know me, your majesty, but I know you. I was your sworn enemy, and I had vowed to take vengeance on you, for during the last war you killed my brother and seized my property. When I learned that you were coming alone to the mountain to meet the hermit, I resolved to surprise you on your way back and kill you. But after waiting a long time there was still no sign of you, and so I left my ambush in order to seek you out. But instead of finding you, I came across your attendants, who recognized me, giving me this wound. Luckily, I escaped and ran here. If I hadn't met you I would surely be dead by now. I had intended to kill you, but instead you saved my life! I am ashamed and grateful beyond words. If I live, I vow to be your servant for the rest of my life, and I will bid my children and grandchildren to do the same. Please grant me your forgiveness."

The emperor was overjoyed to see that he was so easily reconciled with a former enemy. He not only forgave the man but promised to return all the man's property and to send his own physician and servants to wait on the man until he was completely healed. After ordering his attendants to take the man home, the emperor returned to see the hermit. Before returning to the palace the emperor wanted to repeat his three questions one last time. He found the hermit sowing seeds in the earth they had dug the day before.

The hermit stood up and looked at the emperor. "But your questions have already been answered."

"How's that?" the emperor asked, puzzled.

"Yesterday, if you had not taken pity on my age and given me a hand with digging these beds, you would have been attacked by that man on your way home. Then you would have deeply regretted not staying with me. Therefore the most important time was the time you were digging in the beds, the most important person was myself, and the most important pursuit was to help me. Later, when the wounded man ran up here, the most important time was the time you spent dressing his wound, for if you had not cared for him he would have died and you would have lost the chance to be reconciled with him. Likewise, he was the most important person, and the most important pursuit was taking care of his wound. Remember that there is only one important time and that is now. The present moment is the only time over which we have dominion. The most important person is always the person you are with, who is right before you, for who knows if you will have dealings with any other person in the future? The most important pursuit is making the person standing at your side happy, for that alone is the pursuit of life."

Tolstoy's story is like a story out of scripture: it doesn't fall short of any sacred text. We talk about social service, service to the people, service to humanity, service for others who are far away, helping to bring peace to the world—but often we forget that it is the very people around us that we must live for first of all. If you cannot serve your wife or husband or child or parent—how are you going to serve society? If you cannot make your own child happy, how do you expect to be able to make anyone else happy? If all our friends in the peace movement or of service communities of any kind do not love and help one another, whom can we love and help? Are we working for other humans, or are we just working for the name of an organization?

Service

The service of peace. The service of any person in need. The word service is so immense. Let's return first to a more modest scale: our families, our classmates, our friends, our own community. We must live for them—for if we cannot live for them, whom else do we think we are living for?

Tolstoy is a saint—what we Buddhists would call a Bodhisattva. But was the emperor himself able to see the meaning and direction of life? How can we live in the present moment, live right now with the people around us, helping to lessen their suffering and making their lives happier? How? The answer is this: We must practice mindfulness. The principle that Tolstoy gives appears easy. But if we want to put it into practice we must use the methods of mindfulness in order to seek and find the way.

I've written these pages for our friends to use. There are many people who have written about these things without having lived them, but I've only written down those things which I have lived and experienced myself. I hope you and your friends will find these things at least a little helpful along the path of our seeking: the path of our return.

❧ Exercises in Mindfulness

Here are a number of exercises and approaches in meditation which I often have used, adapting them from various methods to fit my own circumstances and preferences. Select the ones you like best and find the most suitable for your own self. The value of each method will vary according to each person's unique needs. Although these exercises are relatively easy, they form the foundations on which everything else is built.

Half-smile when you first wake up in the morning

Hang a branch, any other sign, or even the word "smile" on the ceiling or wall so that you see it right away when you open your eyes. This sign will serve as your reminder. Use these seconds before you get out of bed to take hold of your breath. Inhale and exhale three breaths gently while maintaining the half smile. Follow your breaths.

Half-smile during your free moments

Anywhere you find yourself sitting or standing, half-smile. Look at a child, a leaf, a painting on the wall, anything which is relatively still, and smile. Inhale and exhale quietly three times. Maintain the half smile and consider the spot of your attention as your own true nature.

Half-smile while listening to music

Listen to a piece of music for two or three minutes. Pay attention to the words, music, rhythm, and sentiments. Smile while watching your inhalations and exhalations.

Half-smile when irritated

When you realize you're irritated, half-smile at once. Inhale and exhale quietly, maintaining the half smile for three breaths.

Letting go in a lying-down position

Lie on your back on a flat surface without the support of mattress or pillow. Keep your two arms loosely by your sides and your two legs slightly apart, stretched out before you. Maintain a half smile. Breathe in and out gently, keeping your attention focused on your breath. Let go of every muscle in your body. Relax each muscle as though it were sinking down through the floor or as though it were as soft and yielding as a piece of silk hanging in the breeze to dry. Let go entirely, keeping your attention only on your breath and half smile. Think of yourself as a cat, completely relaxed before a warm fire, whose muscles yield without resistance to anyone's touch. Continue for 15 breaths.

Letting go in the sitting position

Sit in the half or full lotus, or cross-legged, or your two legs folded beneath you, or even on a chair, your two feet touching the floor. Half-smile. Inhale and exhale while maintaining the half smile. Let go.

Deep breathing

Lie on your back. Breathe evenly and gently, focusing your attention on the movement of your stomach. As you begin to breathe in, allow your stomach to rise in order to bring air into the lower half of your lungs. As the upper halves of your lungs begin to fill with air, your chest begins to rise and your stomach begins to lower. Don't tire yourself. Continue for 10 breaths. The exhalation will be longer than the inhalation.

Measuring your breath by your footsteps

Walk slowly and leisurely in a garden, along a river, or on a village path. Breathe normally. Determine the length of your breath, the exhalation and the inhalation, by the number of your footsteps. Continue for a few minutes. Begin to lengthen your exhalation by one step. Do not force a longer inhalation. Let it be natural. Watch your inhalation carefully to see

82

if there is a desire to lengthen it. Continue for 10 breaths.

Now lengthen the exhalation by one more footstep. Watch to see whether the inhalation also lengthens by one step or not. Only lengthen the inhalation when you feel that it will give delight. After 20 breaths, return your breath to normal. About five minutes later, you can begin the practice of lengthened breaths again. When you feel the least bit tired, return to normal. After several sessions of the practice of lengthened breath, your exhalation and inhalation will grow equal in length. Do not practice long, equal breaths for more than 10 to 20 breaths before returning to normal.

Counting your breath

Sit in the half or full lotus or take a walk. As you inhale, be mindful that "I am inhaling, one." When you exhale, be mindful that "I am exhaling, one." Remember to breathe from the stomach. When beginning the second inhalation, be mindful that "I am inhaling, two." And slowly exhaling, be mindful that "I am exhaling, two." Continue on up through 10. After you have reached 10, return to one. Whenever you lose count, return to one.

Following your breath while listening to music

Listen to a piece of music. Breathe long, light, and even breaths. Follow your breath, be master of it while remaining aware of the movement and sentiments of the music. Do not get lost in the music, but continue to be master of your breath and your self.

Following your breath while carrying on a conversation

Breathe long, light, and even breaths. Follow your breath while listening to a friend's words and to your own replies. Continue as with the music.

Following the breath

Sit in a full or half lotus or go for a walk. Begin to inhale gently and normally (from the stomach), mindful that "I am inhaling normally." Exhale in mindfulness, "I am exhaling normally." Continue for three breaths. On the fourth breath, extend the inhalation, mindful that "I am breathing in a long inhalation." Exhale in mindfulness, "I am breathing out a long exhalation." Continue for three breaths.

Now follow your breath carefully, aware of every movement of your stomach and lungs. Follow the entrance and exit of air. Be mindful that "I am inhaling and following the inhalation from its beginning to its end. I am exhaling and following the exhalation from its beginning to its end."

Continue for 20 breaths. Return to normal. After 5 minutes, repeat the exercise. Remember to maintain the half smile while breathing. Once you have mastered this exercise, move on to the next.

Breathing to quiet the mind and body to realize joy

Sit in the full or half lotus. Half-smile. Follow your breath. When your mind and body are quiet, continue to inhale and exhale very lightly, mindful that, "I am breathing in and making the breath-body light and peaceful. I am exhaling and making the breath-body light and peaceful." Continue for three breaths, giving rise to the thought in mindfulness, "I am breathing in and making my entire body light and peaceful and joyous." Continue for three breaths and in mindfulness give rise to the thought, "I am breathing in while my body and mind are peace and joy. I am breathing out while my body and mind are peace and joy."

Maintain this thought in mindfulness from 5 to 30 minutes, or for an hour, according to your ability and to the time available to you. The beginning and end of the practice should be relaxed and gentle. When you want to stop, gently massage your eyes and face with your two hands and then massage the muscles in your legs before returning to a normal sitting position. Wait a moment before standing up.

Mindfulness of the positions of the body

This can be practiced in any time and place. Begin to focus your attention on your breath. Breathe quietly and more deeply than usual. Be mindful of the position of your body, whether you are walking, standing, lying, or sitting down. Know where you walk; where you stand; where you lie; where you sit. Be mindful of the purpose of your position. For example, you might be conscious that you are standing on a green hillside in order to refresh yourself, to practice breathing, or just to stand. If there is no purpose, be mindful that there is no purpose.

Mindfulness while making tea

Prepare a pot of tea to serve a guest or to drink by yourself. Do each movement slowly, in mindfulness. Do not let one detail of your movements go by without being mindful of it. Know that your hand lifts the pot by its handle. Know that you are pouring the fragrant warm tea into the cup. Follow each step in mindfulness. Breathe gently and more deeply than usual. Take hold of your breath if your mind strays.

Washing the dishes

Wash the dishes relaxingly, as though each bowl is an object of contemplation. Consider each bowl as sacred. Follow your breath to prevent your mind from straying. Do not try to hurry to get the job over with. Consider washing the dishes the most important thing in life. Washing the dishes is meditation. If you cannot wash the dishes in mindfulness, neither can you meditate while sitting in silence.

Washing clothes

Do not wash too many clothes at one time. Select only three or four articles of clothing. Find the most comfortable position to sit or stand so as to prevent a backache. Scrub the clothes relaxingly. Hold your attention on every movement of your hands and arms. Pay attention to the soap and water. When you have finished scrubbing and rinsing, your mind and body should feel as clean and fresh as your clothes. Remember to maintain the half smile and take hold of your breath whenever your mind wanders.

Cleaning house

Divide your work into stages: straightening things and putting away books, scrubbing the toilet, scrubbing the bathroom, sweeping the floors and dusting. Allow a good length of time for each task. Move slowly, three times more slowly than usual. Fully focus your attention on each task. For example, while placing a book on the shelf, look at the book, be aware of what book it is, know that you are in the process of placing it on the shelf, intending to put it in that specific place. Know that your hand reaches for the book, and picks it up. Avoid any abrupt or harsh movement. Maintain mindfulness of the breath, especially when your thoughts wander.

A slow-motion bath

Allow yourself 30 to 45 minutes to take a bath. Don't hurry for even one second. From the moment you prepare the bathwater to the moment you put on clean clothes, let every

87

motion be light and slow. Be attentive of every movement. Place your attention to every part of your body, without discrimination or fear. Be mindful of each stream of water on your body. By the time you've finished, your mind should feel as peaceful and light as your body. Follow your breath. Think of yourself as being in a clean and fragrant lotus pond in the summer.

The pebble

While sitting still and breathing slowly, think of yourself as a pebble which is falling through a clear stream. While sinking, there is no intention to guide your movement. Sink toward the spot of total rest on the gentle sand of the river-bed. Continue meditating on the pebble until your mind and body are at complete rest: a pebble resting on the sand. Maintain this peace and joy a half hour while watching your breath. No thought about the past or future can pull you away from your present peace and joy. The universe exists in this present moment. No desire can pull you away from this present peace, not even the desire to become a Buddha or the desire to save all beings. Know that to become a Buddha and to save all beings can only be realized on the foundation of the pure peace of the present moment.

A day of mindfulness

Set aside one day of the week, any day that accords with your own situation. Forget the work you do during the other days. Do not organize any meetings or have friends over. Do only such simple work as house cleaning, cooking, washing clothes, and dusting.

Once the house is neat and clean, and all your things are in order, take a slow-motion bath. Afterwards, prepare and drink tea. You might read scripture or write letters to close friends. Afterwards, take a walk to practice breathing. While reading scripture or writing letters, maintain your mindfulness, don't let the text or letter pull you away to somewhere else. While reading the sacred text, know what you are reading; while writing the letter, know what you are writing. Follow the same procedure as listening to music or conversing with a friend. In the evening prepare yourself a light meal, perhaps only a little fruit or a glass of fruit juice. Sit in meditation for an hour before you go to bed. During the day, take two walks of a half hour to 45 minutes. Instead of reading before you go to bed, practice total relaxation for 5 to 10 minutes. Be master of your breathing. Breathe gently (the breath should not be too long), following the rising, the lowering of your stomach and chest, your eyes closed. Every movement during this day should be at least two times slower than usual.

Contemplation on interdependence

Find a photo of yourself as a child. Sit in the full or half lotus. Begin to follow your breath. After 20 breaths, begin to focus your attention on the photo in front of you. Recreate and live again the five aggregates of which you were made up at the time the photo was taken: the physical characteristics of your body, your feelings, perceptions, mind functionings, and consciousness at that age. Continue to follow your breath. Do not let your memories lure you away or overcome you. Maintain this meditation for 15 minutes. Maintain the half smile. Turn your mindfulness to your present self. Be conscious of your body, feelings, perceptions, mind functionings, and consciousness in the present moment. See the five aggregates which make up yourself. Ask the question, "Who am I?" The question should be deeply rooted in you, like a new seed nestled deep in the soft earth and damp with water. The question "Who am I?" should not be an abstract question to consider with your discursive intellect. The question "Who am I?" will not be confined to your intellect, but to the care of the whole of the five aggregates. Don't try to seek an intellectual answer. Contemplate for 10 minutes, maintaining light but deep breath to prevent being pulled away by philosophical reflection.

Yourself

Sit in a dark room by yourself, or alone by a river at night, or anywhere else where there is solitude. Begin to take hold of your breath. Give rise to the thought, "I will use my finger to point at myself," and then instead of pointing at your body, point away in the opposite direction. Contemplate seeing yourself outside of your bodily form. Contemplate seeing your bodily form present before you—in the trees, the grass and leaves, the river. Be mindful that you are in the universe and the universe is in you: if the universe is, you are; if you are, the universe is. There is no birth. There is no death. There is no coming. There is no going. Maintain the half smile. Take hold of your breath. Contemplate for 10 to 20 minutes.

Your skeleton

Lie on a bed, or on a mat or on the grass in a position in which you are comfortable. Don't use a pillow. Begin to take hold of your breath. Imagine all that is left of your body is a white skeleton lying on the face of the earth. Maintain the half smile and continue to follow your breath. Imagine that all your flesh has decomposed and is gone, that your skeleton is now lying in the earth 80 years after burial. See clearly the bones of your head, back, your ribs, your hip bones, leg and arm bones, finger bones. Maintain the half smile, breathe very lightly, your heart and mind serene. See that your skeleton is not you. Your bodily form is not you. Be at one with life. Live eternally in the trees and grass, in other people, in the birds and other beasts, in the sky, in the ocean waves. Your skeleton is only one part of you. You are present everywhere and in every moment. You are not only a bodily form, or even feelings, thoughts, actions, and knowledge. Continue for 20 to 30 minutes.

Your true visage before you were born

In the full or half lotus follow your breath. Concentrate on the point of your life's beginning—A. Know that it is also the point of beginning of your death. See that both your life and death are manifested at the same time: *this* is because *that* is, this could not have been if that were not. See that the existence of your life and death depend on each other: one is the foundation of the other. See that you are at the same time your life and your death; that the two are not enemies but two aspects of the same reality. Then concentrate on the point of ending of the twofold manifestation—B—which is wrongly called death. See that it is the ending point of the manifestation of both your life and your death.

See that there is no difference before A and after B. Search for your true face in the periods before A and after B.

A loved one who has died

On a chair or bed, sit or lie in a position you feel comfortable in. Begin to take hold of your breath. Contemplate the body of a loved one who has died, whether a few months or several years ago. Know clearly that all the flesh of the person has decomposed and only a skeleton remains lying quietly beneath the earth. Know clearly that your own flesh is still here and in yourself are still converged the five aggregates of bodily form, feeling, perception, mental functionings, and consciousness. Think of your interaction with that person in the past and right now. Maintain the half smile and take hold of your breath. Contemplate this way for 15 minutes.

Emptiness

Sit in the full or half lotus. Begin to regulate your breath. Contemplate the nature of emptiness in the assembly of the five aggregates: bodily form, feeling, perception, mind functionings, and consciousness. Pass from considering one aggregate to another. See that all transform, are impermanent and without self. The assembly of the five aggregates is like the assembly of all phenomena: all obey the law of interdependence. Their coming together and disbanding from one another resembles the gathering and vanishing of clouds around the peaks of mountains. Neither cling to nor reject the five aggregates. Know that like and dislike are phenomena which belong to the assemblage of the five aggregates. See clearly that the five aggregates are without self and are empty, but that they are also wondrous, wondrous as is each phenomenon in the universe, wondrous as the life which is present everywhere. Try to see that the five aggregates do not really undergo creation and destruction for they themselves are ultimate reality. Try to see by this contemplation that impermanence is a concept, nonself is a concept, emptiness is a concept, so that you will not become imprisoned in the concepts of impermanence, non-self, and emptiness. You will see that emptiness is also empty, and that the ultimate reality of emptiness is no different from the ultimate reality of the five aggregates. (*This exercise should* be practiced *only* after the student has thoroughly practiced the previous five exercises. The amount of time will be according to the individual—perhaps one hour, perhaps two.)

Compassion for the person you hate or despise the most

Sit quietly. Breathe and smile the half smile. Contemplate the image of the person who has caused you the most suffering. Regard the features you hate or despise the most or find the most repulsive. Try to examine what makes this person happy and what causes suffering in his daily life. Contemplate the person's perceptions; try to see what patterns of thought and reason this person follows. Examine what motivates this person's hopes and actions. Finally consider the person's consciousness. See whether his views and insights are open and free or not, and whether or not he has been influenced by any prejudices, narrow-mindedness, hatred, or anger. See whether or not he is master of himself. Continue until you feel compassion rise in your heart like a well filling with fresh water and your anger and resentment disappear. Practice this exercise many times on the same person.

Suffering caused by the lack of wisdom

Sit in the full or half lotus. Begin to follow your breath. Choose the situation of a person, family, or society which is suffering the most of any you know. This will be the object of your contemplation.

In the case of a person, try to see every suffering which that person is undergoing. Begin with the suffering of bodily form (sickness, poverty, physical pain) and then proceed to the suffering caused by feelings (internal conflicts, fear, hatred, jealousy, a tortured conscience). Consider next the suffering caused by perceptions (pessimism, dwelling on his problems with a dark and narrow viewpoint). See whether his mind functionings are motivated by fear, discouragement, despair, or hatred. See whether or not his consciousness is shut off because of his situation, because of his suffering, because of the people around him, his education, propaganda, or a lack of control of his own self. Meditate on all these sufferings until your heart fills with compassion like a well of fresh water, and you are able to see that the person suffers because of circumstances and ignorance. Resolve to help that person get out of his present situation through the most silent and unpretentious means possible.

In the case of a family, follow the same method. Go through all the sufferings of one person and then on to the next person until you have examined the sufferings of the entire family. See that their sufferings are your own. See that it is not possible to reproach even one person in that group. See that you must help them liberate themselves from their present situation by the most silent and unpretentious means possible.

In the case of a society, take the situation of a country suffering war or any other situation of injustice. Try to see that every person involved in the conflict is a victim. See that no person, including all those in warring parties or in what appear to be opposing sides, desires the suffering to continue. See that it is not only one or a few persons who are to blame for the situation. See that the situation is possible because of the clinging to ideologies and to an unjust world economic system which is upheld by every person through ignorance or through lack of resolve to change it. See that two sides in a conflict are not really opposing, but two aspects of the same reality. See that the most essential thing is life and that killing or oppressing one another will not solve anything. Remember the Sutra's words:

> In the time of war
> Raise in yourself the Mind of Compassion
> Help living beings
> Abandon the will to fight
> Wherever there is furious battle
> Use all your might
> To keep both sides' strength equal
> And then step into the conflict to reconcile

Vimalakirti Nirdesa

Meditate until every reproach and hatred disappears, and compassion and love rise like a well of fresh water within you. Vow to work for awareness and reconciliation by the most silent and unpretentious means possible.

Detached action

Sit in the full or half lotus. Follow your breath. Take a project in rural development or any other project which you consider important, as the subject of your contemplation. Examine the purpose of the work, the methods to be used, and the people involved. Consider first the purpose of the project. See that the work is to serve, to alleviate suffering, to respond to compassion, not to satisfy the desire for praise or recognition. See that the methods used encourage cooperation between humans. Don't consider the project as an act of charity. Consider the people involved. Do you still see in terms of ones who serve and ones who benefit? If you can still see who are the ones serving and who are the ones benefiting, your work is for the sake of yourself and the workers, and not for the sake of service. The Prajnaparamita Sutra says, "The Bodhisattva helps row living beings to the other shore but in fact no living beings are being helped to the other shore." Determine to work in the spirit of detached action.

Detachment

Sit in the full or half lotus. Follow your breath.
Recall the most significant achievements in
your life and examine each of them. Examine
your talent, your virtue, your capacity, the
convergence of favorable conditions that have
led to success. Examine the complacency and
the arrogance that have arisen from the feeling
that you are the main cause for such success.
Shed the light of interdependence on the whole
matter to see that the achievement is not really
yours but the convergence of various conditions
beyond your reach. See to it that you will not
be bound to these achievements. Only when
you can relinquish them can you really be free
and no longer assailed by them.

Recall the bitterest failures in your life
and examine each of them. Examine your talent,
your virtue, your capacity, and the absence of
favorable conditions that led to the failures.
Examine to see all the complexes that have
arisen within you from the feeling that you are
not capable of realizing success. Shed the light
of interdependence on the whole matter to see
that failures cannot be accounted for by your
inabilities but rather by the lack of favorable
conditions. See that you have no strength to
shoulder these failures, that these failures
are not your own self. See to it that you are free
from them. Only when you can relinquish them
can you really be free and no longer assailed
by them.

Contemplation on non-abandonment

Sit in the full or half lotus. Follow your breath. Apply one of the exercises on interdependence: yourself, your skeleton, or one who has died. See that everything is impermanent and without eternal identity. See that although things are impermanent and without lasting identity, they are nonetheless wondrous. While you are not bound by the conditioned, neither are you bound by the non-conditioned. See that the saint, though he is not caught by the teaching of interdependence, neither does he get away from the teaching. Although he can abandon the teaching as if it were cold ashes, still he can dwell in it and not be drowned. He is like a boat upon the water. Contemplate to see that awakened people, while not being enslaved by the work of serving living beings, never abandon their work of serving living beings.

❀ Nhat Hanh:
Seeing with
the Eyes of Compassion

by James Forest

In 1968, I was traveling with Thich Nhat Hanh on a Fellowship [of Reconciliation] tour during which there were meetings with church and student groups, senators, journalists, professors, business people, and (blessed relief) a few poets. Almost everywhere he went, this brown-robed Buddhist monk from Vietnam (looking many years younger than the man in his forties he was) quickly disarmed those he met.

His gentleness, intelligence, and sanity made it impossible for most who encountered him to hang on to their stereotypes of what the Vietnamese were like. The vast treasury of the Vietnamese and Buddhist past spilled over through his stories and explanations. His interest in Christianity, even his enthusiasm for it, often inspired Christians to shed their condescension toward Nhat Hanh's tradition. He was able to help thousands of Americans glimpse the war through the eyes of peasants laboring in rice paddies and raising their children and grandchildren in villages surrounded by ancient groves of bamboo. He awoke the child within the adult as he described the craft of the village kite-maker and the sound of the wind instruments these fragile vessels would carry toward the clouds.

After an hour with him, one was haunted with the beauties of Vietnam, and filled with anguish at America's military intervention in the political and cultural tribulations of the Vietnamese people. One was stripped of all the ideological loyalties that justified one party or another in their battles, and felt the horror of the skies raked with bombers, houses and humans burned to ash, children left to face life without the presence and love of their parents and grandparents.

But there was one evening when Nhat Hanh awoke not understanding but rather the measureless rage of one American. He had been talking in the auditorium of a wealthy Christian church in a St. Louis suburb. As always, he emphasized the need for Americans to stop their bombing and killing in his country. There had been questions and answers when a large man stood up and spoke with searing scorn of the "supposed compassion" of "this Mr. Hanh."

"If you care so much about your people, Mr. Hanh, why are you here? If you care so much for the people who are wounded, why don't you spend your time with them?" At this point my recollection of his words is replaced by the memory of the intense anger which overwhelmed me.

When he finished, I looked toward Nhat Hanh in bewilderment. What could he—or anyone—say? The spirit of the war itself had suddenly filled the room, and it seemed hard to breathe.

There was a silence. Then Nhat Hanh began to speak—quietly, with deep calm, indeed with a sense of personal caring for the man who had just damned him. The words seemed like rain falling on fire. "If you want the tree to grow," he said, "it won't help to water the leaves. You have to water the roots. Many of the roots of the war are here, in your country. To help the people who are to be bombed, to try to protect them from this suffering, I have to come here."

The atmosphere in the room was transformed. In the man's fury we had experienced our own furies; we had seen the world as through a bomb bay. In Nhat Hanh's response we had experienced an alternate possibility: the possibility (here brought to Christians by a Buddhist and to Americans by an "enemy") of overcoming hatred with love, of breaking the seemingly endless chain reaction of violence throughout human history.

But after his response, Nhat Hanh whispered something to the chairman and walked quickly from the room. Sensing something was wrong, I followed him out. It was a cool, clear night. Nhat Hanh stood on the sidewalk beside the church parking lot. He was struggling for air—like someone who had been deeply underwater and who had barely managed to swim to the surface before gasping for breath. It was several minutes before I dared ask him how he was or what had happened.

Nhat Hanh explained that the man's comments had been terribly upsetting. He had wanted to respond to him with anger. So he had made himself breathe deeply and very slowly in order to find a way to respond with calm and understanding. But the breathing had been too slow and too deep.

"Why not be angry with him," I asked. "Even pacifists have a right to be angry."

"If it were just myself, yes. But I am here to speak for Vietnamese peasants. I have to show them what we can be at our best."

The moment was an important one in my life, one pondered again and again since then. For one thing, it was the first time that I realized there was a connection between the way one breathes and the way one responds to the world around.

Until very recently, Nhat Hanh has made no attempt to teach Western people any of the skills of meditation—what he often calls mindfulness. Only during the past year, first with a few Western friends helping the Vietnamese Buddhist Peace Delegation in Paris, later with a group at that city's Quaker International Center, has he begun to teach meditation. Now he has written a small book on the subject, *The Miracle of Mindfulness*, a manual on meditation.

Nhat Hanh is a poet, Zen Master, and a co-chairman of the Fellowship of Reconciliation. In Vietnam, he played a major role in the creation of "engaged Buddhism"—a profound religious renewal rooted in compassion and service out of which emerged countless projects which combined help to the war's victims with nonviolent opposition to the war itself. For their work, thousands of Buddhists—nuns, monks, and lay people—were shot or imprisoned.

His work in Vietnam gave birth to the School of Youth for Social Service, Van Hanh University, a small monastery that was an early base of the nonviolent movement, a pacifist underground press (led by his co-worker Cao Ngoc Phuong), and the La Boi Press, one of the principal vehicles of cultural and religious renewal.

His poetry provides the words of many of the most popular songs in contemporary Vietnam, songs of hope surviving grief.

Even in exile, representing overseas the Unified Buddhist Church of Vietnam, he has continued to be a force for nonviolence and reconciliation in his homeland and an organizer of supportive responses from other countries. (His friendship with Martin Luther King was a factor in Dr. King's decision to ignore the advice of many colleagues and contributors who opposed his "mixing issues" and to join in the opposition to the Vietnam war. Shortly before his assassination, Dr. King nominated Nhat Hanh for the Nobel Prize for Peace.)

Only a few of his books have been published outside of Vietnam: *Lotus in a Sea of Fire, The Cry of Vietnam, The Path of Return Continues the Journey, Zen Keys,* and *The Raft Is Not the Shore.*

During conversations with Nhat Hanh and his co-workers in Paris, in the apartment of the Vietnamese Buddhist Peace Delegation, our thoughts turned to the absence of a meditative dimension in much of the American peace movement. Its absence helped explain why so much of the "peace" movement (perhaps better called the American-withdrawal movement) had exhibited such slight and superficial interest in the Buddhists' nonviolent campaign against the war. The weaponless Buddhists were not judged truly "political," merely a religious movement: admirable, unusually courageous when compared to other religious groups, but peripheral.

What American peace activists might learn from their Vietnamese counterparts is that, until there is a more meditative dimension in the peace movement, our perceptions of reality (and thus our ability to help occasion understanding and transformation) will be terribly crippled. Whatever our religious or nonreligious background and vocabulary may be, we will be overlooking something as essential to our lives and work as breath itself.

Breath itself. Breathing. It comes to many as astonishing news that something as simple as attention to breathing has a central part to play in meditation and prayer. It is like a mystery novelist's idea of hiding the diamonds in the goldfish bowl: too obvious to notice. But since the news has made its way past my own barriers of skepticism, there has been no end of confirmations—principally, the confirmation of experience.

The problem with meditation is that the contexts for it are too close at hand. The chances, as Nhat Hanh points out, are scattered everywhere: in the bathtub, in the kitchen sink, on a cutting board, a sidewalk or path, on a tenement staircase, on a picket line, at a typewriter . . . literally anywhere. The moments and places of silence and stillness are wondrous and helpful, but not indispensable. The meditative life doesn't require a secluded, greenhouse existence. (It does need occasional periods of time, even a whole day of the week, when special attention can be given to becoming more mindful. But then Christians and Jews ought not to be newcomers to the Sabbath.)

To the skeptic, Nhat Hanh's suggestions will seem quite absurd, a bad joke at the end of history, the latest card trick dealt out of the ancient deck of mystical doubletalk. But the pacifist affirmation itself strikes many as no smaller an absurdity: choosing to nurture life and to live without weapons in a murderous world. The way of meditation only carries that personal disarmament we have already begun an essential step deeper—nonviolence not only in the face of governments and corporations and liberation armies but a nonviolent encounter with reality itself.

This is the way to understand a simple truth

Nhat Hanh has mentioned elsewhere: "Those who are without compassion cannot see what is seen with the eyes of compassion." That more inclusive sight makes the small but crucial difference between despair and hope.

❀

Selection of
Buddhist Sutras

🏶 The Foundation of Mindfulness

(Satipaṭṭhāna Sutta)

Translated from the Pali by Nyānasatta

Thus have I heard. At one time the Blessed One was living among the Kurus, at Kammasadamma—a market town of the Kuru people. There the Blessed One addressed the bhikkhus thus: "Monks," and they replied to him, "Venerable Sir." The Blessed One spoke as follows:

This is the only way, monks, for the purification of beings, for the overcoming of sorrow and lamentation, for the destruction of suffering and grief, for reaching the right path, for the attainment of Nirvāna, namely the four Foundations of Mindfulness. What are the four?

Herein (in this teaching) a monk lives contemplating the body in the body, ardent, clearly comprehending and mindful, having overcome, in this world, covetousness and grief; he lives contemplating feelings in feelings, ardent, clearly comprehending and mindful, having overcome, in this world, covetousness and grief; he lives contemplating consciousness in con-

sciousness, ardent, clearly comprehending and mindful, having overcome, in this world, covetousness and
grief; he lives contemplating mental objects in mental
objects, ardent, clearly comprehending and mindful,
having overcome, in this world, covetousness and
grief.

I. The Contemplation of the Body

1. *Mindfulness of Breathing*

And how does a monk live contemplating the body
in the body?

Herein, monks, a monk having gone to the forest,
to the foot of a tree or to an empty place, sits down,
with his legs crossed, keeps his body erect and his
mindfulness alert.

Ever mindful he breathes in, and mindful he
breathes out. Breathing in a long breath, he knows "I
am breathing in a long breath"; breathing out a long
breath, he knows "I am breathing out a long breath";
breathing in a short breath, he knows "I am breathing
in a short breath"; breathing out a short breath, he
knows "I am breathing out a short breath."

"Experiencing the whole (breath-) body, I shall
breathe in," thus he trains himself. "Experiencing the
whole (breath-) body, I shall breathe out," thus he
trains himself. "Calming the activity of the (breath-)
body, I shall breathe in," thus he trains himself. "Calming the activity of the (breath-) body, I shall breathe
out," thus he trains himself.

Just as a skillful turner or turner's apprentice, making a long turn, knows "I am making a long turn," or
making a short turn, knows, "I am making a short

turn," just so the monk, breathing in a long breath, knows "I am breathing in a long breath"; breathing out a long breath, knows "I am breathing out a long breath"; breathing in a short breath, knows "I am breathing in a short breath"; breathing out a short breath, knows "I am breathing out a short breath." "Experiencing the whole (breath-) body, I shall breathe in," thus he trains himself. "Experiencing the whole (breath-) body, I shall breathe out," thus he trains himself. "Calming the activity of the (breath-) body, I shall breathe in," thus he trains himself. "Calming the activity of the (breath-) body, I shall breathe out," thus he trains himself.

Thus he lives contemplating the body in the body internally, or he lives contemplating the body in the body, internally and externally. He lives contemplating origination-factors in the body, or he lives contemplating origination-and-dissolution factors in the body. Or his mindfulness is established with the thought: "The body exists," to the extent necessary just for knowledge and mindfulness, and he lives detached, and clings to naught in the world. Thus also, monks, a monk lives contemplating the body in the body.

2. The Postures of the Body

And further, monks, a monk knows when he is going "I am going"; he knows when he is standing "I am standing"; he knows when he is sitting "I am sitting"; he knows when he is lying down "I am lying down"; or just as his body is disposed so he knows it.

Thus he lives contemplating the body in the body internally, or he lives contemplating the body in the body externally, or he lives contemplating the body in the body internally and externally. He lives contemplating origination-factors in the body, or he lives contemplating origination-and-dissolution factors in the body. Or his mindfulness is established with the thought: "The body exists," to the extent necessary just for knowledge and mindfulness, and he lives detached, and clings to naught in the world. Thus also, monks, a monk lives contemplating the body in the body.

3. Mindfulness with Clear Comprehension

And further, monks, a monk, in going forward and back, applies clear comprehension; in looking away, he applies clear comprehension; in bending and in stretching, he applies clear comprehension; in wearing robes and carrying the bowl, he applies clear comprehension; in eating, drinking, chewing, and savoring, he applies clear comprehension; in attending to the calls of nature, he applies clear comprehension; in walking, standing, in sitting, in falling asleep, in waking, in speaking and in keeping silence, he applies clear comprehension.

Thus he lives contemplating the body in the body . . .

4. The Reflection on the Repulsiveness of the Body

And further, monks, a monk reflects on this very body enveloped by the skin and full of manifold impurity, from the soles up, and from the top of the head-hair down, thinking thus: "There are in this body hair of the head, hair of the body, nails, teeth, skin, flesh, sinews, bones, marrow, kidneys, heart, liver, midriff, spleen, lungs, intestines, mesentery, gorge, feces, bile, phlegm, pus, blood, sweat, fat, tears, grease, saliva, nasal mucus, synovial fluid, urine."

Just as if there were a double-mouthed provision bag full of various kinds of grain such as hill paddy, paddy, green gram, cow-peas, sesame, and husked rice, and a man with sound eyes, having opened that bag, were to take stock of the contents thus: This is hill paddy, this is paddy, this is green gram, this is cow-pea, this is sesame, this is husked rice. Just so, monks, a monk reflects on this very body enveloped by the skin and full of manifold impurity, from the soles up, and from the top of the head-hair down, thinking thus: "There are in this body hair of the head, hair of the body, nails, teeth, skin, flesh, sinews, bones, marrow, kidneys, heart, liver, midriff, spleen, lungs, intestines, mesentery, gorge, feces, bile, phlegm, pus, blood, sweat, fat, tears, grease, saliva, nasal mucus, synovial fluid, urine."

Thus he lives contemplating the body in the body . . .

5. The Reflection on the Material Elements

And further, monks, a monk reflects on this very body, however it be placed or disposed, by way of the material elements: "There are in this body the element of earth, the element of water, the element of fire, the element of wind."

Just as if, monks, a clever cow-butcher or his apprentice, having slaughtered a cow and divided it into portions, should be sitting at the junction of four high roads, in the same way, a monk reflects on this very body, as it is placed or disposed, by way of the material elements: "There are in this body the elements of earth, water, fire, and wind."

Thus he lives contemplating the body in the body . . .

6. *The Nine Cemetery Contemplations*

And further, monks, as if a monk sees a body dead one, two, or three days; swollen, blue, and festering, thrown in the charnel ground, he then applies this perception to his own body thus: "Verily, also my own body is of the same nature; such it will become and will not escape it."

Thus he lives contemplating the body in the body internally, or lives contemplating the body in the body externally, or lives contemplating the body in the body internally and externally. He lives contemplating origination-factors in the body, or he lives contemplating dissolution-factors in the body, or he lives contemplating origination-and-dissolution-factors in the body. Or his mindfulness is established with the thought: "The body exists," to the extent necessary just for knowledge and mindfulness, and he lives independent, and clings to naught in the world. Thus also, monks, a monk lives contemplating the body in the body.

2. And further, monks, as if a monk sees a body thrown in the charnel ground, being eaten by crows, hawks, vultures, dogs, jackals, or by different kinds of worms, he then applies this perception to his own body thus: "Verily, also my own body is of the same nature; such it will become and will not escape it."

Thus he lives contemplating the body in the body . . .

3. And further, monks, as if a monk sees a body thrown in the charnel ground and reduced to a skeleton with some flesh and blood attached to it, held together by the tendons . . .

4. And further, monks, as if a monk sees a body thrown in the charnel ground, and reduced to a skeleton, blood-besmeared and 'without flesh, held together by the tendons . . .

5. And further, monks, as if a monk sees a body thrown in the charnel ground and reduced to a skeleton without flesh and blood, held together by the tendons . . .

6. And further, monks, as if a monk sees a body thrown in the charnel ground and reduced to disconnected bones, scattered in all directions—here a bone of the hand, there a bone of the foot, a shin bone, a thigh bone, the pelvis, spine and skull . . .

7. And further, monks, as if a monk sees a body thrown in the charnel ground, reduced to bleached bones of conch-like color . . .

8. And further, monks, as if a monk sees a body thrown in the charnel ground, reduced to bones, more than a year old, lying in a heap . . .

9. And further, monks, as if a monk sees a body thrown in the charnel ground, reduced to bones, gone rotten and become dust, he then applies this perception to his own body thus: "Verily, also my own body is of the same nature; such it will become and will not escape it."

Thus he lives contemplating the body in the body internally, or he lives contemplating the body in the body externally, or he lives contemplating the body in the body internally and externally. He lives contemplating origination-factors in the body, or he lives contemplating dissolution-factors in the body, or he lives contemplating origination-and-dissolution-factors in the body. Or his mindfulness is established with the thought: "The body exists," to the extent necessary just for knowledge and mindfulness, and he lives detached, and clings to naught in the world. Thus also, monks, a monk lives contemplating the body in the body.

II. The Contemplation of Feeling

And how, monks, does a monk live contemplating feelings in feelings?

Herein, monks, a monk when experiencing a pleasant feeling knows, "I experience a pleasant feeling"; when experiencing a painful feeling, he knows, "I experience a painful feeling"; when experiencing a neither pleasant nor painful feeling, he knows, "I experience a neither pleasant nor painful feeling"; when experiencing a pleasant worldly feeling, he knows, "I experience a pleasant worldly feeling"; when experiencing a pleasant spiritual feeling, he knows, "I experience a pleasant spiritual feeling"; when experiencing a painful worldly feeling, he knows, "I experience a painful worldly feeling"; when experiencing a painful spiritual feeling, he knows, "I experience a painful spiritual feeling"; when experiencing a neither pleasant nor painful worldly feeling, he knows, "I experience a neither pleasant nor painful worldly feeling"; when experiencing a neither pleasant nor painful spiritual feeling, he knows, "I experience a neither pleasant nor painful spiritual feeling."

Thus he lives contemplating feelings in feelings internally, or he lives contemplating feelings in feelings externally, or he lives contemplating feelings in feelings internally and externally. He lives contemplating origination-factors in feelings, or he lives contemplating dissolution-factors in feelings, or he lives contemplating origination-and-dissolution factors in feelings. Or his mindfulness is established with the thought, "Feeling exists," to the extent necessary just for knowledge and mindfulness, and he lives detached, and clings to naught in the world. Thus, monks, a monk lives contemplating feelings in feelings.

III. The Contemplation of Consciousness

And how, monks, does a monk live contemplating consciousness in consciousness?

Herein, monks, a monk knows the consciousness with lust, as with lust; the consciousness without lust, as without lust; the consciousness with hate, as with hate; the consciousness without hate, as without hate; the consciousness with ignorance, as with ignorance; the consciousness without ignorance, as without ignorance; the shrunken state of consciousness as the shrunken state; the distracted state of consciousness as the distracted state; the developed state of consciousness as the developed state; the undeveloped state of consciousness as the undeveloped state; the state of consciousness with some other mental state superior to it, as the state with something mentally higher; the state of consciousness with no other mental state superior to it, as the state with nothing mentally higher;

the concentrated state of consciousness as the concentrated state; the unconcentrated state of consciousness as the unconcentrated state; the freed state of consciousness as the freed state; and the unfreed state of unconsciousness as the unfreed.

Thus he lives contemplating consciousness in consciousness internally or he lives contemplating consciousness in consciousness externally, or he lives contemplating consciousness in consciousness internally and externally. He lives contemplating origination-factors in consciousness, or he lives contemplating dissolution-factors in consciousness, or he lives contemplating origination-and-dissolution-factors in conousness. Or his mindfulness is established with the thought, "Consciousness exists," to the extent necessary just for knowledge and mindfulness, and he lives detached and clings to naught in the world. Thus, monks, a monk lives contemplating consciousness in consciousness.

IV. The Contemplation of Mental Objects

1. The Five Hindrances

And how, monks, does a monk live contemplating mental objects in mental objects?

Herein, monks, a monk lives contemplating mental objects in the mental objects of the five hindrances.

How, monks, does a monk live contemplating mental objects in the mental objects of the five hindrances?

Herein, monks, a monk, when sense-desire is present, knows, "There is sense-desire in me," or when sense-desire is not present, he knows, "There is no sense desire in me." He knows how the arising of the nonarisen sense-desire comes to be; he knows how the abandoning of the arisen sense-desire comes to be; and he knows how the nonarising in the future of the abandoned sense-desire comes to be.

When anger is present, he knows, "There is anger in me," or when anger is not present, he knows, "There is no anger in me." He knows how the arising of the nonarisen anger comes to be; he knows how the abandoning of the arisen anger comes to be; and he knows how the nonarising in the future of the abandoned anger comes to be.

When sloth and torpor are present, he knows, "There are sloth and torpor in me," and when sloth and torpor are not present, he knows, "There are no sloth and torpor in me." He knows how the arising of the nonarisen sloth and torpor comes to be; he knows how the abandoning of the arisen sloth and torpor comes to be; and he knows how the nonarising in the future of the abandoned sloth and torpor comes to be.

When agitation and scruples are present, he knows, "There are agitation and scruples in me," or when agitation and scruples are not present, he knows, "There are no agitation and scruples in me." He knows how the arising of the nonarisen agitation and scruples comes to be; he knows how the abandoning of the arisen agitation and scruples comes to be; and he knows how the nonarising in the future of the abandoned agitation and scruples comes to be.

When doubt is present, he knows, "There is doubt in me," or when doubt is not present, he knows, "There is no doubt in me." He knows how the arising of the nonarisen doubt comes to be; he knows how the abandoning of the arisen doubt comes to be; he knows how the nonarising in the future of the abandoned doubt comes to be.

Thus he lives contemplating mental objects in mental objects internally, or he lives contemplating mental objects in mental objects externally, or he lives contemplating mental objects in mental objects internally and externally. He lives contemplating origination-factors in mental objects, or he lives contemplating dissolution-factors in mental objects, or he lives contemplating origination-and-dissolution-factors in mental objects. Or his mindfulness is established with the thought, "Mental objects exist," to the extent necessary just for knowledge and mindfulness, and he lives detached, and clings to naught in the world. Thus also, monks, a monk lives contemplating mental objects in the mental objects of the five hindrances.

2. *The Five Aggregates of Clinging*

And further, monks, a monk lives contemplating mental objects in the mental objects of the five aggregates of clinging.

How, monks, does a monk live contemplating mental objects in the mental objects of the five aggregates of clinging?

Herein, monks, a monk thinks, "Thus is material form; thus is the arising of material form; and thus is the disappearance of material form. Thus is feeling; thus is the arising of feeling; thus is the disappearance of feeling. Thus is perception; thus is the arising of perception; thus is the disappearance of perception. Thus are formations; thus is the arising of formations; and thus is the disappearance of formations. Thus is consciousness; thus is the arising of consciousness; and thus is the disappearance of consciousness."

Thus he lives contemplating mental objects in mental objects internally, or he lives contemplating mental objects in mental objects externally, or he lives contemplating mental objects in mental objects internally and externally. He lives contemplating origination-factors in mental objects, or he lives contemplating dissolution-factors in mental objects, or he lives contemplating origination-and-dissolution-factors in mental objects. Or his mindfulness is established with the thought, "Mental objects exist," to the extent necessary just for knowledge and mindfulness, and he lives detached, and clings to naught in the world. Thus also, monks, a monk lives contemplating mental objects in the mental objects of the five aggregates of clinging.

3. *The Six Internal and the Six External Sense-Bases*

And further, monks, a monk lives contemplating mental objects in the mental objects of the six internal and the six external sense-bases.

How, monks, does a monk live contemplating mental objects in the mental objects of the six internal and the six external sense-bases?

Herein, monks, a monk knows the eye and visual forms, and the fetter that arises dependent on both (the eye and forms); he knows how the arising of the nonarisen fetter comes to be; he knows how the abandoning of the arisen fetter comes to be; and he knows how the nonarising in the future of the abandoned fetter comes to be.

He knows the ear and sounds . . . the nose and smells . . . the tongue and flavors . . . the body and tactile objects . . . the mind and mental objects, and the fetter that arises dependent on both; he knows how the abandoning of the nonarisen fetter comes to be; and he knows how the nonarising in the future of the abandoned fetter comes to be.

Thus, monks, the monk lives contemplating mental objects in mental objects internally, or he lives contemplating mental objects in mental objects externally, or he lives contemplating mental objects in mental objects internally and externally. He lives contemplating origination-factors in mental objects, or he lives contemplating dissolution-factors in mental objects, or he lives contemplating origination-and-dissolution-factors in mental objects. Or his mindfulness is established with the thought, "Mental objects exist," to the extent necessary just for knowledge and mindfulness, and he lives detached, and clings to naught in the world. Thus, monks, a monk lives contemplating mental objects in the mental objects of the six internal and the six external sense-bases.

4. *The Seven Factors of Enlightenment*

And further, monks, a monk lives contemplating mental objects in the mental objects of the seven factors of enlightenment.

How, monks, does a monk live contemplating mental objects in the mental objects of the seven factors of enlightenment?

Herein, monks, when the enlightenment-factor of mindfulness is present the monk knows, "The enlightenment-factor of mindfulness is in me," or when the enlightenment-factor of mindfulness is absent, he knows, "The enlightenment-factor of mindfulness is not in me"; and he knows how the arising of the nonarisen enlightenment-factor of mindfulness comes to be; and how perfection in the development of the arisen enlightenment-factor of mindfulness comes to be.

When the enlightenment-factor of the investigation of mental objects is present, the monk knows, "The enlightenment-factor of the investigation of mental objects is in me"; when the enlightenment-factor of the investigation of mental objects is absent, he knows, "The enlightenment-factor of the investigation of mental objects is not in me"; and he knows how the arising of the nonarisen enlightenment-factor of the investigation of mental objects comes to be, and how perfection in the development of the arisen enlightenment-factor of the investigation of mental objects comes to be.

When the enlightenment-factor of energy is present, he knows, "The enlightenment-factor of energy is in me"; when the enlightenment-factor of energy is absent, he knows, "The enlightenment-factor of energy is not in me"; and he knows how the arising of the nonarisen enlightenment-factor of energy comes to be, and how perfection in the development of the arisen enlightenment-factor of energy comes to be.

When the enlightenment-factor of joy is present, he knows, "The enlightenment-factor of joy is in me"; and when the enlightenment-factor of joy is absent, he knows, "The enlightenment-factor of joy is not in me"; and he knows how the arising of the nonarisen enlightenment-factor of joy comes to be, and how perfection in the development of the arisen enlightenment-factor of joy comes to be.

When the enlightenment-factor of tranquility is present, he knows, "The enlightenment-factor of tranquility is in me"; when the enlightenment-factor of tranquility is absent, he knows, "The enlightenment-factor of tranquility is not in me"; and he knows how the arising of the nonarisen enlightenment-factor of tranquility comes to be, and how perfection in the development of the arisen enlightenment-factor of tranquility comes to be.

When the enlightenment-factor of concentration is present, he knows, "The enlightenment-factor of concentration is in me"; when the enlightenment-factor of concentration is absent, he knows, "The enlightenment-factor of concentration is not in me"; and he knows how the arising of the nonarisen enlightenment-factor of concentration comes to be, and how perfection in the development of the arisen enlightenment-factor of concentration comes to be.

When the enlightenment-factor of equanimity is present, he knows, "The enlightenment-factor of equanimity is in me"; when the enlightenment factor of equanimity is absent, he knows, "The enlightenment-factor of equanimity is not in me"; and he knows how the arising of the nonarisen enlightenment-factor of equanimity comes to be, and how perfection in the development of the arisen enlightment-factor of equanimity comes to be.

Thus he lives contemplating mental objects in mental objects internally, or he lives contemplating mental objects in mental objects externally, or he lives contemplating mental objects in mental objects internally and externally. He lives contemplating origination-factors in mental objects, or he lives contemplating dissolution-factors in mental objects, or he lives contemplating origination-and-dissolution-factors in mental objects. Or his mindfulness is established with the thought, "Mental objects exist," to the extent necessary just for knowledge and mindfulness, and he lives detached, and clings to naught in the world. Thus, monks, a monk lives contemplating mental objects in mental objects of the seven factors of enlightenment.

5. The Four Noble Truths

And further, monks, a monk lives contemplating mental objects in the mental objects of the four noble truths.

How monks, does a monk live contemplating mental objects in the mental objects of the four noble truths?

Herein, monks, a monk knows, "This is suffering," according to reality; he knows, "This is the origin of suffering," according to reality; he knows "This is the cessation of suffering," according to reality; he knows, "This is the road leading to the cessation of suffering," according to reality.

Thus he lives contemplating mental objects in mental objects internally, or he lives contemplating mental objects in mental objects externally, or he lives contemplating mental objects in mental objects internally and externally. He lives contemplating origination-factors in mental objects, or he lives contemplating dissolution-factors in mental objects, or he lives contemplating origination-and-dissolution-factors in mental objects. Or his mindfulness is established with the thought, "Mental objects exist," to the extent necessary just for knowledge and mindfulness, and he lives detached, and clings to naught in the world. Thus, monks, a monk lives contemplating mental objects in the mental objects of the four noble truths.

Verily, monks, whosoever practices these four Foundations of Mindfulness in this manner for seven years, then one of these two fruits may be expected by him: Highest Knowledge (Arhatship), here and now, or if some remainder of clinging is yet present, the state of Nonreturning.

O monks, let alone seven years. Should any person practicing these four Foundations of Mindfulness in this manner for six years . . . for five years . . . three years . . . two years . . . one year, then one of these two fruits may be expected by him: Highest Knowledge, here and now, or if some remainder of clinging is yet present, the state of Nonreturning.

O monks, let alone a year. Should any person practice these four Foundations on Mindfulness in this manner for seven months . . . for six months . . . five months . . . four months . . . three months . . . two months . . . a month . . . half a month, then one of these two fruits may be expected by him: Highest Knowledge, here and now, or if some remainder of clinging is yet present, the state of Nonreturning.

O monks, let alone half a month. Should any person practice these four Foundations of Mindfulness in this manner, for a week, then one of these two fruits may be expected by him: Highest Knowledge, here and now, or if some remainder of clinging is yet present, the state of Nonreturning.

Because of this it is said: "This is the only way, monks, for the purification of beings, for the overcoming of sorrow and lamentation, for the destruction of suffering and grief, for reaching the right path, for the attainment of Nirvāna, namely the four Foundations of Mindfulness."

Thus spoke the Blessed One. Satisfied, the monks approved of his words.

The Discourse on Mindfulness of Breathing

(Anāpānasati Sutta)

Translated from the Pali by Nyānaponika

Mindfulness of Breathing, monks, cultivated and regularly practiced, is of great fruit and great benefit. Mindfulness of Breathing, cultivated and regularly practiced, brings to Perfection the four Foundations of Mindfulness. The four Foundations of Mindfulness, cultivated and regularly practiced, bring the seven Factors of Enlightenment to perfection; the seven Factors of Enlightenment, cultivated and regularly practiced, bring wisdom and deliverance to perfection.

And how cultivated and regularly practiced, is Mindfulness of Breathing of great fruit and benefit?

Herein, monks, a monk having gone to the forest, to the foot of a tree, or to an empty place, sits down cross-legged, keeps his body erect and his mindfulness alert. Just mindful he breathes in, mindful he breathes out.

I. The First Tetrad (Contemplation of the Body)

1. Breathing in a long breath, he knows, "I breathe in a long breath"; breathing out a long breath, he knows, "I breathe out a long breath."

2. Breathing in a short breath, he knows, "I breathe in a short breath"; breathing out a short breath, he knows, "I breathe out a short breath."

3. "Experiencing the whole (breath-) body I shall breathe in," thus he trains himself; "Experiencing the whole (breath-) body I shall breathe out," thus he trains himself.

4. "Calming the bodily function (of breathing) I shall breathe in," thus he trains himself; "Calming the bodily function (of breathing) I shall breathe out," thus he trains himself.

II. The Second Tetrad (Contemplation of Feelings)

5. "Experiencing rapture I shall breathe in (I shall breathe out)," thus he trains himself.

6. "Experiencing happiness I shall breathe in (I shall breathe out)," thus he trains himself.

7. "Experiencing the mental functions I shall breathe in (I shall breathe out)," thus he trains himself.

8. "Calming the mental functions I shall breathe in (I shall breathe out)," thus he trains himself.

III. The Third Tetrad (Contemplation of the Mind)

9. "Experiencing the mind I shall breathe in (I shall breathe out)," thus he trains himself.

10. "Gladdening the mind I shall breathe in (I shall breathe out)," thus he trains himself.

11. "Concentrating the mind, I shall breathe in (I shall breathe out)," thus he trains himself.

12. "Liberating the mind I shall breathe in (I shall breathe out)," thus he trains himself.

IV. The Fourth Tetrad (Contemplation of Mind-objects)

13. "Contemplating impermanence I shall breathe in (I shall breathe out)," thus he trains himself.

14. "Contemplating dispassion I shall breathe in (I shall breathe out)," thus he trains himself.

15. "Contemplating cessation I shall breathe in (I shall breathe out)," thus he trains himself.

16. "Contemplating relinquishment I shall breathe in (I shall breathe out)," thus he trains himself.

17. In that way, cultivated and regularly practiced, monks, Mindfulness of Breathing brings great fruit and benefit.

Perfecting the Foundations of Mindfulness

And how cultivated, how regularly practiced brings Mindfulness of Breathing the four Foundations of Mindfulness to perfection?

I. Whenever a monk mindfully breathes in and out a long breath, or a short breath; or when he trains himself to breathe in and out while experiencing the bodily function (of breathing); or while calming that function—at that time, monks, he dwells practicing body-contemplation on the body, ardent, clearly comprehending, and mindful; having overcome covetousness and grief concerning the world. For, breathing in and out, monks, I say, is one of the bodily processes.

II. Whenever the monk trains himself to breathe in and out while experiencing rapture; or while experiencing happiness; or while experiencing the mental functions; or while calming the mental functions—at those times, monks, he dwells practicing feeling-contemplation on feelings, ardent, clearly comprehending, and mindful, having overcome covetousness and grief concerning the world. For the full attention to breathing in and out, I say, is one of the feelings.

III. Whenever a monk trains himself to breathe in and out while experiencing the mind; or while gladdening the mind; or while concentrating the mind; or while liberating the mind—at that time he dwells practicing mind-contemplation on the mind, ardent, clearly comprehending, and mindful, having overcome covetousness and grief concerning the world. For one who lacks mindfulness and clear comprehension, I say, cannot develop Mindfulness of Breathing.

IV. Whenever a monk trains himself to breathe in and out while contemplating impermanence, dispassion, cessation, or relinquishment—at that time he dwells practicing mind-object contemplation on mind-objects, ardent, clearly comprehending, and mindful, having overcome covetousness and grief concerning the world. Having wisely seen the abandoning of covetousness and grief, he looks on with perfect equanimity.

Mindfulness of Breathing, monks, in that way cultivated and regularly practiced, brings the four Foundations of Mindfulness to perfection.

And how do the four Foundations cultivated and regularly practiced, bring the seven Factors of Enlightenment to perfection?

Whenever a monk dwells in the contemplation of

body, feelings, mind, and mind-objects, ardent . . . unclouded mindfulness becomes established in him. And when unclouded mindfulness is established in him, at that time the enlightenment-factor "Mindfulness" is initiated in the monk; at that time the monk develops the enlightenment-factor Mindfulness; at that time he gains perfection in the development of the enlightenment-factor "Mindfulness."

Dwelling mindful in that manner, he wisely investigates, examines, and scrutinizes the respective object; and while doing so, the enlightenment-factor "Investigation of Reality" is initiated in the monk; at that time the monk develops the enlightenment-factor "Investigation of Reality"; at that time he gains perfection in the development of the enlightenment-factor "Investigation of Reality."

While he wisely investigates, examines, and scrutinizes that object, unremitting energy is initiated in him. And when the unremitting factor "Energy" is initiated in him, at that time the monk develops the enlightenment-factor "Energy"; at that time he gains perfection in the development of the enlightenment-factor "Energy."

In him possessed of energy unworldly rapture arises. And when in a monk possessed of energy unworldly rapture arises, at that time the enlightenment-factor "Rapture" is initiated in him; at that time the monk develops the enlightenment-factor "Rapture"; at that time the monk gains perfection in the development of the enlightenment-factor "Rapture."

The body and mind of one who is filled with rapture become tranquil. And when the body and mind of one who is filled with rapture become tranquil, at that time the enlightenment-factor "Tranquility" is initiated in him; at that time the monk develops the enlightenment-factor "Tranquility."

The mind of one who is tranquil and happy becomes concentrated. And when the mind of a monk who is tranquil and happy becomes concentrated, at that time the enlightenment-factor "Concentration" is initiated in him; at that time the monk develops the enlightenment-factor "Concentration"; at that time he gains perfection in the development of the enlightenment-factor "Concentration."

On the mind thus concentrated he looks with perfect equanimity. And when looking on his concentrated mind with perfect equanimity, at that time the enlightenment factor "Equanimity" is initiated in him; at that time the monk develops the enlightenment-factor "Equanimity"; at that time he gains perfection in the development of the enlightenment-factor "Equanimity."

The four Foundations of Mindfulness, in that way cultivated and regularly practiced, bring the seven Factors of Enlightenment to perfection.

And how do the seven Factors of Enlightenment, cultivated and regularly practiced, bring wisdom and deliverance to perfection?

Herein, monks, a monk develops the enlightenment-factors Mindfulness, Investigation of Reality, Energy, Rapture, Tranquility, Concentration, and Equanimity, based on detachment, based on dispassion, based on cessation, resulting in relinquishment.

The seven Factors of Enlightenment, in that way cultivated and regularly practiced, bring wisdom and deliverance to perfection.

Thus spoke the Exalted One. Glad in heart the monks rejoiced in the words of the Blessed One.

Contemplation of Thought

From Siksāsamuccaya

Translated from the Sanskrit by Edward Conze

He searches all around for his thought. But what thought? It is either passionate, or hateful, or confused. What about the past, future, or present? What is past that is extinct, what is future that has not yet arrived, and the present has no stability. For thought, Kasyapa, cannot be apprehended, inside, or outside, or in between both. For thought is immaterial, invisible, nonresisting, inconceivable, unsupported, and homeless. Thought has never been seen by any of the Buddhas, nor do they see it, nor will they see it. And what the Buddhas never see, how can that be an observable process, except in the sense that dharmas proceed by the way of mistaken perception? Thought is like a magical illusion; by an imagination of what is actually unreal it takes hold of a manifold variety of rebirths. A thought is like the stream of a river, without any staying power; as soon as it is produced it breaks up and disappears. A thought is like the flame of a lamp, and it proceeds through causes and conditions. A thought is like lightning, it breaks up in a moment and does not stay on. . . .

Searching for thought all round, he does not see it within or without. He does not see it in the skandhas, or in the elements, or in the sense-fields. Unable to see thought, he seeks to find the trend of thought, and asks himself: Whence is the genesis of thought? And it occurs to him that "where there is an object, there thought arises." Is then the thought one thing, and the object another? No, what is the object, just that is the thought. If the object were one thing, and the thought another, then there would be a double state of thought. So the object itself is just thought. Can then thought review thought? No, thought cannot review thought. As the blade of a sword cannot cut itself, so a thought cannot see itself. Moreover, vexed and pressed hard on all sides, thought proceeds, without any staying power, like a monkey or like the wind. It ranges far, bodiless, easily changing, agitated by the objects of sense, with the six sense-fields for its sphere, connected with one thing after another. The stability of thought, its one-pointedness, its immobility, its undistraughtness, its one-pointed calm, its nondistraction, that is on the other hand called mindfulness as to thought.

❀ Not Dwelling on the Nonconditioned

From the Vimalakirtinirdesa Sutra

Translated from the Chinese by Nhat Hanh

What does it mean, "not dwelling on the Nonconditioned"? The bodhisattva contemplates the reality of Emptiness but does not take Emptiness as an object of attainment. The bodhisattva practices the reality of Nonappearance and Nonpursuit but does not take Nonappearance or Nonpursuit as an object of attainment. He contemplates the reality of Noncreation but does not take Noncreation as an object of attainment. He meditates on the truth of Impermanence but does not abandon his work to serve and save. He meditates on Suffering but does not reject the world of births and deaths. He meditates on Extinction but does not embrace Extinction. He meditates on Detachment but goes on realizing good things in the world. He meditates on the homeless nature of dharmas but continues to orientate himself toward the Good. He meditates on the reality of Neither-creation-nor-destruction but still undertakes the responsibility in the world of creations and destructions. He meditates on the reality of the

Ultimate but still dwells in the world of interdependent origins. He meditates on Nonaction but continues always his acts of service and education. He meditates on Emptiness but does not abandon Great Compassion. He meditates on the Position of the True Dharma but does not follow a rigid path. He meditates on the Unreal, Impermanent, Unoriginated, Nonpossessed, and Markless nature of dharmas but does not abandon his career concerning merits, concentration, and wisdom. Practicing in that way, the bodhisattva is described as "not dwelling on the Nonconditioned." He has wisdom but does not end his action in the realm of the conditioned; he has compassion but does not dwell in the Nonconditioned; he wants to realize his great Vow but he will not abandon the conditioned world.

❀ The Heart of the Prajñāpāramitā

Translated from the Chinese by Nhat Hanh

The bodhisattva Avalokita, while moving in the deep course of the Perfect Wisdom, shed light on the five aggregates and found them equally empty. After this penetration, he overcame all pain.

"Listen, Sāriputra, form is emptiness, emptiness is form, form does not differ from emptiness, emptiness does not differ from form. The same thing is true with feeling, perception, mental functioning, and consciousness.

"Here, Sāriputra, all dharmas are marked with emptiness; they are neither produced nor destroyed, neither defiled nor immaculate, neither increasing nor decreasing. Therefore, in emptiness there is neither form, nor feeling, nor perception, nor mental functioning, nor consciousness; no eye, or ear, or nose, or tongue, or body, or mind; no form, no sound, no smell, no taste, no touchable, no object of mind, no realm of elements (from sight to mind-consciousness), no interdependent origins (from ignorance to death and decay), no extinction of death and decay, no suffering, no origination of suffering, no extinction, no path, no wisdom, no attainment.

"Because there is no attainment, the bodhisattva, basing on the Perfection of Wisdom, finds no obstacles for his mind. Having no obstacles, he overcomes fear, liberating himself forever from illusion and assault and realizing perfect Nirvāna. All Buddhas in the past, present, and future, thanks to this Perfect Wisdom, arrive to full, right, and universal Enlightenment.

"Therefore one should know that the Perfect Wisdom is a great mantra, is the highest mantra, is the unequaled mantra, the destroyer of all suffering, the incorruptible truth. A mantra of Prajñāpāramitā should therefore be proclaimed. It is this: 'Gone, gone, gone to the other shore, gone together to the other shore. O Awakening! All hail!' "

Being Peace

Edited by Arnold Kotler

Illustrations by Mayumi Oda

CONTENTS

EDITOR'S PREFACE

Thich Nhat Hanh was born in central Vietnam in the mid-1920's, and in 1942, at the age of 16, he entered the monkhood. When war came to his country, Nhat Hanh and many of his fellow monks left their monastic isolation and became actively engaged in helping victims of the war and in publicly communicating their desire for peace. In 1966, he was invited by the Fellowship of Reconciliation to tour the United States "to describe to [us] the aspirations and the agony of the voiceless masses of the Vietnamese people." He met with hundreds of groups and individuals, including Secretary of Defense McNamara, Dr. Martin Luther King, Jr., Thomas Merton, and, in Europe, Pope Paul VI. As a result of his outspoken frankness, he was unable to return to Vietnam, threatened with arrest.

After the war ended, Nhat Hanh and his colleagues on the Vietnamese Buddhist Peace Delegation in Paris tried to find legal ways to send funds to Vietnam to help feed hungry children, but they were without success. The following year, the group went to Malaysia and Singapore to try to help insure the safety of boat people on the turbulent Gulf of Siam, but various governments thwarted those efforts as well. Uncertain how to proceed, Thich Nhat Hanh entered a period of retreat, and for more than five

years he remained at his hermitage in France, meditating, writing, gardening, and occasionally seeing
visitors. In 1982, he accepted an invitation to the
Reverence for Life Conference in New York, and I
was fortunate enough to attend that conference and
meet him. Soft, slow-moving, and deeply penetrating, Nhat Hanh was described by fellow conference
participant Richard Baker-roshi, as "a cross between
a cloud, a snail, and a piece of heavy machinery—a
true religious presence."

During that trip, Nhat Hanh became aware of the
tremendous interest in Buddhist meditation among
Americans, and he agreed to return the following
year to lead retreats on Buddhism and peace work. A
monk for more than 40 years, he taught two generations of novices in Vietnam, developing the skill of
expressing the deepest teachings of Buddhism in
straightforward, yet poetic language. Because of his
experience with the war and his willingness to face
the realities of our time, his teachings are also about
suffering, reconciliation, and peace.

Since those visits to North America, Nhat Hanh
has returned annually. *Being Peace* is a collection of
the talks he gave to peaceworkers and meditation
students during his tour of Buddhist centers in the
Fall of 1985. Most of these lectures were delivered to
groups of retreatants who were together for several
days practicing sitting and walking meditation, eating meals silently, and discussing how to create a
more peaceful world. Nhat Hanh invited the children present to sit in front of him for the first 20 or

30 minutes of each lecture, and you may notice passages where he is speaking to children, although he is also addressing the adults through them.

*   *   *

The idea of this book arose during the tour, when several of us saw how deeply Nhat Hanh's words, in fact his entire presence, affected and penetrated his listeners. Thich Nhat Hanh's teachings provide a crucial antidote to our busy lives and to our anthropocentric way of perceiving. It has been a great pleasure to edit this volume, to make these teachings more widely available.

Many people helped create *Being Peace*, more than can be acknowledged here. I especially want to thank the Buddhist Peace Fellowship, for organizing the tour during which these talks were given; the Providence Zen Center, Rocky Mountain Dharma Center, Dharma Sangha, Ojai Foundation, Sonoma Mountain Zen Center, Green Gulch Zen Center, and Diamond Sangha for hosting these retreats; and Mayumi Oda, whose inspiration from meeting Nhat Hanh at Green Gulch gave birth to the illustrations for this book. I also want to thank the many friends of Nancy Wilson Ross, including Paul and Rachel Mellon, Mary Burke, Julius and Cleome Wadsworth, Margot Wilkie, John Bailes, Yvonne Rand, and Bill Sterling, whose generosity allowed work on this book to begin; Tyrone Cashman and Marlow and Cynthia Hotchkiss, whose support as we approached the crucial final stages made completion and publication possible; Carole Melkonian, Trish Farah, Don Stoddard, Sam Rose, and the other transcribers; Gay Reineck, for many hours overseeing the book's production; Jordan Thorn, Therese Fitzgerald, Andy Cooper, Dan Asimov, Paul Rosenblum, Ruth Klein, Tony Husch, Linda Foust, Vanja Palmers, Alan Brilliant, Jack Shoemaker, Brit Pyland, Toinette Lippe, Jean Weininger, Michael Phillips, Randall Goodall, Nelson Foster, Ananda Dalenberg, Gregory Wood, John and Margo Steiner, Rose Kotler, and the many others whose unfailing help have made Parallax Press a reality; and Cao Ngoc Phuong, whose selfless work—feeding hungry children, taking care of Plum Village, and looking after all the details that make Thich Nhat Hanh's work so effective—totally embodies the teachings of understanding and love that are the foundation of "being peace."

Arnold Kotler
Berkeley, California
January 1987

BEING PEACE

"If we are peaceful, if we are happy,
we can blossom like a flower,
and everyone in our family,
our entire society,
will benefit from our peace."

CHAPTER ONE

Suffering is Not Enough

*L*ife is filled with suffering, but it is also filled with many wonders, like the blue sky, the sunshine, the eyes of a baby. To suffer is not enough. We must also be in touch with the wonders of life. They are within us and all around us, everywhere, any time.

If we are not happy, if we are not peaceful, we cannot share peace and happiness with others, even those we love, those who live under the same roof. If we are peaceful, if we are happy, we can smile and blossom like a flower, and everyone in our family, our entire society, will benefit from our peace. Do we need to make a special effort to enjoy the beauty of the blue sky? Do we have to practice to be able to enjoy it? No, we just enjoy it. Each second, each minute of our lives can be like this. Wherever we are, any time, we have the capacity to enjoy the sunshine, the presence of each other, even the sensation of our breathing. We don't need to go to China to enjoy the blue sky. We don't have to travel into the future to enjoy our breathing. We can be in touch with these things right now. It would be a pity if we are only aware of suffering.

We are so busy we hardly have time to look at the people we love, even in our own household, and to look at ourselves. Society is organized in a way that even when we have some leisure time, we don't know how to use it to get back in touch with ourselves. We have millions of ways to lose this precious time—we turn on the TV or pick up the telephone, or start the car and go somewhere. We are not used to being with ourselves, and we act as if we don't like ourselves and are trying to escape from ourselves.

Meditation is to be aware of what is going on—in our bodies, in our feelings, in our minds, and in the world. Each day 40,000 children die of hunger. The superpowers now have more than 50,000 nuclear warheads, enough to destroy our planet many times. Yet the sunrise is beautiful, and the rose that bloomed this morning along the wall is a miracle. Life is both dreadful and wonderful. To practice meditation is to be in touch with both aspects. Please do not think we must be solemn in order to meditate. In fact, to meditate well, we have to smile a lot.

Recently I was sitting with a group of children, and a boy named Tim was smiling beautifully. I said, "Tim, you have a very beautiful smile," and he said, "Thank you." I told him, "You don't have to thank me, I have to thank you. Because of your smile, you make life more beautiful. Instead of saying, 'Thank you,' you should say 'You're welcome.'"

If a child smiles, if an adult smiles, that is very important. If in our daily life we can smile, if we can be peaceful and happy, not only we, but everyone will profit from it. This is the most basic kind of peace work. When I see Tim smiling, I am so happy. If he is aware that he is making other people happy, he can say, "You are welcome."

*   *   *

From time to time, to remind ourselves to relax, to be peaceful, we may wish to set aside some time for a retreat, a day of mindfulness, when we can walk slowly, smile, drink tea with a friend, enjoy being together as if we are the happiest people on Earth. This is not a retreat, it is a treat. During walking meditation, during kitchen and garden work, during sitting meditation, all day long, we can practice smiling. At first you may find it difficult to smile, and we have to think about why. Smiling means that we are ourselves, that we have sovereignty over ourselves, that we are not drowned into forgetfulness. This kind of smile can be seen on the faces of Buddhas and Bodhisattvas.

I would like to offer one short poem you can recite from time to time, while breathing and smiling.

> Breathing in, I calm my body.
> Breathing out, I smile.
> Dwelling in the present moment
> I know this is a wonderful moment.

"Breathing in, I calm my body." This line is like drinking a glass of ice water—you feel the cold, the freshness, permeate your body. When I breathe in and recite this line, I actually feel the breathing calming my body, calming my mind.

"Breathing out, I smile." You know the effect of a smile. A smile can relax hundreds of muscles in your face, and relax your nervous system. A smile makes you master of yourself. That is why Buddhas and Bodhisattvas are always smiling. When you smile, you realize the wonder of the smile.

"Dwelling in the present moment." While I sit here, I don't think of somewhere else, of the future or the past. I sit here, and I know where I am. This is very important. We tend to be alive in the future, not now. We say, "Wait until I finish school and get my Ph.D. degree, and then I will be really alive." When we have it, and it's not easy to get, we say to ourselves, "I have to wait until I have a job in order to be *really* alive." And then after the job, a car. After the car, a house. We are not capable of being alive in the present moment. We tend to postpone being alive to the future, the distant future, we don't know when. Now is not the moment to be alive. We may never be alive at all in our entire life. Therefore, the technique, if we have to speak of a technique, is to *be* in the present moment, to be aware that we are here and now, and the only moment to be alive is the present moment.

"I know this is a wonderful moment." This is the only moment that is real. To be here and now,

and enjoy the present moment is our most important task. "Calming, Smiling, Present moment,
Wonderful moment." I hope you will try it.

*   *   *

Even though life is hard, even though it is sometimes difficult to smile, we have to try. Just as when
we wish each other, "Good morning," it must be a
real "Good morning." Recently, one friend asked
me, "How can I force myself to smile when I am
filled with sorrow? It isn't natural." I told her she
must be able to smile to her sorrow, because we are
more than our sorrow. A human being is like a television set with millions of channels. If we turn
the Buddha on, we are the Buddha. If we turn sorrow on, we are sorrow. If we turn a smile on, we
really are the smile. We cannot let just one chan-
nel dominate us. We have the seed of everything
in us, and we have to seize the situation in our
hand, to recover our own sovereignty.

When we sit down peacefully, breathing and
smiling, with awareness, we are our true selves, we
have sovereignty over ourselves. When we open
ourselves up to a TV program, we let ourselves be
invaded by the program. Sometimes it is good, but
often it is just noisy. Because we want to have
something other than ourselves enter us, we sit
there and let a noisy TV program invade us, assail
us, destroy us. Even if our nervous system suffers,
we don't have the courage to stand up and turn

it off, because if we do that, we will have to return to our self.

Meditation is the opposite. It helps us return to our true self. Practicing meditation in this kind of society is very difficult. Everything seems to work in concert to try to take us away from our true self. We have thousands of things, like video tapes and music, which help us be away from ourselves. Practicing meditation is to be aware, to smile, to breathe. These are on the opposite side. We go back to ourselves in order to see what is going on, because to meditate means to be aware of what is going on. What is going on is very important.

*   *   *

Suppose you are expecting a child. You need to breathe and smile for him or her. Please don't wait until your baby is born before beginning to take care of him or her. You can take care of your baby right now, or even sooner. If you cannot smile, that is very seri- ous. You might think, "I am too sad. Smiling is just not the correct thing to do." Maybe crying or shouting would be correct, but your baby will get it—anything you are, anything you do, is for your baby.

Even if you do not have a baby in your womb, the seed is already there. Even if you are not married, even if you are a man, you should be aware that a baby is already there, the seeds of future generations are already there. Please don't wait until the doctors tell you that you are going to have a baby to begin to take care of it. It is already there. Whatever you are, whatever you do, your baby will get it. Anything you eat, any worries that are on your mind will be for him or her. Can you tell me that you cannot smile? Think of the baby, and smile for him, for her, for the future generations. Please don't tell me that a smile and your sorrow just don't go together. It's your sorrow, but what about your baby? It's not his sorrow, it's not her sorrow.

Children understand very well that in each woman, in each man, there is a capacity of waking up, of understanding, and of loving. Many children have told me that they cannot show me anyone who does not have this capacity. Some people allow it to develop, and some do not, but everyone has it. This capacity of waking up, of being aware of what is going on in your feelings, in your body, in your perceptions, in the world, is called Buddha nature, the capacity of understanding and loving. Since the baby of that Buddha is in us, we should give him or her a chance. Smiling is very important. If we are not able to smile, then the world will not have peace. It is not by going out for a demonstration against nuclear missiles that we can bring about peace. It is with our capacity of smiling, breathing, and being peace that we can make peace.

CHAPTER TWO

The Three Gems

M any of us worry about the situation of the world. We don't know when the bombs will explode. We feel that we are on the edge of time. As individuals, we feel helpless, despairing. The situation is so dangerous, injustice is so widespread, the danger is so close. In this kind of situation, if we panic, things will only become worse. We need to remain calm, to see clearly. Meditation is to be aware, and to try to help.

I like to use the example of a small boat crossing the Gulf of Siam. In Vietnam, there are many people, called boat people, who leave the country in small boats. Often the boats are caught in rough seas or storms, the people may panic, and boats can sink. But if even one person aboard can remain calm, lucid, knowing what to do and what not to do, he or she can help the boat survive. His or her expression—face, voice—communicates clarity and calmness, and people have trust in that person. They will listen to what he or she says. One such person can save the lives of many.

Our world is something like a small boat. Compared with the cosmos, our planet is a very small boat. We are about to panic because our situation is no better than the situation of the small boat in the sea. You know that we have more than 50,000 nuclear weapons. Humankind has become a very dangerous species. We need people who can sit still and be able to smile, who can walk peacefully. We need people like that in order to save us. Mahayana Buddhism says that you are that person, that each of you is that person.

*   *   *

I had one student named Thich Thanh Van, who entered the monastery at the age of six, and at the age of 17, began to study with me. Later he was the first director of the School of Youth for Social Service, where he directed thousands of young people working during the war in Vietnam, rebuilding villages that were destroyed, and resettling tens of thousands of refugees fleeing the war-zones. He was killed in an accident. I was in Copenhagen when I heard of the death of my student. He was a very gentle monk, very brave.

When he was a novice, six or seven years old, he saw people come to the temple and bring cakes and bananas to offer to the Buddha. He wanted to know how the Buddha eats bananas, so he waited until everyone went home and the shrine was closed, and then he peered through the door, waiting for the Buddha to reach out his hand, take a banana, peel it, and eat it. He waited and waited, but nothing happened. The Buddha did not seem to eat bananas, unless he realized that someone was spying on him.

Thich Thanh Van told me several other stories about when he was a young boy. When he discovered that the statue of the Buddha is not the Buddha, he began to ask where the Buddhas are, because it did not seem to him that Buddhas were living among humans. He concluded that Buddhas must not be very nice, because when people became Buddhas, they would leave us to go to a far-away country. I told him that Buddhas are us. They are made of flesh and bones, not copper or silver or gold. The Buddha statue is just a symbol of the Buddha, in the same way the American flag is a symbol of America. The American flag is not the American people.

The root-word *buddh* means to wake up, to know, to understand; and he or she who wakes up and understands is called a Buddha. It is as simple as that. The capacity to wake up, to understand, and to love is called Buddha nature. When Buddhists say "I take refuge in the Buddha," they are expressing trust in their own capacity of understanding, of becoming awake. The Chinese and the Vietnamese say, "I go back and rely on the Buddha in me." Adding "in me" makes it very clear that you yourself are the Buddha.

In Buddhism, there are three gems: Buddha, the awakened one; Dharma, the way of understanding and loving; and Sangha, the community that lives in harmony and awareness. The three are interrelated, and at times it is hard to distinguish one from another. In everyone there is the capacity to wake up, to understand, and to love. So in ourselves we find Buddha, and we also find Dharma and Sangha. I will explain more about Dharma and Sangha, but first I want to say something about Buddha, the one who develops his or her understanding and loving to the highest degree. (In Sanskrit, understanding is *prajña* and love is *karuna* and *maitri*.).

Understanding and love are not two things, but just one. Suppose your son wakes up one morning and sees that it is already quite late. He decides to wake up his younger sister, to give her enough time to eat breakfast before going to school. It happens that she is grouchy and instead of saying, "Thank you for waking me up," she says, "Shut up! Leave me alone!" and kicks him. He will probably get angry, thinking, "I woke her up nicely. Why did she kick me?" He may want to go to the kitchen and tell you about it, or even kick her back. But then he remembers that during the night his sister coughed a lot, and he realizes that she must be sick. Maybe she has a cold, maybe that is why she behaved so meanly. He is not angry any more. At that moment there is *buddh* in him. He understands, he is awake. When you understand, you cannot help but love. You cannot get angry. To develop understanding, you have to practice looking at all living beings with the eyes of compassion. When you understand, you love. And when you love, you naturally act in a way that can relieve the suffering of people.

Someone who is awake, who knows, who understands, is called a Buddha. Buddha is in everyone of us. We can become awake, understanding, and also loving. I often tell children that if their mother or father is very understanding and loving, working, taking care of the family, smiling, being lovely, like a flower, they can say, "Mommy (or Daddy), you are all Buddha today."

*   *   *

Two thousand five hundred years ago there was a person who practiced in a way that his understanding and love became perfected, and everyone in the world recognized this. His name was Siddhartha. When Siddhartha was very young, he began to think that life had a lot of suffering in it, that people do not love each other enough, do not understand each other enough. So he left his home to go to the forest to practice meditating, breathing and smiling. He became a monk, and he tried to practice in order to develop his awakening, his understanding, and his love to the highest levels. He practiced sitting meditation and walking meditation for several years with five friends who were also monks. Although they were intelligent people, they made mistakes. For instance, each day they ate only one piece of fruit—one mango, or one guava, or one star fruit. Sometimes people exaggerate, and say that Siddhartha ate only one sesame seed a day, but I went to the forest in India where he practiced, and I know that is silly because there are no sesame seeds there. I saw also the Anoma River, in which he bathed several times, and the Bodhi tree where he sat and became a Buddha. The Bodhi tree I saw is not the same tree, it is the great-great-great-grandchild of the first Bodhi tree.

One day Siddhartha became so weak that he could not practice, and as he was an intelligent young man, he decided to go to the village and get something to eat—bananas or cake or anything. But as soon as he took four or five steps, he stumbled and fainted; he lost consciousness because he was too hungry. He would have died, but a milk maid carrying milk to the village saw him and came over. She found that he was still alive, still breathing, but very weak, and so she took a bowl and poured some milk into his mouth. At first Siddhartha did not react, but then his lips moved and he began to drink the milk. He drank a whole bowl of milk, and he felt much better and slowly sat up. He looked beautiful, because Siddhartha was a very, very handsome person. Nowadays people make statues of him which are not very handsome. Sometimes they are even grouchy, without any smile on his face. But he was a very beautiful person, and the milk maid thought that he must be the god of the mountain. She kneeled down and was about to worship, but he

stretched out his arm to tell her not to, and he told
her something. What do you think he must have said
to her?

He said, "Please give me another bowl of milk."
Because he saw that the milk was doing wonderful
things, and he knew that once our body is strong
enough, we can succeed in meditation. The young
lady was so happy, she poured him another bowl of
milk. After that, she inquired about him, and he said
that he was a monk, trying to meditate to develop his
compassion and his understanding to the highest level so that he could help other people. She asked if
there was anything she could do to help, and Siddhartha said, "Each day at noon-time, can you give
me a small bowl of rice? That would help me very
much." So from that day on, she brought him some
rice wrapped in banana leaves, and sometimes she
also brought milk.

The five other monks Siddhartha had been practicing with despised him and thought him worthless.
"Let us go somewhere else to practice. He drinks
milk, and he eats rice. He has no perseverance." But
Siddhartha did very well. Day in and day out he
meditated, and he developed his insight, his understanding, and his compassion very, very quickly as
he recovered his health.

One day, after taking a swim in the Anoma River,
he had the impression that he only needed one more
sitting to come to a total breakthrough, to become a
fully enlightened person. When he was about to sit
down, still practicing walking meditation, a buffalo
boy came by. In India 2,500 years ago, buffaloes were

used to pull the plows, and a buffalo boy's job was to watch them, bathe and take care of them, and cut grass for them to eat.

As the buffalo boy came by, he saw Siddhartha walking very peacefully, and he liked him immediately. Sometimes we see someone we like very much, even if we don't know why. The boy wanted to say something, but he was shy, so he came near Siddhartha three or four times before saying, "Gentleman, I like you very much." Siddhartha looked at him and said, "I like you also." Encouraged by this response, the boy told him, "I really want to give you something, but I have nothing I can give you." And Siddhartha said, "You do have something that I need. You have very beautiful green grass that you just cut. If you want to, please give me an armful of that grass." The boy was so happy to be able to give him something, and Siddhartha thanked him very much. After the buffalo boy left, Siddhartha spread the grass into a kind of cushion that he could sit on.

As he sat down, he made a firm vow, "Until I get true enlightenment, I shall not stand up." With this strong determination, he meditated all night, and when the morning star appeared in the sky, he became a fully enlightened person, a Buddha, with the highest capacity to understand and to love.

*   *   *

The Buddha stayed at that spot for two weeks, smiling and enjoying his breathing. Every day the milk

maid brought him rice and the buffalo boy also came
by to see him. He taught them about understanding,
loving, and being awake. There is a scripture in the
Pali Canon called *Sutta of Tending Buffaloes*, which
lists eleven skills a buffalo boy must have, such as
recognizing his own buffaloes, making smoke to keep
mosquitoes away, taking care of wounds on the body
of buffaloes, helping buffaloes cross rivers, and finding places with enough grass and water to eat. After
listing eleven skills, the Buddha tells the monks
that meditation is also like this, and he lists eleven
parallel skills for monks—recognizing the five com-
ponents of a human being, and so on. Most stories of
the life of the Buddha overlook the two weeks he
stayed near the Bodhi tree, meeting with the milk
maid and the buffalo boy, walking slowly, enjoying
themselves. But I am sure it happened this way.
Otherwise how could the Buddha have delivered
the *Sutta of Tending Buffaloes*? In fact, when the
buffalo boy grew up, he must have become a disciple
of the Buddha, and one day, as he sat in the front of
the assembly, the Buddha delivered that sutta.

*   *   *

After two weeks, the Buddha realized he had to get
up from his seat under the Bodhi tree and share his
understanding and compassion with other people.
He told the milk maid and the buffalo boy, "I am
sorry, but I have to leave now. We are so happy together, but I must go and work with the adults."

He thought about who he could share his understanding and compassion with, and he thought of
the five friends who had practiced with him. He
walked an entire day in order to find them, and
when he happened upon their camp, they had just
finished their afternoon sitting meditation. They
sat a lot. They were very thin by now, as you can imagine. One of them saw the Buddha coming and said
to the others, "Don't stand up if he comes. Don't go to
the gate to welcome him. Don't go and fetch water
for him to wash his feet and his hands. He didn't
perservere. He ate rice, and he drank milk." But
when he arrived he was so attractive and so peaceful that they could not help themselves from offering him water to wash his feet and his hands and
giving him a special seat. The Buddha told them,
"Friends, I have found a way to develop understanding and loving. Please sit down, I'll teach you."
They did not believe, at first. They said, "Siddhartha, while we practiced together, you gave up. You
drank milk, you ate rice. How is it possible you have
become a fully enlightened person? Please tell us.
We cannot believe it." The Buddha said, "Friends,
have I ever told you a lie?" In fact, he had never
lied to anyone, and these five friends remembered
that. "I have never told you a lie. Now I am not
telling you a lie. I have become a fully enlightened
person, and I'll be your teacher. Sit down, and listen
to me." And the five of them sat down and listened
to the Buddha. He gave his first Dharma talk for
adults. If you want to read his words, they are

available in a wonderful sutta explaining the basic doctrines of Buddhism: suffering, the causes of suffering, the removal of suffering, and the way to do it.

I have read many accounts of the life of the Buddha, and I see him as a person like us. Sometimes artists draw a Buddha in a way that we cannot recognize him as a human being. In fact, he is a human being. I have seen so many Buddha statues, but not many really beautiful and simple ones. If anytime you want to draw a picture of a Buddha, please sit down and breathe for five or ten minutes, smiling, before you pick up the pen to draw a Buddha. Then draw a simple Buddha, beautiful but simple, with a smile. And if you can, draw some children sitting with him. Buddha is young, not too grim, not too solemn, with a very light smile on his face. We have to go in this direction, because, when we look at the Buddha, we have to like him just as the buffalo boy and the milk maid did.

*   *   *

When we say, "I take refuge in the Buddha," we should also understand that "The Buddha takes refuge in me," because without the second part the first part is not complete. The Buddha needs us for awakening, understanding, and love to be real things and not just concepts. They must be real things that have real effects on life. Whenever I say, "I take refuge in the Buddha," I hear "Buddha takes refuge in me." There is a verse for planting trees and other plants:

> I entrust myself to earth,
> Earth entrusts herself to me.
> I entrust myself to Buddha,
> Buddha entrusts herself to me.

"I entrust myself to earth" is like "I take refuge in the Buddha." (I identify myself with the plant.) The plant will die or be alive because of the earth. The plant takes refuge in the earth, the soil. But earth entrusts herself to me because each leaf that falls down and decomposes makes the soil richer. We know that the layer of soil that is rich and beautiful has been made by the vegetation. If our earth is green and beautiful, it is because of this vegetation. Therefore, while the vegetation needs the earth, the earth also needs the vegetation to express herself as a beautiful planet. So when we say, "I entrust myself to earth," I, the plant, have to hear the other version also: "Earth entrusts herself to me." "I entrust myself to Buddha, Buddha entrusts herself to me." Then it is very clear that the wisdom, the understanding and love of Shakyamuni Buddha needs us to be real again in life. Therefore, we have a very important task: to realize awakening, to realize compassion, to realize understanding.

We are all Buddhas, because only through us can understanding and love become tangible and effective. Thich Thanh Van was killed during his effort to help other people. He was a good Buddhist, he was a good Buddha, because he was able to help tens of thousands of people, victims of the war. Because of him, awakening, understanding, and love were real things. So we can call him a Buddha body, in Sanskrit *Buddhakaya*. For Buddhism to be real, there must be a Buddhakaya, an embodiment of awakened activity. Otherwise Buddhism is just a word. Thich Thanh Van was a Buddhakaya. Shakyamuni was a Buddhakaya. When we realize awakening, when we are understanding and loving, each of us is a Buddhakaya.

*   *   *

The second gem is the Dharma. Dharma is what the Buddha taught. It is the way of understanding and love—how to understand, how to love, how to make understanding and love into real things. Before the Buddha passed away, he said to his students, "Dear people, my physical body will not be here tomorrow, but my teaching body will always be here to help. You can consider it as your own teacher, a teacher who never leaves you." That is the birth of *Dharmakaya*. The Dharma has a body also, the body of the teaching, or the body of the way. As you can see, the meaning of Dharmakaya is quite simple, although people in Mahayana have made it very complicated. Dharmakaya just means the teaching of the Buddha, the way to realize understanding and love. Later it became something like the ontological ground of being.

Anything that can help you wake up has Buddha nature. When I am alone and a bird calls me, I return to myself, I breathe, and I smile, and sometimes it calls me once more. I smile and I say to the bird, "I hear already." Not only sounds, but sights can remind you to return to your true self. In the morning when you open your window and see the light streaming in, you can recognize it as the voice of the Dharma, and it becomes part of the Dharmakaya. That is why people who are awake see the manifestation of the Dharma in everything. A pebble, a bamboo tree, the cry of a baby, anything can be the voice of the Dharma calling. We should be able to practice like that.

One day a monk came to Tue Trung, the most illustrious teacher of Buddhism in Vietnam in the 13th century, a time when Buddhism was flourishing in Vietnam. The monk asked him, "What is the pure, immaculate Dharmakaya?", and Tue Trung pointed to the excrement of a horse. This was an irreverent approach to Dharmakaya, because people were using the word immaculate to describe it. You cannot use words to describe the Dharmakaya. Even though we say that it is immaculate, pure, that does not mean it is separate from things that are impure. Reality, ultimate reality, is free from all adjectives, either pure or impure. So his response was to shake up the mind of the monk, for him to cleanse himself of all these adjectives in order to see into the nature of the Dharmakaya. A teacher is also part of the Dharmakaya because she or he helps us be awake. The way she looks, the way she lives her daily life, the way she deals with people, animals, and plants helps us realize understanding and love in our life.

There are many ways of teaching: teaching by words, teaching by books, teaching by tape recorders. I have a friend who is a Zen teacher in Vietnam, quite well-known, but not many people can come and study with him. Therefore, they make tape recordings of his talks, and he has become known as Cassette Monk! He is still in Vietnam. The government just chased him away from his monastery, so he had to go to another place to teach. He is not allowed to preach in Ho Chi Minh City, because if he teaches there, too many people come to hear him, and the government doesn't like that.

Even if he does not teach, his being is very helpful to us in being awake, for he is part of the Dharmakaya. Dharmakaya is not just expressed in words, in sounds. It can express itself in just being. Sometimes if we don't do anything, we help more than if we do a lot. We call that non-action. It is like the calm person on a small boat in a storm. That person does not have to do much, just to be himself and the situation can change. That is also an aspect of Dharmakaya: not talking, not teaching, just being.

This is true not only of humans, but other species as well. Look at the trees in our yard. An oak tree is an oak tree. That is all it has to do. If an oak tree is less than an oak tree, then we are all in trouble. Therefore, the oak tree is preaching the Dharma. Without doing anything, not serving in the School of Youth for Social Service, not preaching, not even sitting in meditation, the oak tree is very helpful to all of us just by being there. Everytime we look at

the oak tree we have confidence. During the summer
we sit under it and we feel cool, relaxed. We know
that if the oak tree is not there, and all the other
trees are not there, we will not have good air to
breathe.

We also know that in our former lives we were
trees. Maybe we have been an oak tree ourselves.
This is not just Buddhist; this is scientific. The human species is a very young species—we appeared on
the earth only recently. Before that, we were rock,
we were gas, we were minerals, and then we were
single-celled beings. We were plants, we were trees,
and now we have become humans. We have to recall
our past existences. This is not difficult. You just sit
down and breathe and look, and you can see your
past existences. When we shout at the oak tree, the
oak tree is not offended. When we praise the oak
tree, it doesn't raise its nose. We can learn the Dharma from the oak tree; therefore, the oak tree is part
of our Dharmakaya. We can learn from everything
that is around, that is in us. Even if we are not at a
meditation center, we can still practice at home, because around us the Dharma is present. Everything
is preaching the Dharma. Each pebble, each leaf,
each flower is preaching the *Saddharma Pundarika
Sutra*.

*   *   *

The Sangha is the community that lives in harmony
and awareness. Sanghakaya is a new Sanskrit term.

The Sangha needs a body also. When you are with
your family and you practice smiling, breathing, recognizing the Buddha body in yourself and your children, then your family becomes a Sangha. If you
have a bell in your home, the bell becomes part of
your Sanghakaya, because the bell helps you to
practice. If you have a cushion, then the cushion
also becomes part of the Sanghakaya. Many things
help us practice. The air, for breathing. If you have
a park or a river bank near your home, you are very
fortunate because you can enjoy practicing walking
meditation. You have to discover your Sanghakaya,
inviting a friend to come and practice with you,
have tea meditation, sit with you, join you for walking meditation. All those efforts are to establish
your Sanghakaya at home. Practice is easier if you
have a Sanghakaya.

Siddhartha, the Buddha-to-be, while practicing
with other people, began to drink milk, and the five
monks who were with him went away. So he made
the Bodhi tree into his Sanghakaya. He made the
buffalo boy, the milk maid, the river, the trees, and
the birds around him into his Sanghakaya. There
are those in Vietnam who live in re-education
camps. They don't have a Sangha. They don't have
a Zen Center. But they practice. They have to look
upon other things as part of their Sanghakaya. I
know of people who practiced walking meditation
in their prison cells. They told me this after they
got out of the camp. So while we are lucky, while we
are still capable of finding so many elements to set

up our Sanghakaya, we should do so. A friend, our own children, our own brother or sister, our house, the trees in our back yard, all of them can be part of our Sanghakaya.

Practicing Buddhism, practicing meditation is for us to be serene and happy, understanding and loving. In that way we work for the peace and happiness of our family and our society. If we look closely, the Three Gems are actually one. In each of them, the other two are already there. In Buddha, there is Buddhahood, there is the Buddha body. In Buddha there is the Dharma body because without the Dharma body, he could not have become a Buddha. In the Buddha there is the Sangha body because he had breakfast with the bodhi tree, with the other trees, and birds and environment. In a meditation center, we have a Sangha body, Sanghakaya, because the way of understanding and compassion is practiced there. Therefore the Dharma body is present, the way, the teaching is present. But the teaching cannot become real without the life and body of each of us. So the Buddhakaya is also present. If Buddha and Dharma are not present, it is not a Sangha. Without you, the Buddha is not real, it is just an idea.

Without you, the Dharma cannot be practiced. It has to be practiced by someone. Without each of you, the Sangha cannot be. That is why when we say, "I take refuge in the Buddha," we also hear, "the Buddha takes refuge in me." "I take refuge in the Dharma. The Dharma takes refuge in me. I take refuge in the Sangha. The Sangha takes refuge in me."

CHAPTER THREE

Feelings and Perceptions

A ccording to Buddhism, human beings are composed of five aggregates: form, which means
our body, including the five sense organs and the
nervous system; feelings; perceptions; mental formations; and consciousness. I would like to explain
about feelings and perceptions.

Every day we have many feelings. Sometimes we
are happy, sometimes we are sorrowful, sometimes
angry, irritated or afraid; and these feelings fill our
mind and heart. One feeling lasts for a while, and
then another comes, and another, as if there is a
stream of feelings for us to deal with. Practicing
meditation is to be aware of each feeling.

The Abhidharma writings on Buddhist psychology say that feelings are of three kinds: pleasant,
unpleasant, and neutral. When we step on a thorn,
we have an unpleasant feeling. When someone says

something nice to us, "You are very smart," or "You are very beautiful," we have a pleasant feeling. And there are neutral feelings, such as when you sit there and don't feel either pleasant or unpleasant. But I have read the Abhidharma and have practiced Buddhism, and I find this analysis not correct. A so-called neutral feeling can become very pleasant. If you sit down, very beautifully, and practice breathing and smiling, you can be very happy. When you sit in this way, aware that you have a feeling of well-being, that you don't have a toothache, that your eyes are capable of seeing forms and colors, isn't it wonderful?

For some people, working is unpleasant, and they suffer when they have to work. For other people, if they are forbidden from working, it is unpleasant. I do many kinds of work, and if you forbid me from binding books, from gardening, from writing poetry, from practicing walking meditation, from teaching children, I will be very unhappy. To me, work is pleasant. Pleasant or unpleasant depends on our way of looking.

We call seeing a neutral feeling. Yet someone who has lost her sight would give anything to be able to see, and if suddenly she could, she would consider it a miraculous gift. We who have eyes capable of seeing many forms and colors are often unhappy. If we want to practice, we can go out and look at leaves, flowers, children, and clouds, and be happy. Whether or not we are happy depends on our awareness. When you have a toothache, you think that not having toothache will make you very happy. But when you don't have a toothache, often you are still not happy. If you practice awareness, you suddenly become very rich, very very happy. Practicing Buddhism is a clever way to enjoy life. Happiness is available. Please help yourself to it. All of us have the capacity of transforming neutral feelings into pleasant feelings, very pleasant feelings that can last a long time. This is what we practice during sitting and walking meditation. If you are happy, all of us will profit from it. Society will profit from it. All living beings will profit from it.

On the wooden board outside of the meditation hall in Zen monasteries, there is a four-line inscription. The last line is, "Don't waste your life." Our lives are made of days and hours, and each hour is precious. Have we wasted our hours and our days? Are we wasting our lives? These are important questions. Practicing Buddhism is to be alive in each moment. When we practice sitting or walking, we have the means to do it perfectly. During the rest of the day, we also practice. It is more difficult, but it is possible. The sitting and the walking must be extended to the non-walking, non-sitting moments of our day. That is the basic principle of meditation.

*   *   *

Perceiving includes our ideas or concepts about reality. When you look at a pencil, you perceive it, but the pencil itself may be different from the pencil in your mind. If you look at me, the me in myself may be different from the me you perceive. In order to have a correct perception, we need to have a direct encounter.

When you look at the night sky, you might see a very beautiful star, and smile at it. But a scientist may tell you that the star is no longer there, that it was extinct ten million years ago. So our perception is not correct. When we see a very beautiful sunset, we are very happy, perceiving that the sun is there with us. In fact it was already behind the mountain eight minutes ago. It takes eight minutes for the sunshine to reach our planet. The hard fact is that we never see the sun in the present, we only see the sun of the past. Suppose while walking in the twilight, you see a snake, and you scream, but when you shine your flashlight on it, it turns out to be a rope. This is an error of perception. During our daily lives we have many misperceptions. If I don't understand you, I may be angry at you, all the time. We are not capable of understanding each other, and that is the main source of human suffering.

A man was rowing his boat upstream on a very misty morning. Suddenly, he saw another boat coming downstream, not trying to avoid him. It was coming straight at him. He shouted, "Be careful! Be careful!" but the boat came right into him, and his boat was almost sunk. The man became very angry, and began to shout at the other person, to give him a piece of his mind. But when he looked closely, he saw that there was no one in the other boat. It turned out that the boat just got loose and went downstream. All his anger vanished, and he laughed and he laughed. If our perceptions are not correct, they may give us a lot of bad feelings. Buddhism teaches us how to look at things deeply in order to understand their own true nature, so that we will not be misled into suffering and bad feelings.

*   *   *

The Buddha taught that this is like this, because that is like that. You see? Because you smile, I am happy. This is like this, therefore that is like that. And that is like that because this is like this. This is called dependent co-arising.

Suppose you and I are friends. (In fact, I hope we are friends.) My well-being, my happiness depends very much on you, and your well-being, your happiness, depends upon me. I am responsible for you, and you are responsible for me. Anything I do wrong, you will suffer, and anything you do wrong, I have to suffer. Therefore, in order to take care of you, I have to take care of myself.

There is a story in the Pali Canon about a father and a daughter who performed in the circus. The father would place a very long bamboo stick on his forehead, and his daughter would climb to the top of the stick. When they did this, people gave them some money to buy rice and curry to eat. One day the father told the daughter, "My dear daughter, we have to take care of each other. You have to take care of your father, and I have to take care of you, so that we will be safe. Our performance is very dangerous." Because if she fell, both would not be able to earn their living. If she fell, then broke her leg, they wouldn't have anything to eat. "My daughter, we have to take care of each other so we can continue to earn our living."

The daughter was wise. She said, "Father, you should say it this way: 'Each one of us has to take care of himself or herself, so that we can continue to earn our living.' Because during the performance, you take care of yourself, you take care of yourself only. You stay very stable, very alert. That will help me. And if when I climb I take care of myself, I climb very carefully, I do not let anything wrong happen to me. That is the way you should say it, Father. You take good care of yourself, and I take good care of myself. In that way we can continue to earn our living." The Buddha agreed that the daughter was right.

So we are friends, and our happiness depends on each other. According to that teaching I have to take care of myself, and you take care of yourself. That way we help each other. And that is the most correct perception. If I only say, "Don't do this, you have to do that," and I don't take care of myself, I can do many wrong things, and that does not help. I have to take care of myself, knowing that I am responsible for your happiness, and if you do the same, everything will be all right. This is the Buddha's teaching about perception, based on the principle of dependent co-arising. Buddhism is easy to learn!

The Buddha had a special way to help us understand the object of our perception. He said that in order to understand, you have to be one with what you want to understand. This is a way that is practice-able. About fifteen years ago, I used to help a committee for orphans, victims of the war in Vietnam. From Vietnam, they sent out applications, one sheet of paper with a small picture of a child in the corner, telling the name, the age, and the conditions of the orphan. We were supposed to translate it from Vietnamese into French, English, Dutch, or German, in order to seek a sponsor, so that the child would have food to eat and books for school, and be put into the family of an aunt or an uncle or a grandparent. Then the committee could send the money to the family member to help take care of the child.

Each day I helped translate about 30 applications into French. The way I did it was to look at the picture of the child. I did not read the application, I just took time to look at the picture of the child. Usually after only 30 or 40 seconds, I became one with the child. I don't know how or why, but it's always like that. Then I would pick up the pen and translate the words from the application onto another sheet. Afterwards I realized that it was not me who had translated the application; it was the child and me, who had become one. Looking at his face or her face, I got motivated and I became him and he became me, and together we did the translation. It is very natural. You don't have to practice a lot of meditation to be able to do that. You just look, you allow yourself to be, and then you lose yourself in the child, and the child in you. This is one example which illustrates the way of perception recommended by Buddha. In order to understand something, you have to be one with that something.

The French language has the word *comprendre*, which means to understand, to know, to comprehend. *Com* means to be one, to be together, and *prendre* means to take or to grasp. To understand something is to take that thing up and to be one with it. The Indians have a wonderful example. If a grain of salt would like to measure the degree of saltiness of the ocean, to have a perception of the saltiness of the ocean, it drops itself into the ocean and becomes one with it, and the perception is perfect.

Nowadays, nuclear physicists have begun to feel the same way. When they get deeply into the world of subatomic particles, they see their mind in it. An electron is first of all your concept of the electron. The object of your study is no longer separated from your mind. Your mind is very much in it. Modern physicists think that the word *observer* is no longer valid, because an observer is distinct from the object he observes. They have discovered that if you retain that kind of distinction, you cannot go very far in subatomic nuclear science. So they have proposed the word *participant*. You are not an observer, you are a participant. That is the way I always feel when I give a lecture. I don't want the audience to be outside, to observe, to listen only. I want them to be one with me, to practice, to breathe. The speaker and the people who listen must become one in order for right perception to take place. Non-duality means "not two," but "not two" also means "not one." That is why we say "non-dual" instead of "one." Because if there is one, there are two. If you want to avoid two, you have to avoid one also.

In the *Satipatthana Sutta*, the basic manual on meditation from the time of the Buddha, it is recorded, "The practitioner will have to contemplate body in the body, feelings in the feelings, mind in the mind, objects of mind in the objects of mind." The words are clear. The repetition, "body in the body," is not just to underline the importance of it. Contemplating body in the body means that you do not stand outside of something to contemplate it. You must be one with it, with no distinction between the contemplator and the contemplated. Contemplating body in the body means that you should not look on your body as the object of your contemplation. You have to be one with it. The message is clear. Non-duality is the key word for Buddhist meditation.

*   *   *

To sit is not enough. We have to *be* at the same time. To be what? To be is to be a something, you cannot be a nothing. To eat, you have to eat something, you cannot just eat nothing. To be aware is to be aware of something. To be angry is to be angry at something. So to be is to be something, and that something is *what is going on*: in your body, in your mind, in your feelings, and in the world.

While sitting, you sit and you are. You are what?
You are the breathing. Not only the one who
breathes—you *are* the breathing and the smiling. It
is like a television set of one million channels.
When you turn the breathing on, you *are* the breathing. When you turn the irritation on, you are the irritation. You are one with it. Irritation and breathing are not things outside of you. You contemplate
them in them, because you are one with them.

If I have a feeling of anger, how would I meditate
on that? How would I deal with it, as a Buddhist, or
as an intelligent person? I would not look upon anger
as something foreign to me that I have to fight, to
have surgery in order to remove it. I know that anger
is me, and I am anger. Non-duality, not two. I have
to deal with my anger with care, with love, with
tenderness, with nonviolence. Because anger is me, I
have to tend my anger as I would tend a younger
brother or sister, with love, with care, because I myself am anger, I am in it, I am it. In Buddhism we do
not consider anger, hatred, greed as enemies we have
to fight, to destroy, to annihilate. If we annihilate
anger, we annihilate ourselves. Dealing with anger
in that way would be like transforming yourself into
a battlefield, tearing yourself into parts, one part
taking the side of Buddha, and one part taking the
side of Mara. If you struggle in that way, you do violence to yourself. If you cannot be compassionate to
yourself, you will not be able to be compassionate to
others. When we get angry, we have to produce
awareness: "I am angry. Anger is in me. I am anger."
That is the first thing to do.

In the case of a minor irritation, the recognition of the presence of the irritation, along with a smile and a few breaths will usually be enough to transform the irritation into something more positive, like forgiveness, understanding, and love. Irritation is a destructive energy. We cannot destroy the energy; we can only convert it into a more constructive energy. Forgiveness is a constructive energy. Understanding is a constructive energy. Suppose you are in the desert, and you only have one glass of muddy water. You have to transform the muddy water into clear water to drink, you cannot just throw it away. So you let it settle for a while, and clear water will appear. In the same way, we have to convert anger into some kind of energy that is more constructive, because anger is you. Without anger you have nothing left. That is the work of meditation.

Earlier I gave the example of a big brother who got angry at his sister at first and then found out that she has a fever, and he understood and became concerned, and he tried to help her. So the destructive energy of anger, because of understanding, is transformed into the energy of love. Meditation on your anger is first of all to produce awareness of anger, "I am the anger," and then to look deeply into the nature of anger. Anger is born from ignorance, and is a strong ally of ignorance.

*   *   *

Perceptions are perceptions of our body, feelings, mind, nature, and society. We should have a good perception of the oak tree in order to see its Buddha nature, its function as a Dharma teacher. We have to perceive our political and economic systems correctly in order to see what is going wrong. Perception is very important for our well-being, for our peace. Perception should be free from emotions and ignorance, free from illusions.

In Buddhism, knowledge is regarded as an obstacle to understanding, like a block of ice that obstructs water from flowing. It is said that if we take one thing to be the truth and cling to it, even if truth itself comes in person and knocks at our door, we won't open it. For things to reveal themselves to us, we need to be ready to abandon our views about them.

The Buddha told a story about this. A young widower, who loved his five-year-old son very much, was away on business, and bandits came, burned down his whole village, and took his son away. When the man returned, he saw the ruins, and panicked. He took the charred corpse of an infant to be his own child, and he began to pull his hair and beat his chest, crying uncontrollably. He organized a cremation ceremony, collected the ashes and put them in a very beautiful velvet bag. Working, sleeping, eating, he always carried the bag of ashes with him.

One day his real son escaped from the robbers and found his way home. He arrived at his father's new cottage at midnight, and knocked at the door. You can imagine at that time, the young father was still carrying the bag of ashes, and crying. He asked,

"Who is there?" And the child answered, "It's me Papa. Open the door, it's your son." In his agitated state of mind the father thought that some mischievous boy was making fun of him, and he shouted at the child to go away, and he continued to cry. The boy knocked again and again, but the father refused to let him in. Some time passed, and finally the child left. From that time on, father and son never saw one another. After telling this story, the Buddha said, "Sometime, somewhere you take something to be the truth. If you cling to it so much, when the truth comes in person and knocks at your door, you will not open it."

Guarding knowledge is not a good way to understand. Understanding means to throw away your knowledge. You have to be able to transcend your knowledge the way people climb a ladder. If you are on the fifth step of a ladder and think that you are very high, there is no hope for you to climb to the sixth. The technique is to release. The Buddhist way of understanding is always letting go of our views and knowledge in order to transcend. This is the most important teaching. That is why I use the image of water to talk about understanding. Knowledge is solid; it blocks the way of understanding. Water can flow, can penetrate.

The Heart of Practice

Meditation is not to get out of society, to escape from society, but to prepare for a re-entry into society. We call this "engaged Buddhism." When we go to a meditation center, we may have the impression that we leave everything behind—family, society, and all the complications involved in them—and come as an individual in order to practice and to search for peace. This is already an illusion, because in Buddhism there is no such thing as an individual.

Just as a piece of paper is the fruit, the combination of many elements that can be called non-paper elements, the individual is made of non-individual elements. If you are a poet, you will see clearly that there is a cloud floating in this sheet of paper. Without a cloud there will be no water; without water, the trees cannot grow; and without trees, you cannot make paper. So the cloud is in here. The existence of this page is dependent on the existence of a cloud. Paper and cloud are so close. Let us think of other things, like sunshine. Sunshine is very important because the forest cannot grow without sunshine, and we humans cannot grow without sunshine. So the logger needs sunshine in order to cut the tree, and the tree needs sunshine in order to be a tree. Therefore you can see sunshine in this sheet of paper. And if you look more deeply, with the eyes of a bodhisattva, with the eyes of those who are awake, you see not only the cloud and the sunshine in it, but that everything is here: the wheat that became the bread for the logger to eat, the logger's father—everything is in this sheet of paper.

The *Avatamsaka Sutra* tells us that you cannot point to one thing that does not have a relationship with this sheet of paper. So we say, "A sheet of paper is made of non-paper elements." A cloud is a non-paper element. The forest is a non-paper element. Sunshine is a non-paper element. The paper is made of all the non-paper elements to the extent that if we return the non-paper elements to their sources, the cloud to the sky, the sunshine to the sun, the logger to his father, the paper is empty. Empty of what? Empty of a separate self. It has been made by all the non-self elements, non-paper elements, and if all these non-paper elements are taken out, it is truly empty, empty of an independent self. Empty, in this sense, means that the paper is full of everything, the entire cosmos. The presence of this tiny sheet of paper proves the presence of the whole cosmos.

In the same way, the individual is made of non-individual elements. How do you expect to leave everything behind when you enter a meditation center? The kind of suffering that you carry in your heart, that is society itself. You bring that with you, you bring society with you. You bring all of us with you. When you meditate, it is not just for yourself, you do it for the whole society. You seek solutions to your problems not only for yourself, but for all of us.

Leaves are usually looked upon as the children of the tree. Yes, they are children of the tree, born from the tree, but they are also mothers of the tree. The leaves combine raw sap, water, and minerals, with sunshine and gas, and convert it into a variegated sap that can nourish the tree. In this way, the leaves become the mother of the tree. We are all children of society, but we are also mothers. We have to nourish society. If we are uprooted from society, we cannot transform it into a more livable place for us and for our children. The leaves are linked to the tree by a stem. The stem is very important.

I have been gardening in our community for many years, and I know that sometimes it is difficult to transplant cuttings. Some plants do not transplant easily, so we use a kind of vegetable hormone to help them be rooted in the soil more easily. I wonder whether there is a kind of powder, something that

may be found in meditation practice that can help
people who are uprooted be rooted again in society.
Meditation is not an escape from society. Meditation
is to equip oneself with the capacity to reintegrate
into society, in order for the leaf to nourish the tree.

*   *   *

Something has happened in some meditation centers. A number of young people found themselves ill
at ease with society, so they left in order to come to
a meditation center. They ignored the reality that
they did not come to the meditation center as an individual. Coming together in a meditation center,
they form another kind of society. As a society, it
has problems like other societies. Before entering
the meditation center, they had hoped that they
could find peace in meditation. Now, practicing and
forming another kind of society, they discover that
this society is even more difficult than the larger society. It is composed of alienated people. After some
years, they feel frustrated, worse than before coming
to the meditation center. This is because we misunderstand meditation, we misunderstand the purpose
of meditation. Meditation is for everyone and not
just for the person who meditates.

Bringing children into a meditation center is very
natural. In Plum Village, children practice with
adults. From time to time, we open the door for
guests to come and practice with us, and bring their
children. We especially take care of the children.

When the children are happy, the adults are happy. One day I overheard the children telling each other, "How come our parents are so nice here?" I have a friend who has been practicing meditation for fourteen years, and he has never shown his daughter how to meditate. You cannot meditate alone. You have to do it with your children. If your children are not happy, do not smile, you cannot smile. When you make a peaceful step, that is for you, but it is also for the children, and for the world.

*   *   *

I think that our society is a difficult place to live. If we are not careful, we can become uprooted, and once uprooted, we cannot help change society to make it more livable. Meditation is a way of helping us stay in society. This is very important. We have seen people who are alienated from society and cannot be reintegrated into society. We know that this can happen to us if we are not careful.

I have learned that many of the Buddhist practitioners in America are young and intellectual, and have come to Buddhism not by the door of faith, but by the door of psychology. I know people in the Western world suffer a great deal psychologically, and that is why many have become Buddhists, practicing meditation in order to solve psychological problems. Many are still in society, but some have been uprooted. Having lived for quite some time in

this society, I myself feel that I cannot get along
with this society very well. There are so many
things that make me want to withdraw, to go back
to myself. But my practice helps me remain in society, because I am aware that if I leave society, I will
not be able to help change it. I hope that those who
are practicing Buddhism succeed in keeping their
feet on earth, staying in society. That is our hope for
peace.

*   *   *

I wrote a poem over 30 years ago, when I was 27 or 28,
about a brother who suffered so much he had to drop
out of society and go to a meditation center. Since the
Buddhist Temple is a place of compassion, they welcomed him. When someone is suffering so much,
when he or she comes to a meditation center, the
first thing is to give some kind of comfort. The people in the Temple were compassionate enough to let
him come and have a place to cry. How long, how
many days, how many years did he need to cry? We
don't know. But finally he took up refuge in the meditation center and did not want to go back to society.
He had had enough of it. He thought that he had
found some peace, but one day I myself came and
burned his meditation center, which was only a
small hut: his last shelter! In his understanding, he
had nothing else outside of that small cottage. He
had nowhere to go because society was not his. He
thought he had come to seek his own emancipation,

but, in the light of Buddhism, there is no such thing
as individual self. As we know, when you go into a
Buddhist center, you bring with you all the scars, all
the wounds from society, and you bring the whole society as well. In this poem, I am the young man, and
I am also the person who came and burned down the
cottage.

I shall say that I want it all.
If you ask me how much I want,
I shall tell you that I want it all.
You and I and everyone are flowing this
        morning
Into the marvelous stream of oneness.
Small pieces of imagination as we are,
We have come a long way to find ourselves,
And for ourselves in the dark,
The illusion of emancipation.

This morning my brother is back from his
        long adventure.
He kneels before the altar and his eyes are
        filled with tears.
His soul is looking for a shore to put an
        anchor,
My own image of long ago.
Let him kneel there and weep,
Let him cry his heart out.
Let him have his refuge for a thousand years.
Enough to dry all his tears.

Because one of these nights I shall come.
I have to come and set fire to this small
      cottage of his on a hill.
His last shelter.
My fire will destroy,
Destroy everything.
Taking away from him the only life raft he
      has, after a shipwreck.
In the utmost anguish of his soul,
The shell will break.
The light of the burning hut will witness,
      gloriously, his deliverance.
I will wait for him beside the burning cottage,
Tears will run down my cheeks.
I shall be there to contemplate his new
      existence,
And hold his hands in mine,
And ask him how much he would want.
He will smile at me and say that he wants it
      all.
Just as I did.

To me, a meditation center is where you get back
to yourself, you get a clearer understanding of reality, you get more strength in understanding and love,
and you prepare for your re-entry into society. If it is
not like that, it is not a real meditation center. As
we develop real understanding, we can re-enter society and make a real contribution.

*   *   *

We have many compartments in our lives. When we practice sitting meditation and when we do not practice sitting, these two periods of time are so different from each other. While sitting, we practice intensively and while we are not sitting, we do not practice intensively. In fact, we practice non-practice intensively. There is a wall which separates the two, practicing and non-practicing. Practicing is only for the practice period and non-practicing is only for non-practicing period. How can we mix the two together? How can we bring meditation out of the meditation hall and into the kitchen, and the office? How can the sitting influence the non-sitting time? If a doctor gives you an injection, not only your arm but your whole body benefits from it. If you practice one hour of sitting a day, that hour should be all 24 hours, and not just for that hour. One smile, one breath should be for the benefit of the whole day, not just for that moment. We must practice in a way that removes the barrier between practice and non-practice.

When we walk in the meditation hall, we make careful steps, very slowly. But when we go to the airport, we are quite another person. We walk very differently, less mindfully. How can we practice at the airport and in the market? That is engaged Buddhism. Engaged Buddhism does not only mean to use Buddhism to solve social and political problems, protesting against the bombs, and protesting against social injustice. First of all we have to bring Buddhism into our daily lives. I have a friend who breathes between telephone calls, and it helps her very much. Another friend does walking meditation between business appointments, walking mindfully between buildings in downtown Denver. Passers-by smile at him, and his meetings, even with difficult persons, often turn out to be very pleasant, and very successful.

We should be able to bring the practice from the meditation hall into our daily lives. How can we practice to penetrate our feelings, our perceptions during daily life? We don't deal with our perceptions and our feelings only during sitting practice. We have to deal with them all the time. We need to discuss among ourselves how to do it. Do you practice breathing between phone calls? Do you practice smiling while cutting carrots? Do you practice relaxation after hours of hard work? These questions are very practical. If you know how to apply Buddhism to dinner time, leisure time, sleeping time, I think Buddhism will become engaged in your daily life. Then it will have a tremendous effect on social concerns. Buddha, Dharma, and Sangha become the matters of everyday life, each minute, each hour of our daily life, and not just a description of something far away.

*   *   *

Our mind is like a river, with many thoughts and feelings flowing along. From time to time, it is helpful to recite a gatha, a short verse, to remind us what is going on. When we focus our mind on a gatha, the gatha is our mind at that moment. The gatha fills our mind for half a second, or ten seconds, or one minute, and then we may have another gatha a little further downstream. While eating a silent meal, I recite a gatha to myself, and then I eat something. When the plate is empty, I recite another gatha, and drink a cup of tea. Suppose there is one hour of sitting in meditation, and then five hours of non-sitting, followed by three more hours of sitting, intensive practice. What is the relationship between the practice time and the non-practice time, the practice mind and the non-practice mind? Sitting is like a gatha, a long silent gatha. (Maybe it's not so silent.) My main concern is the effect the gatha has on the non-gatha state of mind.

An automobile driver will need signs from time to time to show him the way. The sign and the road are one, because you don't see the sign only where it appears, you see it all along the way, until the next sign. There is no difference between the signs and the road. That is what we should do while practicing gathas and sitting. Gathas help us get back to ourselves, and as soon as the gatha ends, we continue along the stream. If we do not realize the unity of the gathas and the rest of our life, between the signs and the road, then we would have in ourselves what the French call *cloisons etanches*. It means absolute compartmentalization, with no communication whatsoever between the two compartments. Not permeable. Between the gatha and the non-gatha state of mind is an absolute distinction, like the sitting and the non-sitting.

How can the gathas affect the non-gatha moments? How will the sitting permeate the non-sitting hours? We must learn to practice so that one gatha, one minute of sitting will influence the rest of the day, one step made in walking meditation will have an effect on the rest of the day. Every action, every thought has an effect. Even if I just clap my hands, the effect is everywhere, even in far away galaxies. Every sitting, every walking, every smile will have an effect on your own daily life, and the life of other people also, and practice must be based on that.

*   *   *

When we practice sitting and walking, we must pay attention to the quality of the sitting and the walking, not the quantity. We have to practice intelligently. We need to create the kind of practice that will fit our circumstance.

There is a story I would like to tell you about a woman who practices the invocation of the Buddha Amitabha's name. She is very tough, and she practices the invocation three times daily, using a wooden drum and a bell, reciting, "Namo Amitabha Buddha" for one hour each time. When she arrives at one thousand times, she invites the bell to sound. (In Vietnamese, we don't say "strike" or "hit" a bell.) Although she has been doing this for ten years, her personality has not changed. She is still quite mean, shouting at people all the time.

A friend wanted to teach her a lesson, so one afternoon when she had just lit the incense, invited the bell to sound three times, and was beginning to recite "Namo Amitabha Buddha," he came to her door, and said, "Mrs. Nguyen, Mrs. Nguyen!" She found it very annoying because this was her time of practice, but he just stood at the front gate shouting her name. She said to herself, "I have to struggle against my anger, so I will ignore that," and she went on, "Namo Amitabha Buddha, Namo Amitabha Buddha."

The gentleman continued to shout her name, and her anger became more and more oppressive. She struggled against it, wondering, "Should I stop my recitation and go and give him a piece of my mind?" But she continued chanting, and she struggled very hard. Fire mounted in her, but she still tried to chant "Namo Amitabha Buddha." The gentleman knew it, and he continued to shout, "Mrs. Nguyen! Mrs. Nguyen!"

She could not bear it any longer. She threw away the bell and the drum. She slammed the door, went out to the gate and said, "Why, why do you behave like that? Why do you call my name hundreds of times like that?" The gentleman smiled at her and said, "I just called your name for ten minutes, and you are so angry. You have been calling the Buddha's name for ten years. Think how angry he must be by now!"

The problem is not to do a lot, but to do it correctly. If you do it correctly, you become kinder, nicer,
more understanding and loving. When we practice
sitting or walking we should pay attention to the
quality and not the quantity. If we practice only for
the quantity, then we are not very different from
Mrs. Nguyen. I think she learned her lesson. I think
she did better after that.

CHAPTER FIVE

Working for Peace

*I*n Plum Village in France, we receive many letters from the refugee camps in Singapore, Malaysia, Indonesia, Thailand, and the Philippines, hundreds each week. It is very painful to read them, but we have to do it, we have to be in contact. We try our best to help, but the suffering is enormous, and sometimes we are discouraged. It is said that half the boat people die in the ocean; only half arrive at the shores in Southeast Asia.

There are many young girls, boat people, who are raped by sea pirates. Even though the United Nations and many countries try to help the government of Thailand prevent that kind of piracy, sea pirates continue to inflict much suffering on the refugees. One day we received a letter telling us about a young girl on a small boat who was raped by a Thai pirate.

She was only twelve, and she jumped into the ocean and drowned herself.

When you first learn of something like that, you get angry at the pirate. You naturally take the side of the girl. As you look more deeply you will see it differently. If you take the side of the little girl, then it is easy. You only have to take a gun and shoot the pirate. But we cannot do that. In my meditation I saw that if I had been born in the village of the pirate and raised in the same conditions as he was, I am now the pirate. There is a great likelihood that I would become a pirate. I cannot condemn myself so easily. In my meditation, I saw that many babies are born along the Gulf of Siam, hundreds every day, and if we educators, social workers, politicians, and others do not do something about the situation, in 25 years a number of them will become sea pirates. That is certain. If you or I were born today in those fishing villages, we might become sea pirates in 25 years. If you take a gun and shoot the pirate, you shoot all of us, because all of us are to some extent responsible for this state of affairs.

After a long meditation, I wrote this poem. In it, there are three people: the twelve-year-old girl, the pirate, and me. Can we look at each other and recognize ourselves in each other? The title of the poem is *Please Call Me By My True Names*, because I have so many names. When I hear one of these names, I have to say, "Yes."

Do not say that I'll depart tomorrow
because even today I still arrive.

Look deeply: I arrive in every second
to be a bud on a spring branch,
to be a tiny bird, with wings still fragile,
    learning to sing in my new nest,
to be a caterpillar in the heart of flower,
to be a jewel hiding itself in a stone.

I still arrive, in order to laugh and to cry,
    in order to fear and to hope,
the rhythm of my heart is the birth and
    death of all that are alive.

I am the mayfly metamorphosing on the
    surface of the river,
and I am the bird which, when spring comes,
    arrives in time to eat the mayfly.

I am the frog swimming happily in the
    clear water of a pond,
and I am also the grass-snake who,
    approaching in silence,
    feeds itself on the frog.

I am the child in Uganda, all skin and bones,
    my legs as thin as bamboo sticks,
and I am the arms merchant, selling deadly
    weapons to Uganda.

I am the 12-year-old girl, refugee
    on a small boat,
who throws herself into the ocean after
    being raped by a sea pirate,
and I am the pirate, my heart not yet capable
    of seeing and loving.

I am a member of the politburo, with
    plenty of power in my hands,
and I am the man who has to pay his
    "debt of blood" to my people,
dying slowly in a forced labor camp.

My joy is like spring, so warm it makes
    flowers bloom in all walks of life.
My pain is like a river of tears, so full it
    fills up the four oceans.

Please call me by my true names,
so I can hear all my cries and my laughs
    at once,
so I can see that my joy and pain are one.

Please call me by my true names,
    so I can wake up,
and so the door of my heart can be left open,
the door of compassion.

*   *   *

There is a Zen story about a man riding a horse which is galloping very quickly. Another man, standing alongside the road, yells at him, "Where are you going?" and the man on the horse yells back, "I don't know. Ask the horse." I think that is our situation. We are riding many horses that we cannot control. The proliferation of armaments, for instance, is a horse. We have tried our best, but we cannot control these horses. Our lives are so busy.

In Buddhism, the most important precept of all is to live in awareness, to know what is going on. To know what is going on, not only here, but there. For instance, when you eat a piece of bread, you may choose to be aware that our farmers, in growing the wheat, use chemical poisons a little too much. Eating the bread, we are somehow co-responsible for the destruction of our ecology. When we eat a piece of meat or drink alcohol, we can produce awareness that 40,000 children die *each day* in the third world from hunger and that in order to produce a piece of meat or a bottle of liquor, we have to use a lot of grain. Eating a bowl of cereal may be more reconciling with the suffering of the world than eating a piece of meat. An authority on economics who lives in France told me that if only the people in Western countries would reduce the eating of meat and the drinking of alcohol by 50%, that would be enough to change the situation of the world. Only 50% less.

Every day we do things, we are things, that have to do with peace. If we are aware of our lifestyle, our way of consuming, of looking at things, we will know how to make peace right in the moment we are alive, the present moment. When we pick up the Sunday newspaper, for instance, we may be aware that it is a very heavy edition, maybe three or four pounds. To print such a paper, a whole forest may be needed. When we pick up the paper, we should be aware. If we are very aware, we can do something to change the course of things.

*   *   *

In my temple, I was the first monk to ride a bicycle. At that time, there were no gathas to recite while riding on a bicycle. We have to practice intelligently, to keep the practice up to date, so recently I wrote a gatha you can use before you start your car. I hope you will find it helpful:

> Before starting the car,
> I know where I am going.
> The car and I are one.
> If the car goes fast, I go fast.

Sometimes we don't really need to use the car, but because we want to get away from ourselves, we go down and start the car. If we recite the gatha, "Before starting the car, I know where I am going," it can be like a flashlight—we may see that we don't need to go anywhere. Anywhere we go, we will have our self with us; we cannot escape ourselves. Sometimes it is better to turn the engine off and go out for a walking meditation. It may be more pleasant to do that.

It is said that in the last few years, two million square miles of forest land have been destroyed by acid rain, and that is partly because of our cars. "Before starting the car, I know where I am going," is a very deep question. "Where shall I go? To my own destruction?" If the trees die, humans are going to die also. If trees and animals are not alive, how can we be alive?

"The car and I are one." We have the impression that we are the boss, and the car is only an instrument, but that is not true. With the car, we become something different. With a gun, we become very dangerous. With a flute, we become pleasant. With 50,000 atomic bombs, humankind has become the most dangerous species on earth. We were never so dangerous as we are now. We should be aware. The most basic precept of all is to be aware of what we do, what we are, each minute. Every other precept will follow from that.

*   *   *

We have to look deeply at things in order to see. When a swimmer enjoys the clear water of the river, he or she should also be able to *be* the river. One day I was having lunch at Boston University with some friends, and I looked down at the Charles River. I had been away from home for quite a long time, and seeing the river, I found it very beautiful. So I left

my friends and went down to wash my face and dip
my feet in the water, as we used to do in our country.
When I returned, a professor said, "That's a very
dangerous thing to do. Did you rinse your mouth in
the river?" When I told him, "Yes," he said, "You
should see a doctor and get a shot."

I was shocked. I didn't know that the rivers here
are so polluted. You may call them dead rivers. In
our country the rivers get very muddy sometimes, but
not that kind of dirt. Someone told me that there are
so many chemicals in the Rhine River in Germany
that it is possible to develop photographs in it. We
can be good swimmers, but can we be a river and experience the fears and hopes of a river? If we cannot,
then we do not have the chance for peace. If all the
rivers are dead, then the joy of swimming in the river will no longer exist.

If you are a mountain climber or someone who enjoys the countryside, or the green forest, you know
that the forests are our lungs outside of our bodies.
Yet we have been acting in a way that has allowed
two million square miles of forest land to be destroyed by acid rain. We are imprisoned in our small
selves, thinking only of the comfortable conditions
for this small self, while we destroy our large self.
One day I suddenly saw that the sun is my heart, my
heart outside of this body. If my body's heart ceases
to function I cannot survive; but if the sun, my other
heart, ceases to function, I will also die immediately. We should be able to be our true self. That means
we should be able to be the river, we should be able

to be the forest, we should be able to be a Soviet citizen. We must do this to understand, and to have
hope for the future. That is the non-dualistic way of
seeing.

*   *   *

During the war in Vietnam we young Buddhists organized ourselves to help victims of the war rebuild
villages that had been destroyed by the bombs.
Many of us died during service, not only because of
the bombs and the bullets, but because of the people
who suspected us of being on the other side. We were
able to understand the suffering of both sides, the
Communists and the anti-Communists. We tried to
be open to both, to understand this side and to understand that side, to be one with them. That is why
we did not take a side, even though the whole world
took sides. We tried to tell people our perception of
the situation: that we wanted to stop the fighting,
but the bombs were so loud. Sometimes we had to
burn ourselves alive to get the message across, but
even then the world could not hear us. They thought
we were supporting a kind of political act. They
didn't know that it was a purely human action to be
heard, to be understood. We wanted reconciliation,
we did not want a victory. Working to help people
in a circumstance like that is very dangerous, and
many of us got killed. The Communists killed us because they suspected that we were working with the
Americans, and the anti-Communists killed us be-

cause they thought that we were with the Communists. But we did not want to give up and take one
side.

The situation of the world is still like this. People completely identify with one side, one ideology.
To understand the suffering and the fear of a citizen
of the Soviet Union, we have to become one with
him or her. To do so is dangerous—we will be suspected by both sides. But if we don't do it, if we
align ourselves with one side or the other, we will
lose our chance to work for peace. Reconciliation is to
understand both sides, to go to one side and describe
the suffering being endured by the other side, and
then to go to the other side and describe the suffering being endured by the first side. Doing only that
will be a great help for peace.

During a retreat at the Providence Zen Center, I
asked someone to express himself as a swimmer in a
river, and then after 15 minutes of breathing, to express himself as the river. He had to become the
river to be able to express himself in the language
and feelings of the river. After that a woman who
had been in the Soviet Union was asked to express
herself as an American, and after some breathing
and meditation, as a Soviet citizen, with all her
fears and her hope for peace. She did it wonderful-
ly. These are exercises of meditation related to non-
duality.

The young Buddhist workers in Vietnam tried to
do this kind of meditation. Many of them died during service. I wrote a poem for my young brothers and

sisters on how to die nonviolently, without hatred.
It is called *Recommendation*:

> Promise me,
> promise me this day
> while the sun is just overhead
> even as they strike you down
> with a mountain of hate and violence,
> remember, brother,
> man is not our enemy.
>
> Just your pity,
> just your hate
> invincible, limitless,
> hatred will never let you face
> the beast in man.
> And one day, when you face this
> beast alone, your courage intact,
> your eyes kind,
> out of your smile
> will bloom a flower
> and those who love you
> will behold you
> across 10,000 worlds of birth and dying.
>
> Alone again
> I'll go on with bent head
> but knowing the immortality of love.
> And on the long, rough road
> both sun and moon will shine,
> lighting my way.

To practice meditation is to be aware of the existence of suffering. The first Dharma Talk that the Buddha gave was about suffering, and the way out of suffering. In South Africa, the black people suffer enormously, but the white people also suffer. If we take one side, we cannot fulfill our task of reconciliation in order to bring about peace.

Are there people who can be in touch with both the black community and the white community in South Africa? If there are not many of them, the situation is bad. There must be people who can get in touch with both sides, understanding the suffering of each, and telling each side about the other. Are there people doing that kind of understanding and mediation and reconciliation between the two major political blocs on the earth? Can you be more than Americans? Can you be people who understand deeply the suffering of both sides? Can you bring the message of reconciliation?

*   *   *

You may not be aware that your country has been manufacturing a lot of conventional weapons to sell to third world countries for their people to kill each other. You know very well that children and adults in these countries need food more than these deadly weapons. Yet no one has the time to organize a national debate to look at the problem of manufacturing and selling these deadly things. Everyone is too busy. Conventional weapons have been killing in the

last 30, 40, 50 years, very much. If we only think of
the nuclear bombs that may explode in the future
and do not pay attention to the bombs that are ex-
ploding in the present moment, we commit some kind
of error. I believe President Reagan said that the
U.S. has to continue to make conventional weapons
to sell because if you don't, someone else will and the
U.S. will lose its interest. This is not a good thing to
say. It is off course. This statement is just an excuse,
but there are real factors that push him and push
the whole nation to continue to manufacture conventional weapons to sell. For instance, many people
will lose their jobs if they stop. Have we thought
about the kind of work that will help these people
if the weapons industry stops?

Not many Americans are aware that these weapons are killing people in the third world every
day. The Congress has not debated this issue seriously. We have not taken the time to see this situation
clearly, so we have not been able to change our government's policy. We are not strong enough to pressure the government. The foreign policy of a government is largely dictated by its people and their way
of life. We have a large responsibility as citizens.
We think that the government is free to make policy, but that freedom depends on our daily life. If we
make it possible for them to change policies, they
will do it. Now it is not possible yet. Maybe you
think that if you get into government and obtain
power, you can do anything you want, but that is not
true. If you become President, you will be confronted

by this hard fact. You will probably do just the same thing, a little better or a little worse.

Therefore we have to see the real truth, the real situation. Our daily lives, the way we drink, what we eat, has to do with the world's political situation. Meditation is to see deeply into things, to see how we can change, how we can transform our situation. To transform our situation is also to transform our minds. To transform our minds is also to transform our situation, because the situation is mind, and mind is situation. Awakening is important. The nature of the bombs, the nature of injustice, the nature of the weapons, and the nature of our own beings are the same. This is the real meaning of engaged Buddhism.

*   *   *

During the last 2,500 years in Buddhist monasteries, a system of seven practices of reconciliation has evolved. Although these techniques were formulated to settle disputes within the circle of monks, I think they might also be of use in our households and in our society.

The first practice is **Face-to-Face Sitting**. In a convocation of the whole sangha, everyone sits together, mindfully, breathing and smiling, with the willingness to help, and not with the willingness to fight. This is basic. The two conflicting monks are present, and they know that everyone in the community expects them to make peace. Even before anything is said, the atmosphere of peace is already present. People refrain from listening to stories outside of the assembly, spreading news about this monk or other monks, commenting on the behavior of this monk or the other monks. That would not help. Everything must be said in public, in the community. So the two monks are sitting facing each other, breathing and, how hard, smiling.

The second practice is **Remembrance**. Both monks try to remember the whole history of the conflict, every detail of the life having to do with the conflict, while the whole assembly just sits patiently and listens: "I remember that that day it was rainy, and I went to the kitchen and you were there. . . ," telling as much he can recall. This is quite important, because the monks are trying to mend the things of the past. The principle of sangha life is to be aware of what is going on every day. If you are not aware of what is going on, one day things will explode, and it will be too late. If the community is sitting in assembly and there are two monks confronting each other, already the conflict has exploded into the open. To sit and try to recall details from the past is the only thing to do now, as far as the past is concerned.

Suppose a woman and a man get married and then live a neglectful life, not knowing what is really going on subconsciously. Their feelings and their perceptions are creating a dangerous situation. Sometimes things occur beneath the surface which will eventually explode, and by then it is too late to deal with, so the only recourse is divorce or fighting or even killing each other. To meditate is to be aware of what is going on in yourself, your feelings, your body, your perceptions, your family. This is very important for any kind of life. The second technique is to recall, and the more details which the community has, the easier it is to help.

The third principle is **Non-stubbornness**. Everyone in the community expects the two monks not to be stubborn, to try their best for reconciliation. The outcome is not important. The fact that each monk is doing his best to show his willingness for reconciliation and understanding is most important. When you do your best, trying to be your best in understanding and accepting, you don't have to worry about the outcome. You do your best, and that is enough. The other person will do his or her best. The atmosphere of the assembly is crucial. Because everyone has high expectations for the two monks, they know they must act well or they will not be recognized as brothers.

The fourth practice is **Covering Mud with Straw**. You know when you walk in the countryside after a rain, it is very muddy. If you have straw to spread over the mud, you can walk safely. One respected senior monk is appointed to represent each side of the conflict. These two monks then address the assembly, trying to say something to de-escalate the feeling in the concerned people. In a Buddhist sangha, people respect the high monks. We call them ancestral

teachers. They don't have to say very much; whatever they say is taken very seriously by the rest of
the community. One says something concerning this
monk, and what he says will cause the other monk
to understand better and de-escalate his feeling, his
anger or his resistance. Then the other high monk
says something to protect the other monk, saying it
in a way that the first monk feels better. By doing
so, they dissipate the hard feelings in the hearts of
the two monks and help them to accept the verdict
proposed by the community. Putting straw on mud—
the mud is the dispute, and the straw is the loving-
kindness of the Dharma.

The next stage is **Voluntary Confession**. Each monk
reveals his own shortcomings, without waiting for
others to say them. If the others say them, you feel
differently. If you yourself say them, it is wonderful. First you reveal a minor weakness. You may
have a big weakness, but you tell only of some minor
transgression. (There is an art in all that.) As you
make a confession, you might say, "On that day, I
was not very mindful. I said such and such a thing.
That is horrible. I am sorry." Even though it is a
very minor confession, it helps the other person feel
better. It encourages him to confess something of the
same magnitude. (Imagine the Soviet Union and the
United States trying to slowly de-escalate the small
things.)

This atmosphere is encouraging. Everyone is
supportive, expecting that de-escalation will be

realized. The Buddha nature in each monk has the opportunity to come out, and the pressure on each monk from his anger or resentment will lighten. In this kind of atmosphere, the capacity of mutual understanding and acceptance will be born. Then the senior monks remind the feuding monks, "First of all you are part of the community. The well-being of the community is most important. Don't think only of your own feeling. Think of the well-being of the community." And then each monk will be ready to make a sacrifice, and get ready to accept the verdict or decision made by the community.

The sixth and seventh practices are **Decision by Consensus** and **Accepting the Verdict**. It is agreed in advance that the two monks will accept whatever verdict is pronounced by the whole assembly, or they will have to leave the community. So, after exploring every detail of the conflict, after realizing the maximum of reconciliation, a committee presents a verdict. It is announced three times. The head of the community reads the decision in this way: "After meditation, after exploration, after discussion, after all efforts have been made, it is suggested that this monk will do so and so, that monk will do so and so, this should be repaired in this way, that should be repaired in that way. Does the assembly of monks accept this verdict?" If the community remains silent, that means, "Okay." Then he repeats exactly the same words, "Does the noble assembly accept this verdict?" And then, silence. And a third time,

"Does the community accept this verdict?" After a
third time of silence, he pronounces, "The noble community of monks and nuns has accepted the verdict.
Please, both sides carry out the decision." This is
the end of the session. There may be many sessions to
solve one case. If one of the monks rebels against the
verdict, his voice is of no weight, because he has
already agreed to obey any verdict made by the
assembly.

These seven methods of settling disputes have
been adopted by Buddhist monks and nuns in India,
China, Vietnam, Japan, Korea, and many other
countries for more than 2,500 years. I think we can
learn something from them to apply in our own
households and society.

*   *   *

In the peace movement there is a lot of anger, frustration, and misunderstanding. The peace movement
can write very good protest letters, but they are not
yet able to write a love letter. We need to learn to
write a letter to the Congress or to the President of
the United States that they will want to read, and
not just throw away. The way you speak, the kind of
understanding, the kind of language you use should
not turn people off. The President is a person like
any of us.

Can the peace movement talk in loving speech,
showing the way for peace? I think that will depend on whether the people in the peace movement

can be peace. Because without being peace, we cannot do anything for peace. If we cannot smile, we cannot help other people to smile. If we are not peaceful, then we cannot contribute to the peace movement.

I hope we can bring a new dimension to the peace movement. The peace movement is filled with anger and hatred. It cannot fulfill the path we expect from them. A fresh way of being peace, of doing peace is needed. That is why it is so important for us to practice meditation, to acquire the capacity to look, to see, and to understand. It would be wonderful if we could bring to the peace movement our contribution, our way of looking at things, that will diminish aggression and hatred. Peace work means, first of all, being peace. Meditation is meditation for all of us. We rely on each other. Our children are relying on us in order for them to have a future.

CHAPTER SIX

Interbeing

I believe that the encounter between Buddhism and the West will bring about something very exciting, very important. There are important values in Western society, such as the scientific way of looking at things, the spirit of free inquiry, and democracy. An encounter between Buddhism and these values will give humankind something very new, very exciting. Let us look at some examples: Printing was invented in China and movable metal type was invented in Korea, but when the West began printing, it became a very important means for communication. Gun powder was discovered by the Chinese, but when it came to be manufactured by Westerners, it changed the face of the Earth. And the tea that we discovered in Asia, when brought to the West, has become tea bags.

When combined with the Western way of doing
things, the Buddhist principle of seeing and acting
non-dualistically will totally change our way of
life. The role of American Buddhists in bringing
Buddhism into the encounter with Western civilization is very important for all of us.

Buddhism is not one. The teaching of Buddhism is
many. When Buddhism enters one country, that
country always acquires a new form of Buddhism.
The first time I visited Buddhist communities in
this country I asked a friend, "Please show me your
Buddha, your American Buddha." The question surprised my friend, because he thought that the Buddha is universal. In fact, the Chinese have a Chinese Buddha, Tibetans have a Tibetan Buddha, and
also the teaching is different. The teaching of Buddhism in this country is different from other countries. Buddhism, in order to be Buddhism, must be
suitable, appropriate to the psychology and the culture of the society that it serves.

My question was a very simple question. "Where
is your Bodhisattva? Show me an American Bodhisattva." My friend was not capable of doing that.
"Show me an American monk, an American nun, or an
American Buddhist Center." All these things are not
apparent yet. I think we can learn from other Buddhist traditions, but you have to create your own
Buddhism. I believe that out of deep practice you
will have your own Buddhism very soon.

*   *   *

I would like to present to you a form of Buddhism
that may be accepted here in the West. In the past
20 years we have been experimenting with this form
of Buddhism, and it seems that it may be suitable
for our modern society. It is called the Tiep Hien Order, the Order of "Interbeing."

The Tiep Hien Order was founded in Vietnam
during the war. It derives from the Zen School of Lin
Chi, and is the 42nd generation of this school. It is a
form of engaged Buddhism, Buddhism in daily life,
in society, and not just in a retreat center. *Tiep* and
hien are Vietnamese words of Chinese origin. I
would like to explain the meaning of these words,
because understanding them helps in understanding
the spirit of this order.

Tiep means "to be in touch." The notion of engaged
Buddhism already appears in the word tiep. First of
all, to be in touch with oneself. In modern society
most of us don't want to be in touch with ourselves;
we want to be in touch with other things like religion, sports, politics, a book—we want to forget ourselves. Anytime we have leisure, we want to invite
something else to enter us, opening ourselves to the
television and telling the television to come and
colonize us. So first of all, "in touch" means in touch
with oneself in order to find out the source of wisdom, understanding, and compassion in each of us.
Being in touch with oneself is the meaning of meditation, to be aware of what is going on in your body,
in your feelings, in your mind. That is the first meaning of tiep.

Tiep also means to be in touch with Buddhas and Bodhisattvas, the enlightened people in whom full understanding and compassion are tangible and effective. Being in touch with oneself means being in touch with this source of wisdom and compassion. You know that children understand that the Buddha is in themselves. One young boy claimed to be a Buddha on the first day of the retreat in Ojai, California. I told him that this is partly true, because sometimes he is Buddha, but sometimes he is not; it depends on his degree of being awake.

The second part of the meaning of tiep is "to continue," to make something more long-lasting. It means that the career of understanding and compassion started by Buddhas and Bodhisattvas should be continued. This is possible only if we get in touch with our true self, which is like digging deep into the soil until we reach a hidden source of fresh water, and then the well is filled. When we are in touch with our true mind, the source of understanding and compassion will spring out. This is the basis of everything. Being in touch with our true mind is necessary for the continuation of the career started by the Buddhas and Bodhisattvas.

Hien means "the present time." We have to be in the present time, because only the present is real, only in the present moment can we be alive. We do not practice for the sake of the future, to be reborn in a paradise, but to be peace, to be compassion, to be joy right now. Hien also means "to make real, to manifest, realization." Love and understanding are

not only concepts and words. They must be real
things, realized, in oneself and in society. That is
the meaning of the word hien.

It is difficult to find English or French words
which convey the same meaning as *Tiep Hien*. There
is a term from the *Avatamsaka Sutra*, "interbeing,"
which conveys the spirit, so we have translated
Tiep Hien as interbeing. In the sutra it is a compound
term which means "mutual" and "to be." Interbeing
is a new word in English, and I hope it will be accepted. We have talked about the many in the one,
and the one containing the many. In one sheet of paper, we see everything else, the cloud, the forest,
the logger. I am, therefore you are. You are, therefore I am. That is the meaning of the word
"interbeing." We inter-are.

In the Order of Interbeing, there are two communities. The Core Community consists of men and
women who have taken the vow to observe the 14
precepts of the Order. Before being ordained as a
brother or a sister of the Order of Interbeing, one
should practice at least one year in this way. Upon
ordination, the person has to organize a community
around himself or herself in order to continue the
practice. That community is called the Extended
Community. This means all those who practice exactly the same way, but have not taken the vow,
have not been ordained into the Core Community.

The people who are ordained into the Core Community do not have any special sign at all. They
don't shave their heads, they do not have a special

robe. What makes them different is that they observe a number of rules, one of them is to practice at least 60 days of retreat, days of mindfulness, each year, whether consecutively or divided into several periods. If they practice every Sunday, for instance, they will have 52 already. The people in the Extended Community can do that, or more, even if they don't want to be ordained. In the Core Community people can choose to observe celibacy, or lead a family life.

At least once every two weeks, members and friends come together and recite the 14 precepts. They begin with the three refuges and the two promises for children. These two promises envelop all the precepts of the adults. The first promise is: "I vow to develop my compassion in order to love and protect the life of people, animals, and plants." The second promise is: "I vow to develop understanding in order to be able to love and to live in harmony with people, animals, and plants." So the two promises are compassion, or love, and understanding. They are the essence of the Buddha's teaching. After the children recite the three refuges and these two promises, they can go outside and play; and the adults recite their 14 precepts.

Usually precepts begin with admonitions concerning the body, such as "not to kill." The Tiep Hien precepts are in a kind of reverse order—the ones concerning the mind come first. In Buddhism, the mind is the root of everything else. These then are the precepts of the Order of Interbeing:

First: Do not be idolatrous about or bound to any doctrine, theory, or ideology, even Buddhist ones. All systems of thought are guiding means; they are not absolute truth.

This precept is the roar of the lion. Its spirit is characteristic of Buddhism. It is often said that the Buddha's teaching is only a raft to help you cross the river, a finger pointing to the moon. Don't mistake the finger for the moon. The raft is not the shore. If we cling to the raft, if we cling to the finger, we miss everything. We cannot, in the name of the finger or the raft, kill each other. Human life is more precious than any ideology, any doctrine.

The Order of Interbeing was born in Vietnam during the war, which was a conflict between two world ideologies. In the name of ideologies and doctrines, people kill and are killed. If you have a gun, you can shoot one, two, three, five people; but if you have an ideology and stick to it, thinking it is the absolute truth, you can kill millions. This precept includes the precept of not killing in its deepest sense. Humankind suffers very much from attachment to views. "If you don't follow this teaching, I will cut off your head." In the name of the truth we kill each other. The world now is stuck in that situation. Many people think that Marxism is the highest product of the human mind, that nothing can compare with it. Other people think that it's crazy, and that we have to destroy those people. We are caught in this situation.

Buddhism is not like that. One of the most basic teachings of Shakyamuni is that life is the most precious. It is an answer to our main problem of war and peace. Peace can only be achieved when we are not attached to a view, when we are free from fanaticism. The more you decide to practice this precept, the deeper you will go into reality and understand the teaching of Buddhism.

Second: Do not think that the knowledge you presently possess is changeless, absolute truth. Avoid being narrow-minded and bound to present views. Learn and practice non-attachment from views in order to be open to receive others' viewpoints. Truth is found in life and not merely in conceptual knowledge. Be ready to learn throughout your entire life and to observe reality in yourself and in the world at all times.

This precept springs from the first one. Remember the young father who refused to open the door to his own son, thinking the boy was already dead. The Buddha said, "If you cling to something as the absolute truth and you are caught in it, when the truth comes in person to knock on your door, you will refuse to let it in." A scientist with an open mind, who can question the present knowledge of science, will have more of a chance to discover a higher truth. A Buddhist, also, in her meditation, in her quest for higher understanding has to question her present

view concerning reality. The technique of understanding is to overcome views and knowledge. The
way of non-attachment from views is the basic
teaching of Buddhism concerning understanding.

**Third: Do not force others, including children, by
any means whatsoever, to adopt your views,
whether by authority, threat, money, propaganda,
or even education. However, through compassionate
dialogue, help others renounce fanaticism and
narrowness.**

This also springs from the first precept. It is the
spirit of free inquiry. I think Westerners can accept
this, because you understand it. If you can find a way
to organize it globally, it will be a happy event for
the world.

**Fourth: Do not avoid contact with suffering or close
your eyes before suffering. Do not lose awareness of
the existence of suffering in the life of the world.
Find ways to be with those who are suffering by all
means, including personal contact and visits, images,
sound. By such means, awaken yourself and others to
the reality of suffering in the world.**

The first Dharma Talk given by the Buddha was on
the Four Noble Truths. The first truth is the existence of suffering. This kind of contact and awareness

is needed. If we don't encounter pain, ills, we won't look for the causes of pain and ills to find a remedy, a way out of the situation.

America is somehow a closed society. Americans are not very aware of what is going on outside of America. Life here is so busy that even if you watch television and read the newspaper, and the images from outside flash by, there is no real contact. I hope you will find some way to nourish the awareness of the existence of suffering in the world. Of course, inside America there is also suffering, and it is important to stay in touch with that. But much of the suffering in the West is "useless" and can vanish when we see the real suffering of other people. Sometimes we suffer because of some psychological fact. We cannot get out of our self, and so we suffer. If we get in touch with the suffering in the world, and are moved by that suffering, we may come forward to help the people who are suffering, and our own suffering may just vanish.

Fifth: Do not accumulate wealth while millions are hungry. Do not take as the aim of your life fame, profit, wealth, or sensual pleasure. Live simply and share time, energy, and material resources with those who are in need.

The *Eight Realizations of Great Beings Sutra* says, "The human mind is always searching for possessions, and never feels fulfilled. Bodhisattvas move

in the opposite direction and follow the principle of
self-sufficiency. They live a simple life in order to
practice the Way, and consider the realization of
perfect understanding as their only career." In the
context of our modern society, simple living also
means to remain as free as possible from the destructive social and economic machine, and to avoid
stress, depression, high blood pressure, and other
modern diseases. We should make every effort to
avoid the pressures and anxieties that fill most
modern lives. The only way out is to consume less.
Once we are able to live simply and happily, we are
better able to help others.

**Sixth: Do not maintain anger or hatred. As soon as
anger and hatred arise, practice the meditation on
compassion in order to deeply understand the persons
who have caused anger and hatred. Learn to look at
other beings with the eyes of compassion.**

We have to be aware of irritation or anger as it
arises, and try to understand it. Once we understand,
we are better able to forgive and love. Meditation on
compassion means meditation on understanding. If
we do not understand, we cannot love.
    "Learn to look at other beings with the eyes of
compassion" is directly quoted from *The Lotus Sutra*,
the chapter on Avalokitesvara. You might like to
write this down and put it in your sitting room. The
original Chinese is only five words: "compassionate

eyes looking living beings." The first time I recited
The Lotus Sutra, when I came to these five words, I
was silenced. I knew that these five words are
enough to guide my whole life.

**Seventh: Do not lose yourself in dispersion and in
your surroundings. Learn to practice breathing in order to regain composure of body and mind, to practice
mindfulness, and to develop concentration and understanding.**

This precept is in the middle. It is the heart of the
14 precepts, the most important precept: to live in
awareness. Without this precept, without mindfulness, the other precepts cannot be observed completely. It is like a carrying pole. In Asia they used to
carry things with a pole, and put the middle of the
pole on their shoulders. This precept is like the
middle of the pole that you carry on your shoulders.

**Eighth: Do not utter words that can create discord
and cause the community to break. Make every effort
to reconcile and resolve all conflicts, however small.**

We now come to the second set of precepts, concerning
speech. The first seven precepts deal with mind,
then two with speech, and five with body. This precept is about reconciliation, the effort to make
peace, not only in your family, but in society as well.

In order to help reconcile a conflict, we have to be in touch with both sides. We must transcend the conflict; if we are still in the conflict, it is difficult to reconcile. We have to have a non-dualistic viewpoint in order to listen to both sides and understand. The world needs persons like this for the work of reconciliation, persons with the capacity of understanding and compassion.

Ninth: Do not say untruthful things for the sake of personal interest or to impress people. Do not utter words that cause division and hatred. Do not spread news that you do not know to be certain. Do not critize or condemn things that you are not sure of. Always speak truthfully and constructively. Have the courage to speak out about situations of injustice, even when doing so may threaten your own safety.

The words we speak can create love, trust, and happiness around us, or create a hell. We should be careful about what we say. If we tend to talk too much, we should become aware of it and learn to speak less. We must become aware of our speech and the results of our speaking. There is a gatha which can be recited before picking up the telephone:

> Words can travel across thousands of miles.
> They are intended to build up understanding
>   and love.
> Each word should be a jewel,
> A beautiful tapestry.

We should speak constructively. In our speech we can try not to cause misunderstanding, hatred, or jealousy, rather to increase understanding and mutual acceptance. This may even help reduce our telephone bills. The ninth precept also requires frankness and courage. How many of us are brave enough to denounce injustice in a situation where speaking the truth might threaten our own safety?

Tenth: Do not use the Buddhist community for personal gain or profit, or transform your community into a political party. A religious community should, however, take a clear stand against oppression and injustice, and should strive to change the situation without engaging in partisan conflicts.

This does not mean that we must be silent about injustice. It just means we should do it with awareness and not take sides. We should speak the truth and not just weigh the political consequences. If we take sides, we will lose our power to help mediate the conflict.

During one visit to America, I met with a group of people who wanted to raise funds to help the government of Vietnam rebuild the country. I asked whether they would also like to do something for the boat people, and they said no. They thought that politically it is not good to talk about the boat people, because that would discredit the government of Vietnam. In order to succeed in one thing, they

have to refrain from doing something that they
think is right.

Eleventh: Do not live with a vocation that is harmful to humans and nature. Do not invest in companies that deprive others of their chance to life. Select a vocation which helps realize your ideal of compassion.

This is an extremely hard precept to observe. If you
are lucky enough to have a vocation that helps you
realize your ideal of compassion, you still have to
understand more deeply. If I am a teacher, I am very
glad to have this job helping children. I am glad
that I am not a butcher who kills cows and pigs. Yet
the son and the daughter of the butcher come to my
class, and I teach them. They profit from my right
livelihood. My son and daughter eat the meat that
the butcher prepares. We are linked together. I cannot say that my livelihood is perfectly right. It cannot be. Observing this precept includes finding ways
to realize a collective right livelihood.
   You may try to follow a vegetarian diet, to lessen
the killing of animals, but you cannot completely
avoid the killing. When you drink a glass of water,
you kill many tiny living beings. Even in your dish of
vegetables, there are quite a lot of them, boiled or
fried. I am aware that my vegetarian dish is not
completely vegetarian, and I think that if my
teacher, the Buddha, were here, he could not avoid

that either. The problem is whether we are determined to go in the direction of compassion or not. If
we are, then can we reduce the suffering to a minimum? If I lose my direction, I have to look for the
North Star, and I go to the north. That does not
mean I expect to arrive at the North Star. I just want
to go in that direction.

**Twelfth: Do not kill. Do not let others kill. Find
whatever means possible to protect life and to prevent war.**

The defense budgets in Western countries are enormous. Studies show that by stopping the arms race,
we will have more than enough money to erase poverty, hunger, illiteracy, and many diseases from the
world. This precept applies not only to humans, but
to all living beings. As we have seen, no one can observe this precept to perfection; however, the essence is to respect and protect life, to do our best to
protect life. This means not killing, and also not letting other people kill. It is difficult. Those who try
to observe this precept have to be working for peace
in order to have peace in themselves. Preventing
war is much better than protesting against the war.
Protesting the war is too late.

**Thirteenth: Possess nothing that should belong to
others. Respect the property of others but prevent**

**others from enriching themselves from human suf-
fering or the suffering of other beings.**

Bringing to our awareness the pain caused by social
injustice, the thirteenth precept urges us to work for
a more livable society. This precept is linked with
the fourth precept (the awareness of suffering), the
fifth precept (lifestyle), the eleventh precept
(right livelihood), and the twelfth precept (the
protection of life). In order to deeply comprehend
this precept, we must also meditate on these four
precepts.

To develop ways to prevent others from enriching
themselves on human suffering and the suffering of
other beings is the duty of legislators and politicians. However, each of us can also act in this direction. To some degree, we can be close to oppressed
people and help them protect their right to life and
defend themselves against oppression and exploitation. Letting people enrich themselves from human
suffering or the suffering of other beings is something
we cannot do. As a community we must try to prevent
this. How to work for justice in our own city is a problem that we have to consider. The Bodhisattvas'
vows—to help all sentient beings—are immense.
Each of us can vow to sit in their rescue boats.

**Fourteenth: Do not mistreat your body. Learn to
handle it with respect. Do not look on your body as
only an instrument. Preserve vital energies (sexual,**

breath, spirit) for the realization of the Way. Sexual expression should not happen without love and commitment. In sexual relationships be aware of future suffering that may be caused. To preserve the happiness of others, respect the rights and commitments of others. Be fully aware of the responsibility of bringing new lives into the world. Meditate on the world into which you are bringing new beings.

You may have the impression that this precept discourages having children, but it is not so. It only urges us to be aware of what we are doing. Is our world safe enough to bring in more children? If you want to bring more children into the world, then do something for the world.

This precept also has to do with celibacy. Traditionally, Buddhist monks were celibate for at least three reasons. The first is that the monks in the time of the Buddha were urged to practice meditation for most of the day. They had to be in contact with the people in the village in order to teach them the Dharma, and in order to ask for some food for the day. If a monk had to support a family, he would not be able to perform his duties as a monk.

The second reason is that sexual energy had to be be preserved for meditation. In the religious and medical traditions of Asia, the human person was said to have three sources of energy: sexual, breath, and spirit. Sexual energy is what you spend during sexual intercourse. Breath energy is the kind of energy you spend when you talk too much and breathe

too little. Spirit energy is energy that you spend
when you worry too much, and do not sleep well. If
you spend these three sources of energy, your body is
not strong enough for the realization of the Way and
a deep penetration into reality. Buddhist monks observed celibacy, not because of moral admonition, but
for conservation of energy. Someone on a long fast
knows how important it is to preserve these three
sources of energy.

The third reason Buddhist monks observed celibacy is the question of suffering. At that time, and
even today, if we go to India we see many children
without food, so many children sick without medicine, and one woman can give birth to ten, twelve
children, without being able to feed two or three
properly. "Life is suffering" is the first truth in
Buddhism. To bring a child into the world is a great
responsibility. If you are wealthy, maybe you can do
it with no problem. But if you are poor, this is a real
concern. To be reborn means first to be reborn in your
children. Your children are a continuation of yourself. You are reborn in them. You continue the cycle of
suffering. Aware that having more children in his
society would be to make them suffer, the Buddha
urged the monks not to have children. I think that
during the past 2,500 years, Buddhist monks in many
countries have helped curb the birth rate. That is
quite important.

The fourteenth precept urges us to respect our own
body, to maintain our energy for the realization of
the Way. Not only meditation, but any kind of

efforts that are required to change the world require energy. We should take good care of ourselves.

In my opinion, the liberation of sexual behavior in the West has caused a number of good results, but has also caused some problems. The liberation of women, because of modern birth control methods, has been something very real. In the past, young girls, in Asia as well as Europe, had enormous problems and some even committed suicide when they became pregnant. Since the discovery of birth control, these kinds of tragedies have lessened considerably. But the liberation of sexual behavior has also caused much stress, much trouble. I think the fact that many people suffer from depression is partly because of that. Please meditate on the problem. It is a very important problem for Western society.

If you wish to have children, please do something for the world you bring them into. That will make you someone who works for peace, in one way or another.

CHAPTER SEVEN

Meditation in Daily Life

*D*uring retreats, from time to time a Bell Master invites the bell to sound, silently reciting this poem first:

Body, speech, and mind in perfect oneness,
I send my heart along with the sound of the bell.
May the hearer awaken from forgetfulness
And transcend all anxiety and sorrow.

Then he or she breathes three times, and invites the bell to sound. When the rest of us hear the bell, we stop our thinking and breathe in and out three times, reciting this verse:

Listen, listen,
This wonderful sound
brings me back to my true self.

Meditation is to be aware of what is going on: in your body, in your feelings, in your mind, and in the world. The most precious practice in Buddhism is meditation, and it is important to practice meditation in a joyful mood. We have to smile a lot in order to be able to meditate. The Bell of Mindfulness helps us to do this.

*   *   *

Suppose we have a son who becomes an unbearable young man. It may be hard for us to love him. That is natural. In order to be loved, a person should be lovable. If our son has become difficult to love, we will be very unhappy. We wish we could love him, but the only way we can is to understand him, to understand his situation. We have to take our son as the subject of our meditation. Instead of taking the concept of emptiness or some other subject, we can take our son as a concrete subject for our meditation.

First we need to stop the invasion of feelings and thoughts, which deplete our strength in meditation, and cultivate the capacity, the power of concentration. In Sanskrit this is called *samadhi*. For a child to do his homework he has to stop chewing gum and stop listening to the radio, so he can concentrate on the homework. If we want to understand our son, we have to learn to stop the things that divert our attention. Concentration, samadhi, is the first practice of meditation.

When we have a light bulb, for the light to con-

centrate on our book, we need a lamp shade to keep
the light from dispersing, to concentrate the light so
that we can read the book more easily. The practice
of concentration is like acquiring a lamp shade to
help us concentrate our mind on something. While
doing sitting or walking meditation, cutting the future, cutting the past, dwelling in the present time,
we develop our own power of concentration. With
that power of concentration, we can look deeply into
the problem. This is insight meditation. First we are
aware of the problem, focusing all our attention on
the problem, and then we look deeply into it in order
to understand its real nature, in this case the nature
of our son's unhappiness.

We don't blame our son. We just want to understand why he has become like that. Through this
method of meditation, we find out all the causes,
near and far, that have led to our son's present state
of being. The more we see, the more we understand.
The more we understand, the easier it is for us to
have compassion and love. Understanding is the
source of love. Understanding is love itself. Understanding is another name for love; love is another
name for understanding. When we practice Buddhism, it is helpful to practice in this way.

When you grow a tree, if it does not grow well,
you don't blame the tree. You look into the reasons it
is not doing well. You may need fertilizer, or more
water, or less sun. You never blame the tree, yet we
blame our son. If we know how to take care of him,
he will grow well, like a tree. Blaming has no effect

at all. Never blame, never try to persuade using reason and arguments. They never lead to any positive effect. That is my experience. No argument, no reasoning, no blame, just understanding. If you understand, and you show that you understand, you can love, and the situation will change.

*   *   *

The Bell of Mindfulness is the voice of the Buddha calling us back to ourselves. We have to respect that sound, stop our thinking and talking, and go back to ourselves, with a smile and breathing. It is not a Buddha from the outside. It is our own Buddha calling us. If we cannot hear the sound of the bell, then we cannot hear other sounds which also come from the Buddha, like the sound of the wind, the sound of the bird, even the sounds of cars or a baby crying. They are all calls from the Buddha to return to ourselves. Practicing with a bell is helpful, and once you can practice with a bell, you can practice with the wind and other sounds. After that you can practice not only with the sounds, but with forms. The sunlight coming through your window is also a calling from Dharmakaya for the Buddhakaya to be, and also for the Sanghakaya to be real.

"Calming, Smiling, Present moment, Wonderful moment." When you sit you can recite this, and while doing walking meditation you can use it, or other methods, like counting: Breathing in, one. Breathing out, one. Breathing in, two. Out, two.

In, three; out, three. Until ten, and then you de-
crease: ten, and then nine, eight, seven. Counting the
breath is one of the ways to educate yourself for concentration, samadhi.

If you do not have enough concentration, you cannot be strong enough to break through, to have a
breakthrough into a subject of your meditation.
Therefore breathing, walking, sitting, and other
practices are primarily for you to realize some degree of concentration. This is called *Stop*. Stop, in order to concentrate. Just as the lamp shade stops the
light from dispersing so you can read your book more
easily, the first step of meditation is stopping, stopping the dispersion, concentrating on one subject. The
best subject, the most available subject is your
breathing. Breathing is wonderful. It unites body
and mind. Whether you count breaths or just follow
them, it is for stopping.

Stopping and seeing are very close. As soon as you
stop, the words on the page become clear, the problem of our son becomes clear. Stop and look, that's
meditation, insight meditation. Insight means you
have a vision, an insight into reality. Stopping is
also to see, and seeing helps to stop. The two are one.
We do so much, we run so quickly, the situation is
difficult, and many people say, "Don't just sit there,
do something." But doing more things may make the
situation worse. So you should say, "Don't just do
something, sit there." Sit there, stop, be yourself
first, and begin from there. That is the meaning of
meditation. When you sit in the meditation hall or

at home or wherever you are, you can do that. But
you have to really sit. Just sitting is not enough. Sit
and *be*. Sitting without being is not sitting. Be stopping and seeing.

There are so many methods of stopping and seeing, and intelligent teachers will be able to invent
ways to help you. In Buddhism it is said that there
are 84,000 Dharma doors for you to enter reality.
Dharma doors are means of practice, ways of practice. When we ride on a horse which is out of control,
I think our deepest wish is to stop. How can we stop?
We have to resist the speed, the losing of ourselves,
and therefore we must organize a resistance. Spend-
ing two hours on one cup of tea during a tea meditation is an act of resistance, nonviolent resistance. We
can do it because we have a Sanghakaya. We can do
it together, we can resist a way of life that makes us
lose ourselves. Walking meditation is also resistance. Sitting is also resistance. So if you want to
stop the course of armaments, you have to resist, and
begin by resisting in your own daily life. I saw a car
from New York with a bumper sticker, "Let peace
begin with me." That's correct. And let me begin
with peace. That is also correct.

*   *   *

Walking meditation can be very enjoyable. We walk
slowly, alone or with friends, if possible in some
beautiful place. Walking meditation is really to enjoy the walking. Walking not in order to arrive, just
for walking. The purpose is to be in the present

moment and enjoy each step you make. Therefore you have to shake off all worries and anxieties, not thinking of the future, not thinking of the past, just enjoying the present moment. You can take the hand of a child as you do it. You walk, you make steps as if you are the happiest person on Earth.

We walk all the time, but usually it is more like running. When we walk like that, we print anxiety and sorrow on the Earth. We have to walk in a way that we only print peace and serenity on Earth. Everyone of us can do that provided that we want it very much. Any child can do that. If we can take one step like that, we can take two, three, four, and five. When we are able to take one step peacefully, happily, we are for the cause of peace and happiness for the whole of humankind. Walking meditation is a wonderful practice.

*   *   *

The Buddha's basic Dharma Talk concerning meditation, *The Satipatthana Sutta*, is available in Pali, Chinese, and many other languages, including English and French. According to this text, to meditate is to be aware of what is going on in your body, in your feelings, in your mind, and in the objects of your mind, which are the world. If you are aware of what is going on, then you can see problems as they unfold, and you can help prevent many of them. When things explode, it is too late. How we deal with our daily lives is the most important question.

How we deal with our feelings, our speaking, with ordinary things everyday is just meditation. We must learn to apply meditation in our daily lives.

There are many easy things to do. For instance, before eating the evening meal, everyone can sit around the table, and practice breathing, three slow breaths. You breathe to recover yourself, to be yourself. I am sure that every time you breathe deeply like that, you become entirely yourself again. Then before eating you can look at everyone and smile, just two or three seconds, not much, for each person. We never have time to look at each other, even those we love, and soon it will be too late. It is wonderful to do that, to openly appreciate everyone in our own household.

In Plum Village, it is a child who reads the gatha before eating. Holding up a bowl of rice, he knows he is very lucky. Being a refugee he knows that in many countries of Southeast Asia, children do not have enough to eat. The kind of rice that they buy in the West is the best kind of rice imported from Thailand. The children know that even in Thailand, Thai children do not have the opportunity to eat such rice. They eat poorer quality rice. The good rice is exported for the country to get foreign currency. When a refugee boy holds up a bowl of rice, he has to remember that he is lucky. He knows that 40,000 children his age die in the world each day because of hunger. Then the child says something like this: "Today, on the table there are good things that Mommy just cooked. There I see Papa, there I

see my brother, there I see my sister, it is so good to
be together and eat together like this, while there
are many who are hungry. I feel very thankful."

There are so many practices we can do to bring
awareness into our everyday lives: breathing between telephone calls, walking meditation between
business meetings, practicing meditation while
helping hungry children or war victims. Buddhism
must be engaged. What is the use of practicing meditation if it does not have anything to do with our
daily lives?

*   *   *

You can feel very happy while practicing breathing
and smiling. The conditions are available. You can
do it in a meditation hall. You can do it at home.
You can do it in a park, along the riverside, anywhere. I would like to suggest that in each home we
have a tiny room for breathing. We have a room for
sleeping, a room for eating, and a room for cooking,
why not have one room for breathing? Breathing is
very important.

I suggest that that room be decorated very simply, and not be too bright. You may want to have a
small bell, one with a beautiful sound, a few cushions or chairs, and perhaps a pot of flowers to remind us of our true nature. Children can arrange
flowers in mindfulness, smiling. If your household
has five members, you can have five cushions or
chairs, plus a few for guests. From time to time, you

might like to invite a guest to come and sit and breathe with you for five minutes, or three minutes.

If you want to have a statue or a painting of a Buddha, please be choosy. Many times I see Buddhas who are not relaxed and peaceful. The artists who make them do not practice breathing, smiling. Be choosy if you ask a Buddha to come home. A Buddha should be smiling, happy, beautiful, for the sake of our children. If they look at the Buddha and don't feel refreshed and happy, then it is not a good statue. If you don't find a beautiful Buddha, wait, and have a flower instead. A flower is a Buddha. A flower has Buddha nature.

I know of families where children go into a room like that after breakfast, sit down and breathe for ten times, in-out-one, in-out-two, in-out-three, ten times, and then they go to school. This is a very beautiful practice. If your child doesn't wish to breathe ten times, how about three times? Beginning the day with being a Buddha is a very nice way to start the day. If we are a Buddha in the morning and we try to nourish the Buddha throughout the day, we may be able to come home at the end of a day with a smile—the Buddha is still there.

When you become agitated, you do not have to do or say anything. Just follow your breathing and walk slowly into that room. (The room for breathing also symbolizes our own inner Buddha Land, so we can enter it whenever we need to, even if we are not at home). I have a friend who, whenever he becomes agitated, enters the breathing room in his home. He sits down respectfully, breathes in and out three times, invites the bell to sound, and recites the gatha. Immediately he feels better. If he needs to sit longer, he stays there. From time to time, while his wife is preparing dinner, she hears the sound of the bell, and it reminds her to be mindful in her work. At such times, she deeply appreciates her husband. "He is so wonderful, quite different from others. He knows how to deal with anger." If she has been irritated, her own resentment subsides. Sometimes she stops cutting vegetables and goes into the breathing room to sit with him. This picture is so lovely, more beautiful than an expensive painting. Doing things in this way has a good effect on everyone, teaching by example, not just with words. When your child is agitated, you don't have to say, "Go to that room!" You can take his or her hand and walk together into the room for breathing, and sit quietly together. This is the best education for peace.

It is really beautiful to begin the day by being a Buddha. Each time we feel ourselves about to leave our Buddha, we can sit and breathe until we return to our true self. There are three things I can recommend to you: arranging to have a breathing room in your home, a room for meditation; practicing breathing, sitting, for a few minutes every morning at home with your children; and going out for a slow walking meditation with your children before going to sleep, just ten minutes is enough. These things are very important. They can change our civilization.

The Sun My Heart

From Mindfulness to Insight Contemplation

Contents

Introduction

M editors since the beginning of time have known that they must use their own eyes and the language of their own times to express their insight. Wisdom is a living stream, not an icon to be preserved in a museum. Only when a practitioner finds the spring of wisdom in his or her own life can it flow to future generations. Keeping the torch of wisdom glowing is the work of all of us who know how to clear a path through the forest in order to walk on ahead.

Our insight and our language are inseparable from the times in which we live. For many years now, the East has followed the West down the path of technological and material development, to the point of neglecting its own spiritual values. In our world, technology is the main force behind economics and politics, but those in the forefront of science have begun to see something similar to what the spiritual disciplines of the East discovered long ago. If we can survive our times, the gap that separates science and spirituality will close, and East and West will meet one another on the path to discover true mind. Those in whom the seeds of this important endeavor have already been sown can start working towards that convergence right now, using their own daily mindful lives.

This small book was written not to show off any knowledge of the author. (In fact, there is not much for him to show off.) It prefers to be a friend rather than a book. You can take it with you on the bus or subway as you do your coat or your scarf. It can give you small moments of joy at any time. You may like to read a few lines, then close it and put it back in your pocket, and read another few lines sometime later. If you find a paragraph that is difficult or complicated, just skip over it and try the next one. You can return to it later and maybe you will find that it is not so complicated after all. Chapter Five, which is the last one, is quite pleasant to read. You can start there if you like.

Please draw on your own experience to understand this book. Do not be intimidated by any of the words or ideas. Only as author of the text yourself will you find the joy and the strength necessary to journey from mindfulness to insight.

Nhat Hanh
January 1988

THE SUN MY HEART

Sunshine and Green Leaves

Thanh Thuy's Apple Juice

Today three children, two girls and a little boy, came from the village to play with Thanh Thuy (pronounced "Tahn Tui"). The four of them ran off to play on the hillside behind our house and were gone for about an hour when they returned to ask for something to drink. I took the last bottle of homemade apple juice and gave them each a full glass, serving Thuy last. Since her juice was from the bottom of the bottle, it had some pulp in it. When she noticed the particles, she pouted and refused to drink it. So the four children went back to their games on the hillside, and Thuy had not drunk anything.

Half an hour later, while I was meditating in my room, I heard her calling. Thuy wanted to get herself a glass of cold water, but even on tiptoes she couldn't reach the faucet. I reminded her of the glass of juice on the table and asked her to drink that first. Turning to look at it, she saw that the pulp had settled and the juice looked clear and delicious. She went to the table and took the glass with both hands. After drinking half of it, she put it down and asked, "Is this a different glass, Uncle Monk?" (a common term for Vietnamese children to use when addressing an older monk.)

"No," I answered. "It's the same one as before. It sat quietly for a bit, and now it's clear and delicious." Thuy looked at the glass again. "It really is good. Was it meditating like you, Uncle Monk?" I laughed and patted her head. "Let's say that I imitate the apple juice when I sit; that is closer to the truth."

Every night at Thuy's bedtime, I sit in meditation. I let her sleep in the same room, near where I am sitting. We have agreed that while I am sitting, she will go to bed without talking. In that peaceful atmosphere, rest comes easily to her, and she is usually asleep within 5 or 10 minutes. When I finish sitting, I cover her with a blanket.

Thanh Thuy is the child of "boat people." She is not yet 4 1/2 years old. She crossed the seas with her father and arrived in Malaysia in April of last year. Her mother stayed in Vietnam. When her father arrived here in France, he left Thuy with us for several months while he went to Paris to look for a job. I taught her the Vietnamese alphabet and some popular folk songs from our country. She is very intelligent, and after two weeks she was able to spell out and slowly read *The Kingdom of Fools*, by Leo Tolstoy, which I translated into Vietnamese from the French.

Every night Thanh Thuy sees me sit. I told her that I am "sitting in meditation" without explaining what it means or why I do it. Every night when she sees me wash my face, put on my robes, and light a stick of incense to make the room fragrant, she knows that soon I will begin "meditating." She also knows that it is time for her to brush her teeth, change into pajamas, and go quietly to bed. I have never had to remind her.

Without a doubt, Thuy thought that the apple juice was sitting for a while to clear itself, just like her Uncle Monk. "Was it meditating like you?" I think that Thanh Thuy, not yet 4 1/2, understands the meaning of meditation without any explanation. The apple juice became clear after resting awhile. In the same way, if we rest in meditation awhile, we too become clear. This clarity refreshes us and gives us strength and serenity. As we feel ourselves refreshed, our surroundings also become refreshed. Children like to be near us, not just to get candy and hear stories. They like to be near us because they can feel this "freshness."

Tonight a guest has come. I fill a glass with the last of the apple juice and put it on the table in the middle of the meditation room. Thuy is already fast asleep, and I invite my friend to sit very quietly, just like the apple juice.

A River of Perceptions

We sit for about 40 minutes. I notice my friend smiling as he looks at the juice. It has become very clear. "And you, my friend, are you? Even if you have not settled as thoroughly as the apple juice, don't you feel a little less agitated, less fidgety, less disturbed? The smile on your lips hasn't faded yet, but I think you doubt that you might become as clear as the apple juice, even if we continue to sit for hours.

"The glass of juice has a very stable base. But you, your sitting is not so sure. Those tiny bits of pulp only have to follow the laws of nature to fall gently to the bottom of the glass. But your thoughts obey no such law. To the contrary, they buzz feverishly, like a swarm of bees, and so you think you cannot settle like the apple juice.

"You tell me that people, living beings with the capacity to think and to feel, cannot be compared with a glass of juice. I agree, but I also know that we can do what the apple juice does, and more. We can be at peace, not only while sitting, but also while walking and working.

"Perhaps you don't believe me, because 40 minutes have passed and you tried so hard but weren't able to achieve the peace you hoped for. Thuy is sleeping peacefully, her breathing is light. Why don't we light another candle before continuing our conversation?"

"Little Thuy sleeps this way effortlessly. You know those nights when sleep eludes you, and the harder you try to sleep the less you can. You are trying to force yourself to be peaceful, and you feel the resistance inside of you. This same sort of resistance is felt by many people during their first experiences with meditation. The more they try to calm themselves, the more restless they become. The Vietnamese think this is because they are victims of demons or bad karma, but really this resistance is born out of our very efforts to be peaceful. The effort itself becomes oppressive. Our thoughts and feelings flow like a river. If we try to stop the flow of a river, we will meet the resistance of the water. It is better to flow with it, and then we may be able to guide it in ways we want it to go. We must not attempt to halt it.

"Keep in mind that the river must flow and that we are going to follow it. We must be aware of every little stream that joins it. We must be aware of all the thoughts, feelings, and sensations that arise in us—of their birth, duration, and disappearance. Do you see? Now the resistance begins to disappear. The river of perceptions is still flowing, but no longer in darkness. It is now flowing in the sunlight of awareness. To keep this sun always shining inside of us, illuminating each rivulet, each pebble, each bend in the river, is the practice of meditation. To practice meditation is, first of all, to observe and to follow these details.

"At the moment of awareness we feel we are in control, even though the river is still there, still flowing. We feel ourselves at peace, but this isn't the 'peace' of the apple juice. Being at peace doesn't mean our thoughts and feelings are frozen. Being at peace is not the same as being anesthetized. A peaceful mind does not mean a mind empty of thoughts, sensations, and emotions. A peaceful mind is not an absent one. It is clear that thoughts and feelings alone do not comprise the whole of our being. Fury, hatred, shame, faith, doubt, impatience, disgust, desire, sorrow, and anguish are also mind. Hope, inhibition, intuition, instinct, subconscious and unconscious minds are equally part of the self. Vijñanavada Buddhism discusses at length the eight principal and 51 subordinate mental conditions. If you have the time, you may want to look at these writings. They embrace all psychological phenomena."

Sunshine and Green Leaves

Beginning meditators usually think they must suppress all thoughts and feelings (often called "false mind") in order to create conditions favorable to concentration and understanding (called "true mind"). They use methods such as focusing their attention on an object or counting their breaths to try to block out thoughts and feelings. Concentrating on an object and counting the breath are excellent methods, but they should not be used for suppression or repression. We know that as soon as there is repression, there is rebellion—repression entails rebellion. True mind and false mind are one. Denying one is denying the other. Suppressing one is suppressing the other. Our mind is our self. We cannot suppress it. We must treat it with respect, with gentleness, and absolutely without violence. Since we do not even know what our "self" is, how can we know if it is true or false, and whether or what to suppress? The only thing we can do is to let the sunlight of awareness shine on our "self" and en-lighten it, so we can look at it directly.

Just as flowers and leaves are only part of a plant, and just as waves are only part of the ocean, perceptions, feelings, and thoughts are only part of the self. Blossoms and leaves are a natural manifestation of plants, and waves are a natural expression of oceans. It is useless to try to repress or stifle them. It is impossible. We can only observe them. Because they exist, we can find their source, which is exactly the same as our own.

The sun of awareness originates in the heart of the self. It enables the self to illuminate the self. It lights not only all thoughts and feelings present. It lights itself as well.

Let us return to the apple juice, quietly "resting." The river of our perceptions continues to flow, but now, in the sunlight of awareness, it flows peacefully, and we are serene. The relation between the river of perceptions and the sun of awareness is not the same as that of an actual river and the actual sun. Whether it is midnight or noon, whether the sun is absent or its penetrating rays are beaming down, the waters of the Mississippi River continue to flow, more or less the same. But when the sun of awareness shines on the river of our perceptions, the mind is transformed. Both river and sun are of the same nature.

Let us consider the relationship between the color of leaves and sunlight, which also have the same nature. At midnight, the starlight and moonlight reveal only the form of the trees and leaves. But if the sun were suddenly to shine, the green color of the leaves would immediately appear. The tender green of the leaves in April exists because the sunlight exists. One day, while sitting in a forest, mimicking the *Prajña Paramita Heart Sutra*, I wrote:

> Sunshine is green leaves
> Green leaves are sunshine
> Sunshine is not different from green leaves
> Green leaves are not different from sun-
> shine
> The same is true of all forms and colors.[1]

As soon as the sun of awareness shines, at that very moment a great change takes place. Meditation lets the sun of awareness rise easily, so we can see more clearly. When we meditate, we seem to have two selves. One is the flowing river of thoughts and feelings, and the other is the sun of awareness that shines on them. Which is our own self? Which is true? Which false? Which is good? Which bad? Please calm down, my friend. Lay down your sharp sword of conceptual thinking. Don't be in such a hurry to cut your "self" in two. Both are self. Neither is true. Neither is false. They are both true and both false.

We know that light and color are not separate phenomena. In the same way, the sun of self and the river of self are not different. Sit with me, let a smile form on your lips, let your sun shine, close your eyes, if need be, to see your self more clearly. Your sun of awareness is only part of your river of self, isn't it? It follows the same laws as all psychological phenomena: it arises and vanishes away. To examine something with a microscope, a scientist must shine light on the object being observed. To observe the self, you must shine light on it too, the light of awareness.

I just told you to put down your sword of conceptualization and not cut your self into sections. Actually, you couldn't, even if you wanted to. Do you think you can separate the sunshine from the green color of the leaves? You can no more separate the observing self from the self observed. When the sun of awareness shines, the nature of thoughts and feelings is transformed. It is one with the observing mind, but they remain different, like the green of the leaves and the sunshine. Don't rush from the concept of "two" to the concept of "one." This ever-present sun of awareness is at the same time its own object. When a lamp is turned on, the lamp itself is also brought to light. "I know that I know." "I am conscious of being conscious." When you think, "The sun of awareness has gone out in me," at that moment it re-lights itself, faster than the speed of light.

Darkness Becomes Light

Observe the changes that take place in your mind under the light of awareness. Even your breathing has changed and become "not-two" (I don't want to say "one") with your observing self. This is also true of your thoughts and feelings, which, together with their effects, are suddenly transformed. When you do not try to judge or suppress them, they become intertwined with the observing mind.

From time to time you may become restless, and the restlessness will not go away. At such times, just sit quietly, follow your breathing, smile a half-smile, and shine your awareness on the restlessness. Don't judge it or try to destroy it, because this restlessness is you yourself. It is born, has some period of existence, and fades away, quite naturally. Don't be in too big a hurry to find its source. Don't try too hard to make it disappear. Just illuminate it. You will see that little by little it will change, merging, becoming connected, with you, the observer. Any psychological state which you subject to this illumination will eventually soften and acquire the same nature as the observing mind.

Throughout your meditation, keep the sun of your awareness shining. Like the physical sun, which lights every leaf and every blade of grass, our awareness lights our every thought and feeling, allowing us to recognize them, be aware of their birth, duration, and dissolution, without judging or evaluating, welcoming or banishing them. It is important that you do not consider awareness to be your "ally," called on to suppress the "enemies" that are your unruly thoughts. Do not turn your mind into a battlefield. Do not have a war there; for *all* your feelings—joy, sorrow, anger, hatred—are part of yourself. Awareness is like an elder brother or sister, gentle and attentive, who is there to guide and enlighten. It is a tolerant and lucid presence, never violent or discriminating. It is there to recognize and identify thoughts and feelings, not to judge them as good or bad, or place them into opposing camps in order to fight with each other. Opposition between good and bad is often compared to light and dark, but if we look at it in a different way, we will see that when light shines, darkness does not disappear. It doesn't leave; it merges with the light. It becomes the light.

A while ago I invited my guest to smile. To meditate does not mean to fight with a problem. To meditate means to observe. Your smile proves it. It proves that you are being gentle with yourself, that the sun of awareness is shining in you, that you have control of your situation. You are yourself, and you have acquired some peace. It is this peace that makes a child love to be near you.

A Poem for Buttoning Your Jacket

We can be better than a glass of apple juice. Not only can we settle peacefully while sitting still, we can also do it while standing, lying down, walking, or even working. What prevents you from allowing the sun of awareness to shine while you take a walk, make a cup of tea or coffee, or wash your clothes? When I first became a student at the Tu Hieu Monastery, I learned to maintain awareness during all activities—weeding the garden, raking leaves around the pond, washing dishes in the kitchen. I practiced mindfulness in the way taught by Zen Master Doc The in his little manual, *Essentials of the Practice to Apply Each Day*. According to this small book, we must be fully aware of all our actions. While waking up we know that we are waking up; while buttoning our jacket, we know that we are buttoning our jacket; while washing our hands we know that we are washing our hands. Master Doc The composed short poems for us to recite while washing our hands or buttoning our jackets to help us remain firmly rooted in awareness. Here is the poem he wrote for us to recite while buttoning our jacket:

> While buttoning my jacket
> I hope that all beings
> Will keep their hearts warm
> And not lose themselves.

With the aid of verses like this, it is easy for the the sun of awareness to shine its light on our physical actions as well as our thoughts and feelings. When I was a child I often heard my mother tell my elder sister that a girl must pay attention to her every movement. I was glad I was a boy who didn't have to pay attention like that. It was only when I began to practice meditation that I realized that I had to pay a thousand times more attention to my movements than my sister had. And not only to my movements, but also to my thoughts and feelings! My mother, like all mothers, knew that a girl who pays attention to her movements becomes more beautiful. Her movements are not jerky, rushed, or clumsy; they become gentle, calm, and graceful. Without knowing it, my mother taught my sister meditation.

In the same way, someone who practices awareness becomes beautiful to see. A Zen master, observing a student ringing the bell, sweeping the yard, setting the table, can guess how ripe that student is, can measure the student's "level of meditation" in his or her manners and personality. This "level" is the fruit of the practice of awareness, and the master calls it "the flavor of Zen."

Three Hours for a Cup of Tea

The secret of meditation is to be conscious of each second of your existence and to keep the sun of awareness continually shining—in both the physical and psychological realms, in all circumstances, on each thing that arises. While drinking a cup of tea, our mind must be fully present in the act of drinking the tea. Drinking tea or coffee can be one of our daily pleasures if we partake of it fully. How much time do you set aside for one cup of tea? In coffee shops in New York or Tokyo, people come in, order their coffee, drink it quickly, pay, and rush out to do something else. This takes a few minutes at most. Often there is loud music playing, and your ears hear the music, your eyes watch others gulping down their coffee, and your mind is thinking of what to do next. You can't really call this drinking coffee.

Have you ever participated in a tea ceremony? It may take two or three hours just being together and drinking one or two cups of tea. The time is not spent talking—only being together and drinking tea. Perhaps you think this is irresponsible because the participants are not worrying about the world situation, but you must admit that people who spend their time this way know how to drink tea, know the pleasure of having tea with a friend.

Devoting two hours to a cup of tea is, I agree, a little extreme. There are many other things to do: gardening, laundry, washing dishes, binding books, writing. Perhaps these other tasks are less pleasant than drinking tea or walking in the hills, but if we do them in full awareness, we will find them quite agreeable. Even washing the dishes after a big meal can be a joy.

Bathing a Newborn Buddha

To my mind, the idea that doing dishes is unpleasant can occur only when you aren't doing them. Once you are standing in front of the sink with your sleeves rolled up and your hands in warm water, it really isn't so bad. I enjoy taking my time with each dish, being fully aware of the dish, the water, and each movement of my hands. I know that if I hurry in order to go and have a cup of tea, the time will be unpleasant, and not worth living. That would be a pity, for each minute, each second of life is a miracle. The dishes themselves and the fact that I am here washing them are miracles! I wrote about this in *The Miracle of Mindfulness*. Each bowl I wash, each poem I compose, each time I invite a bell to sound is a miracle, and each has exactly the same value. One day, while washing a bowl, I felt that my movements were as sacred and respectful as bathing a newborn Buddha. If he were to read this, that newborn Buddha would certainly be happy for me, and not at all insulted at being compared with a bowl.

Each thought, each action in the sunlight of awareness becomes sacred. In this light, no boundary exists between the sacred and the profane. I must confess it takes me a bit longer to do the dishes, but I live fully in every moment, and I am happy. Washing the dishes is at the same time a means and an end—that is, not only do we do the dishes in order to have clean dishes, we also do the dishes just to do the dishes, to live fully in each moment while washing them.

If I am incapable of washing dishes joyfully, if I want to finish them quickly so I can go and have a cup of tea, I will be equally incapable of drinking the tea joyfully. With the cup in my hands I will be thinking about what to do next, and the fragrance and the flavor of the tea, together with the pleasure of drinking it, will be lost. I will always be dragged into the future, never able to live in the present moment.

Nourishing Awareness While Working

Our work, which lets us "earn our daily bread," can be done in the same way as the dishes. In my community, I bind books. Using a toothbrush, a small wheel, and a very heavy fire-proof brick (about 4 or 5 pounds), I can bind 200 books in a day. Before binding, I gather all the pages and arrange them numerically around a long table. Then I walk around the table, and when I have walked all around it, I know that I have the correct number of pages for one signature. Walking around the table, I know that I am not going anywhere in particular, so I walk slowly, gathering each page, conscious of each movement, breathing softly, conscious of each breath. I am at peace while assembling the pages, gluing them, and putting the cover on the book. I know I cannot produce as many books in a day as a professional bookbinder or a machine, but I also know that I do not hate my job. If you want a lot of money to spend, you must work hard and quickly, but if you live simply, you can work gently and in full awareness. I know many young people who prefer to work less, perhaps four hours a day, earning a small livelihood, so they can live simply and happily. This may be a solution to our society's problems—reducing the production of useless goods, sharing work with those who have none, and living simply and happily. Some individuals and communities have already proved that it is possible. This is a promising sign for the future, isn't it?

You may ask how you can nourish awareness while washing dishes, binding books, or working in a factory or an office. I think you have to find your own answer. Do whatever you can to keep the light of awareness shining inside yourself. You will discover ways that suit you, or you can try some techniques that others have tried—like reciting the short poems of Zen master Doc The, or concentrating on your breathing. You can maintain awareness of each inhalation and exhalation, of each movement of your lungs. When a thought or feeling arises, allow it to flow naturally with your breath. It may help to breathe lightly and a little more slowly than usual as a reminder that you are following your breathing.

The Precious Smile

While following your breathing, you have been able to stay fully conscious for some time. You have succeeded a bit, haven't you? So why not smile? A tiny bud of a smile, just to prove you have succeeded. Seeing you smile, I know immediately that you are dwelling in awareness. Keep this smile always blooming, the half-smile of a Buddha.

This tiny budding smile, how many artists have labored to bring it to the lips of countless statues of the Buddha? Perhaps you have seen them on the faces at Angkor Wat in Kampuchea, or those from Gandhara in northwest India. I am sure the same smile must have been on the faces of the sculptors as they worked. Can you imagine an angry sculptor giving birth to such a smile? Surely not! I know the sculptor who created the "Parinirvana" statue on Tra Cu Mountain in Vietnam. During the six months it took him to create that statue, he remained vegetarian, practicing sitting meditation and studying sutras. Mona Lisa's smile is light, just a hint of a smile. Yet even a smile like that is enough to relax all the muscles on your face, to banish all worries and fatigue. A tiny bud of a smile on your lips nourishes awareness and calms you miraculously. It returns you to the peace you had lost.

When you walk in the hills, or in a park, or along a river bank, you can follow your breath, with a half-smile blooming on your lips. When you feel tired or irritated, you can lie down with your arms at your sides, allowing all your muscles to relax, maintaining awareness of just your breath and your smile. Relaxing in this way is wonderful, and quite refreshing. You will benefit a lot if you practice it several times a day. Your mindful breath and your smile will bring happiness to you and to those around you. Even if you spend a lot of money on gifts for everyone in your family, nothing you could buy them can give as much true happiness as your gift of awareness, breathing, and smiling, and these precious gifts cost nothing.

Breathing Rhythmically

When you are too restless or under too much strain to follow your breathing, you can count your breath instead. Count "one" during the first inhalation and exhalation. Do not lose the thought "one." During the next inhalation and exhalation, count "two," and do not lose it. Continue in this way until you reach "ten," and then start again with "one." If you lose the thread of concentration at any time, you can start again at "one." When you are calm and concentrated, you will be able to follow your breath without counting.

Have you ever cut grass with a scythe? Five or six years ago, I brought a scythe home and tried to cut the grass around my cottage with it. It took more than a week before I found the best way to use it. The way you stand, the way you hold the scythe, the angle of the blade on the grass are all important. I found that if I coordinated the movement of my arms with the rhythm of my breathing, and worked unhurriedly, while maintaining awareness of my activity, I was able to work for a longer period of time. When I didn't do this, I became tired in just ten minutes. One day a Frenchman of Italian descent was visiting my neighbor, and I asked him to show me how to use a scythe. He was much more adept than I, but for the most part he used the same position and movements. What surprised me was that he too coordinated his movements with his breathing. Since then, whenever I see a neighbor cutting his grass with a scythe, I know they are practicing awareness.

Even before having a scythe, I used other tools—picks, shovels, rakes—coordinating my breath and my movement. I have found that except for very heavy labor, such as moving boulders or pushing full wheelbarrows (which make full awareness difficult), most jobs—turning the soil, making furrows, sowing seeds, spreading manure, watering—can be done in a relaxed and mindful way. During the past few years I have avoided tiring myself and losing my breath. I think it is better not to mistreat my body. I must take care of it, treat it with respect as a musician does his instrument. I apply "nonviolence" to my body, for it is not merely a means to practice the Way, it itself is the Way. It is not only the temple, it is also the sage. My gardening and bookbinding tools, I like and respect them very much. I use them while following my breathing, and I feel that these tools and I breathe together in rhythm.

A Poem and a Peppermint Plant

I don't know what job you do every day, but I do know that some tasks lend themselves to awareness more easily than others. Writing, for example, is difficult to do mindfully. I have now reached the point when I know that a sentence is finished. But while writing the sentence, even now, I sometimes forget. That is why I have been doing more manual work and less writing these past few years. Someone said to me, "Planting tomatoes and lettuce may be the gateway to everything, but not everyone can write books and stories and poems as well as you do. Please don't waste your time with manual work!" I have not wasted any of my time. Planting a seed, washing a dish, cutting the grass are as eternal, as beautiful, as writing a poem! I do not understand how a poem can be better than a peppermint plant. Planting seeds gives me as much pleasure as writing a poem. For me, a head of lettuce or a peppermint plant has as much everlasting effect in time and space as a poem.

When I helped found the University of Advanced Buddhist Studies in 1964, I made a grave error. The students, who included young monks and nuns, studied only books, scriptures, and ideas.

At the end they had gathered nothing more than a handful of knowledge and their diplomas. In the past, when novices were accepted into a monastery, they would be taken immediately into the garden to learn weeding, watering, and planting in full awareness. The first book they read was the collection of *gathas* by Master Doc The, the book which included the poems for buttoning your jacket, washing your hands, crossing a stream, carrying water, finding your slippers in the morning, practical things, so they could practice awareness all day long. Only later would they begin to study *sutras* and participate in group discussions and private interviews with the master, and even then the scholarly studies would always go hand in hand with the practical ones. If I were to help found another university, I would model it on the old monasteries. It would be a community where all the students would eat, sleep, work, and live everyday life in the sunlight of awareness, perhaps like the Ark Community in France or the Shanti Niketan or Phuong Boi communities. I am sure that in all the world's religions, meditation and study centers resemble one another. These are good models for universities as well.

Establishing a Spiritual Homeland

Each of us needs to "belong to" a place, such as a retreat center or a monastery, where each feature of the landscape, the sounds of the bell, and even the buildings are designed to remind us to return to awareness. It is helpful to go there from time to time for several days or several weeks to renew ourselves. Even when we cannot actually go there, we only need to think of it, and we can feel ourselves smile and become peaceful and happy.

The people who live there should emanate peace and freshness, the fruits of living in awareness. They must always be there to care for us, console and support us, help us heal our wounds. Each of us must find a spiritual homeland where we can retreat from time to time, much as we ran to our mothers for refuge when we were young.

In the late 1950's, several of us built the Fragrant Palm Hermitage (Phuong Boi) in the Dalat Forest in central Vietnam. It was our spiritual homeland. Later when some of us left to form La Boi Press, the School of Youth for Social Service, Van Hanh University, and Thuong Chieu Monastery, we were able to recall Phuong Boi, and make each of these new institutions in its own way a spiritual homeland. Many of you are involved in working for social change and have a great need for such a healing place. When we were prevented by the war from returning to Phuong Boi, we went to Thuong Chieu Monastery, and when Thuong Chieu became inaccessible, we prepared for the birth of Plum Village in France.

Singing, Really Singing

We lead extremely busy lives. Even though we do not have to do as much manual labor as people in former times, we never seem to have enough time for ourselves. I know people who say they do not even have enough time to eat or breathe, and it appears to me to be true! What can we do about this? Can we take hold of time with both hands and slow it down?

First, let us light the torch of our awareness and learn again how to drink tea, eat, wash dishes, walk, sit, drive, and work in awareness. We do not have to be swept along by circumstances. We are not just a leaf or a log in a rushing river. With awareness, each of our daily acts takes on a new meaning, and we discover that we are more than machines, that our activities are not just mindless repetitions. We find that life is a miracle, the universe is a miracle, and we too are a miracle.

When we are invaded by confusion and dispersion, we can ask ourselves, "What exactly am I doing right now? Am I wasting my life?" These questions immediately relight our awareness and return our attention to our breathing. A small smile naturally appears on our lips, and each second of our work becomes alive. If you want to sing, please sing! Really sing!

From Sleep to Awakening

A political science professor asked me what I think about when I meditate. I told him, "I don't think about anything." I said that I am only attentive to what is there, what is going on. He appeared skeptical, but it is the truth. While sitting, I make almost no use of my intellect. I don't try to analyze things or solve complex problems, like math problems or riddles. Even if I am examining a *kung-an* (Japanese: *koan*), I just allow it to be there and I contemplate it, without seeking to explain or interpret it, because I know that a *kung-an* is not a puzzle to solve. Examination, in the sense of awareness, does not mean analysis. It only means continuous recognition. Thinking requires strenuous mental work, and makes us tired. This is not the case while resting in awareness or "recognizing." We have a tendency to think that meditation demands a great mobilization of "gray matter," but that is really not the case. A meditator is not a thinker; a meditator does not do mental labor. On the contrary, meditation rests the mind.

Since our conversation began, I haven't once asked my friend to use his "gray matter." I have only invited him to "see," to "recognize" things with me. To do that, we must concentrate, but not analyze. We must be attentive, without speculation or interpretation. Being attentive means giving only bare attention. It is a vehicle which can take you from sleep to awakening. If you do not *know* you are angry, feeling, thinking, sitting, and so forth, you are asleep. In his novel *The Stranger*, Albert Camus describes his anti-hero as a man who "lives as though dead." This is like living in a dark room with no light of awareness. When you light the lamp of awareness, you pass from sleep to awakening. The verb *buddh* in Sanskrit means "to wake up," and one who wakes up is called a Buddha. A Buddha is a person who is always awake. From time to time we have this awareness, so we are "from-time-to-time" Buddhas.

Awareness, Concentration, Understanding

Awareness (*sati* in Pali, *smrti* in Sanskrit) simply means "being conscious of," "remembering," or "becoming acquainted with." But we must use it in the sense of "being in the process of being conscious of," or "being in the process of remembering." We have learned the word awareness in the sense of recognition, or bare attention, but the meaning doesn't stop there. In awareness, there are also the elements concentration (*samadhi*) and understanding (*prajña*). Concentration and understanding together are both the intensity of awareness and the fruit of awareness. Every time the lamp of awareness is lit, concentration (one-pointedness) and understanding (clear-seeing) are naturally present. The words concentration and understanding are often used as terms of consequence or effect. In terms of antecedent or cause, we may use the words "stopping" and "looking." If we can stop and look attentively, we succeed in seeing clearly. But what has to stop? Forgetfulness, dispersion, and confusion—the state of lost awareness, the absence of consciousness must stop. Stopping does not mean suppression. There is only the transformation of forgetfulness into remembrance, the absence of awareness into the presence of awareness.[2]

Cooking a Pot of Corn

The practice of meditation is not an exercise in analysis or reasoning. The sword of logic has no place in the practices of awareness, concentration, and understanding, and those of stopping and looking. In Vietnam, when we cook a pot of dried corn, we concentrate the fire under the pot and several hours later the kernels come loose and split open. When the sun's rays beat down on the snow, the snow slowly melts. When a hen sits on her eggs, the chicks inside gradually take form until they are ready to peck their way out. These are images which illustrate the effect of practicing meditation.

The aim of this practice is to see the true face of reality, which is mind and mind-object. When we speak of mind and of the outside world, we immediately are caught in a dualistic conception of the universe. If we use the words mind and mind-object, we can avoid the damage done by the sword of conceptualized discrimination. The effect of meditation is like the fire under the pot, the sun's rays on the snow, and the hen's warmth on her eggs. In these three cases, there is no attempt at reasoning or analysis, just patient and continuous concentration. We can allow the truth to appear, but we cannot describe it using math, geometry, philosophy, or any other image of our intellect.

Examining a Kung-an

"Truth cannot be captured by concepts." I wonder who said this first. We too have this perception when we concentrate ourselves in order to observe. The sword of conceptual thinking only cuts truth into small, lifeless pieces all seemingly independent of each other. Many scientists acknowledge that great discoveries are often realized through intuition. For them, reason is not an agent of discovery but a tool to explain and support it afterwards. These discoveries often occur at the most unexpected times, times when the scientist is not actively engaged in thinking, analyzing, or reasoning. An illuminating perception comes about because the scientist has been paying continual silent attention to the problem—while eating, walking, talking, even sleeping, every moment of the day. People working with kung-ans do so in exactly the same way. We speak of "meditating on" a kung-an, but a more precise description would be "examining" or "looking at" it. All the problems of life, all feelings such as passion, hatred, sadness, and suffering, as well as thoughts such as birth, death, form, emptiness, existence, and non-existence can be used equally well as "objects of examination."

Awareness is Both Cause and Effect

Awareness is at the same time cause and effect, concentration and understanding, stopping and looking. As soon as the light of awareness is lit, we concentrate, we are peaceful, we see ourselves more clearly. When a generator is running, the current flows and the bulb lights. When it keeps running while charging a battery, energy accumulates in the battery. In the same way, when awareness is maintained continuously, concentration and understanding accumulate. This is what we call "working intensively." Even in sleep, awareness does not cease and the kung-an continues to be examined, even without the knowledge of the sleeper. Sometimes we even continue in awareness while dreaming. When I practice intensively, I can see even in my dreams that I maintain awareness.

Conceiving the Inconceivable

The scientific method involves limiting as much as possible the field of observation in order to see clearly. The smaller the field, the greater the attention. However, at the level of subatomic particles, scientists have discovered that each particle is affected by all other particles, and even by the mind of the observing scientist. A school of theoretical physicists has developed the "bootstrap" concept, which suggests that every thing and every being in the universe depend on every other thing and every other being for their existence. We are used to believing that particles form "things," but in fact *all* particles are dependent upon *all* other particles and none have a separate individuality—"every particle is made up of all the others." This concept is quite similar to that expressed in the *Avatamsaka Sutra*, "All is one."[3]

If reality is an interaction, an "interbeing," how can we penetrate its essence? The *Tsao-tung* (Japanese: *Soto*) Zen sect teaches its practitioners just to observe, without judgment, without speculation. They say, "How can one conceive the inconceivable? Not thinking, that is the essence of Zen."[4] I like the Vietnamese words *quan chieu* because they include the idea of shining light on something in order to look at it—a looking free of all speculation, reasoning, interpretation, or evaluation. When the sun shines continuously on a lotus flower, it opens widely, revealing its seedheart. In the same way, through the activity of looking, reality gently reveals itself. In meditation, the subject and object of pure observation are inseparable.

A Grain of Salt Enters the Sea

In science before the twentieth century, a line was always drawn between the researcher and the object of his or her study. Even today, except in the atomic realm, this is often true. A virologist and the virus under the microscope are regarded as two separate and independent entities.[5]

The attitude of meditation is exactly the opposite. Remember the relationship between the sunshine and the green leaf. When we illuminate something with our awareness, it changes, it blends and merges with the awareness. For example, when you are aware that you are happy, you may say, "I am aware that I am happy." If you go a step further, you may say, "I am aware of being aware that I am happy." There are three levels: The happiness, the awareness of happiness, and the awareness of being aware. I am offering this sword of conceptual thinking in order to demonstrate a point; but in truth, in you these three levels are one.

The Satipatthana Sutta,[6] a Buddhist scripture which teaches awareness, uses expressions such as "observing the body in the body," "observing the feelings in the feelings," "observing the mind in the mind," "observing the objects of mind in the objects of mind." Why are the words, body, feelings, mind, and objects of mind repeated? Some masters of the Abhidhamma say that the purpose of this repetition is to underline the importance of these words. I see it otherwise. I think that these words are repeated in order to remind us not to separate the meditator and the object of meditation. We must live with the object, identify with it, merge with it, like a grain of salt entering the sea in order to measure the saltiness of the sea.

It is the same with a kung-an. A kung-an is not a problem to be solved with the intellect. A kung-an is not a kung-an if it is someone else's. A kung-an is only a kung-an when it is our own. It must be our own question of life and death—it cannot be apart from our daily life. It must be planted in our flesh and bones; we must be the soil which nourishes it. Only then will its fruit and flowers be our own fruit and flowers.

The word "comprehend" is formed by combining two Latin roots: *com* (together) and *prehendere* (take, or grasp). To understand means to *take* something and *join together* with it. If we only analyze someone from the outside, without becoming one with them, without entering their shoes, their skin, we will never really understand them. The theologian Martin Buber has said that the relation between a person and God is not one of subject and object, because God cannot be the object of our knowledge. Twentieth century physicists have come to realize that "no totally objective phenomenon can exist, that is to say, independent of the observer's mind. And correlatively, all subjective phenomena present an objective fact."[7]

The Dance of the Bees

Don't Leave Your Fate in the Hands of Others

One evening I returned to my hermitage from a walk in the hills, and I found that all the doors and windows of the hermitage had been blown open. When I left the house, I hadn't secured them, and a cold wind blew through the house, opened the windows, and scattered the papers from my desk all over the room. Immediately I closed the doors and windows, lit a lamp, picked up the papers, and arranged them neatly on my desk. Then I started a fire in the fireplace, and soon the crackling logs brought warmth back to the room.

Sometimes in a crowd we feel tired, cold, and lonely. We may wish to withdraw to be by ourselves and become warm again, as I did at the hermitage, sitting by the fire, protected from the cold, damp wind. Our senses are our windows to the outside world, and sometimes the wind blows and disturbs everything within us. Many of us leave our windows open all the time, allowing the sights and sounds of the world to invade us, penetrate us, and expose our sad, troubled selves. We feel so cold and lonely and afraid. Do you ever find yourself watching an awful TV program, unable to turn it off? The raucous noises, explosions of gunfire, are upsetting. Yet you don't get up and turn it off. Why do you torture yourself in this way? Don't you want to close your windows? Are you afraid of solitude—the emptiness and the loneliness you may find when you face yourself alone.

We are what we feel and perceive. If we are angry, we are the anger. If we are in love, we are the love. If we look at a snowy mountain peak, we are the mountain. Watching a bad TV program, we are the TV program. While dreaming, we are the dream. We can be anything we want, even without a magic wand. So why do we open our windows to bad movies and TV programs, movies made by sensationalist producers in search of easy money, movies which make our hearts pound, our fists tighten, and send us back into the streets exhausted. Who allows such movies and TV programs to be made? Especially for the very young. We do! We are too undemanding, too ready to watch whatever is on the screen, too lonely, lazy, or bored to create our own lives. We turn on the TV and leave it on, allowing someone else to guide us, shape us, and destroy us. Losing ourselves in this way is leaving our fate in the hands of others who may not be acting responsibly. We must be aware of what kinds of programs do harm to our nervous systems, our minds, and our hearts, and which programs and films benefit us.

I am not just talking about movies and TV programs. All around us, how many lures are set there by our fellows and ourselves? In a single day, how many times do we become lost and scattered because of them? We must be very careful to protect our fate and our peace. That does not mean shutting all our windows, for there are many miracles in the world we call "outside." Open your windows to these miracles. Look at any one of them with the light of awareness. Even while sitting beside a clear, flowing stream, listening to beautiful music, or watching an excellent movie, do not entrust yourself entirely to the stream, the music, or the film. Continue to be aware of yourself and your breathing. With the sun of awareness shining in us, we can avoid most dangers—the stream will be purer, the music more harmonious, and the soul of the artist completely visible in the film.

A beginning meditator may want to leave the city and go off to the countryside to help close those windows that would trouble his spirit if left open. There he or she can become one with the quiet forest, and rediscover and restore himself or herself, without being carried away by the chaos of "the outside world." The fresh and silent woods help you remain in awareness. When awareness is well-rooted, when you can maintain it without faltering, then you may wish to return to the city and remain there, less troubled. But before you reach this point, you must be very careful, nourishing your awareness moment by moment, choosing the surroundings and sustenance that assist you the most.

Do Not Take a Cold Shower When You Have the Flu

If you are a professional critic, you read a book or watch a movie with an observing mind. While reading or watching you are aware of your responsibility as a critic and you do not become the "victim" of the book or film. You remain in control of yourself. When you live in awareness, you also remain in control of yourself. Though your windows are open on the world, you are not compelled by it. If we need to protect our senses, it is because we are not yet strong enough to fully encounter the world, just as someone with a cold or a flu may not be strong enough to take a cold shower.

I remember one day at La Boi Press, a small book publishing company several of us started in Vietnam, I was invited to say something about arts and letters. I said that they must both reveal and heal. To reveal means to show the true situation of people and society. To heal means to show ways to cure them. The Buddha is often called the Medicine King because his teaching is adapted to each particular being and situation. Prince Siddhartha retired to the forest to sit beside a stream for many years before returning to the world of people. Today we live in noisy and polluted societies, filled with injustice, but we can take refuge in a public park or along a river bank for a moment. Contemporary music, literature, and entertainment do little to help with healing; to the contrary much of it compounds the bitterness, desperation, and weariness we all feel. We need to find ways to protect ourselves, to learn when to open and when to close our sense-windows. This is the first step for a beginning meditator.

I find that I need surroundings and objects that fit me, that contribute to my happiness, peace, and health. Where are they? They are right there in the "outside world." A stream in a forest, the eyes of a child, a dear friend, an excellent book, a concert, a delicious, healthy meal, I know these things are available. But without awareness, I am not fully able to enjoy and appreciate them.

Taking Care of the Apple Tree in Your Yard

As we sit down next to a stream, we can listen to its laughter and watch its sparkling waters, noticing the pebbles glistening and the fresh green plants nearby, and we may be overcome with happiness. We are one with the stream's freshness, purity, and clarity. But in just an instant we may find we've had enough. Our heart is troubled, and we think of other things. We are no longer at one with the stream. It is of no use to sit in a peaceful forest if our mind is lost in the city. When we live with a child or a friend, their freshness and warmth can relax us. But if our heart is not with them, their precious presence is neglected, and they no longer exist. We must be aware of them to appreciate their value, to allow them to be our happiness. If through carelessness and forgetfulness we become dissatisfied with them, and begin asking too much of them or reprimanding them, we will lose them. Only after they are gone will we realize their preciousness and feel regret. But once they are gone, all our regrets are in vain.

Around us, life bursts forth with miracles—a glass of water, a ray of sunshine, a leaf, a caterpillar, a flower, laughter, raindrops. If you live in awareness, it is easy to see miracles everywhere. Each human being is a multiplicity of miracles. Eyes that see thousands of colors, shapes, and forms; ears that hear a bee flying or a thunderclap; a brain that ponders a speck of dust as easily as the entire cosmos; a heart that beats in rhythm with the heartbeat of all beings. When we are tired and feel discouraged by life's daily struggles, we may not notice these miracles, but they are always there.

Have a look at the apple tree in your yard. Look at it with complete attention. It is truly a miracle. If you notice it, you will take good care of it, and you too are part of its miraculousness. Even after caring for it for only a week, its leaves are already greener and shinier. It is exactly the same with the people who are around you. Under the influence of awareness, you become more attentive, understanding, and loving, and your presence not only nourishes you and makes you lovelier, it enhances them as well. Our entire society can be changed by one person's peaceful presence.

Our minds create everything. The majestic mountain top, brilliant with snow, is you yourself when you contemplate it. Its existence depends on your awareness. When you close your eyes, as long as your mind is present, the mountain is there. Sitting in meditation, with several sense-windows closed, you feel the presence of the whole universe. Why? Because the mind is there. If your eyes are closed, it is so that you can see better. The sights and sounds of the world are not your "enemies." Your "enemy" is forgetfulness, the absence of mindfulness.

Don't Become a Colony

As I write, French workers are struggling to reduce their work week from 40 hours to 35. They are working hard to accomplish this, but these five hours, how will they use them? If they use them the way they spend their Saturday nights, sitting at a bar or in front of a TV, it will be a terrible waste. We all need time to relax and to live, but how? Usually when we have some free time, we watch whatever is on TV in order to avoid "having nothing to do," which means staying home alone with ourselves. Watching TV may make us more tired, more nervous, more unbalanced, but we rarely notice these results. The free time we struggle so hard for is seized by TV broadcasting companies and the products of their advertisers. We end up being their colony. We have to find ways to use our precious time to rest and be happy.

We can choose good TV shows to watch, beautiful places to go, meetings with dear friends, books and records that suit us well. And we can live in a relaxed, contented way with what we have chosen. Remember we are whatever we choose. Have you ever been on a beach when the sun rises, or on a mountain top at noon? Did you stretch your arms wide and breathe deeply, filling your lungs with pure, clean air, with unbounded immensity? Did you feel as if you were just the sky, the sea, the mountain? If you are too far away from the sea or a mountain, you can sit cross-legged and breathe gently and deeply, and the sea, the mountain, the entire universe will enter you.

The Known is Not Separate from the Knower

To be aware is to be aware of something. When the mind settles on the mountain, it becomes the mountain. When it settles on the sea, it becomes the sea. When we say "know," both the known and the knower are included. When we meditate on our body, we are our body; we limit our observations to our body, even though we realize that our body is not separate from the rest of the universe. If we meditate on limitless space, we become limitless space (*akasanantyayatana*). If we meditate on the consciousness which includes both space and time, we reach the state of limitless consciousness (*vijñananantyayatana*). If we meditate on the absence of identity of all things, we enter the state of nothingness (*akiñcanyayatana*). If we meditate on the non-distinction between knower and known, we come to the state of "neither perception nor nonperception" (*naivasañjñanasañjñayatana*). The Four Formless States of Consciousness are not as difficult to reach as you might think, provided awareness is there to shine on every movement of the mind.

You may try to experience one of these—which, if any, is not important. The key point is never to let your awareness stand apart from whatever you regard as the object of awareness. Once you are aware, body, mountain top, or flowing river, all become your mind.

Letting Go of "In" and "Out"

You may have noticed that each time I use the expression "outside world," I put it in quotes. This is because to me it is not really "outside." Look deeply at this: Is the world outside your body? Is it outside your mind? Our body—blood, flesh, bones—belongs to this "outside world." In fact, our brain and nervous system do not escape it either. Perhaps the several hundred square centimeters that comprise our brain can be considered "inside." But no, the brain occupies space, and space is part of the "outside world," isn't it?

Is our mind in the "inner" world? Where is mind to be found? Can you identify it in space? No, all you can do is observe it, observe it observing itself. Please try looking at your mind as though it were something physical. We know that the mind is related to the brain and to the nervous system. It is memory, feeling, thought, perception, knowledge. These mental phenomena have physiological roots; they are born and they die; they have intensity. Can we locate them in space and time? In space, the nervous system serves as their base. In time, they may appear yesterday or today or tomorrow. So mind itself may be regarded as part of the so-called "outer" world. Continue to examine and you will find that everything seems to belong to the "outside" world. But outside of what? How can there be an "outer" without an "inner"?

Do not jump to the conclusion that the "outer" world is located in the mind and that the mind encloses the entire universe. That conclusion continues to accept the distinction between "inside" and "outside." To say, "Everything is found inside the mind; there is nothing outside the mind," is as absurd as saying, "It is mind that realizes the outer world."

Our confusion stems from the habit of distinguishing "in" and "out." In normal daily life, this distinction is necessary. If we stay indoors, we may be comfortable dressing lightly, even on a cold winter day. But if we go outside without dressing more warmly, we may catch a cold. Concepts such as high and low, one and many, coming and going, birth and death, are all important in everyday life. But when we leave the realm of the practical to meditate on the true nature of the universe, we must also leave behind these concepts. For example, when you raise your eyes to look up at the stars and the moon, you say that they are "above." But at the very same moment, for someone standing on the opposite side of the planet, the direction you are looking is "below" for them. When looking at the entire universe, we have to abandon all these concepts of high and low, and so forth.

Reality Cannot Be Contained

Abandoning concepts is of prime importance for a meditator. When we observe our body, our feelings, our thoughts, our perceptions, we situate them in space and time just as when we observe physical phenomena. We see psychological phenomena and physical, physiological phenomena.

You may ask, "When mind becomes the object of its own observation, is that which is grasped mind itself or only a projection or reflection of mind?" This is a good question. You may also want to ask, "When physiological and physical phenomena are observed as objects, do they keep their true nature or do they become just a projection or reflection of reality, transformed by becoming objects of observation?" Our mind creates categories—space and time, above and below, inside and outside, myself and others, cause and effect, birth and death, one and many—and puts all physical and psychological phenomena into categories like these before examining them and trying to find their true nature. It is like filling many different shapes and sizes of bottles with water in order to find out the shape and size of water. Truth itself transcends these concepts, so if you want to penetrate it you must break all the conceptual categories you use in normal daily life. The Theory of Relativity recognizes that if you do not abandon the idea that space and time are absolute and independent of one another, you cannot make progress in understanding the universe. Quantum Theory says that if you want to understand the world of subatomic particles, you must leave behind matter and empty space, cause and effect, front and back, concepts so useful in daily life.

Understanding is the Fruit of Meditation, Not of Thought

Quantum theorists today know that the consciousness of the observer is in a very close relationship with the object observed, and they are directing more and more of their attention to that consciousness. In 1979, France-Culture organized a one-week meeting in Córdoba, Spain, on "Mind and Science." Many renowned scholars were present, and a number of them affirmed their conviction that the world and mind have the same nature.

Although some scientists have seen the fundamental characteristic of mind, I am afraid that most still want to study it like any other object in their laboratories. Then it is no longer mind, but the projection or reflection of it, framed by conceptions. Remember the phrase from the *Satipatthana Sutta*: "Observe the body in the body, observe the feelings in the feelings, observe the mind in the mind, observe the objects of mind in the objects of mind." This means that you must live in the body in full awareness of it, and not just study it like a separate object. Live in awareness with feelings, mind, and objects of mind. Do not just study them. When we meditate on our body, we live with it as truth and give it our most lucid attention; we become one with it. The flower blossoms because sunlight touches and warms its bud, becoming one with it. Meditation reveals not a concept of truth, but a direct view of truth itself. This we call *Insight*, the kind of understanding based on attention and concentration.

Thinking is to take cinder blocks of concepts from the memory warehouse and build monuments. We call these hovels and palaces "thoughts." But such thinking, by itself, has no creative value. It is only when lit by understanding that thinking takes on real substance. Understanding does not arise as a result of thinking. It is a result of the long process of conscious awareness. Sometimes understanding can be translated into thoughts, but often thoughts are too rigid and limited to carry much understanding. Sometimes a look or a laugh expresses understanding much better than words or thoughts.

The Dance of the Bees

Have you ever read a book or seen a film about bees? When a worker bee finds a hillside covered with flowers, she flies back to the hive to tell her mates exactly where the flowers are, and she does it with a dance. She can even tell them of places quite far away. K. von Frisch revealed this to us after studying the language of the dance of the bees.[8]

We humans also know how to dance. Some of us dance with our bodies, others with painting or music. Even our spoken and written words are no more than the steps of a dance, the notes of a song, the strokes of a painting. They may be more or less skillful. They may translate our vision poorly or well. The skill is not only in the hands of the artist or the words of the speaker; the listener too must be skillful and perceptive. With words it is especially difficult to escape from conceptual categorizations; and even if the speaker skillfully avoids them, the listener can still fall into their traps. Remember the empty bottles? They had definite shapes and sizes even before being filled. People who practice Zen often advise not using words. This is not to discredit words, but to avoid the danger of becoming stuck in them. It is to encourage us to use words as skillfully as possible for the sake of those who hear them.

In the second century, Nagarjuna wrote *The Madhyamika Sastra*, in which he used concepts to destroy concepts. He was not trying to create a new doctrine, but to break *all* the bottles, *all* the flasks, *all* the vases, *all* the containers, to prove that water needs no form to exist. He outlined a dance for us, a dance for us to drop our categories and barriers so that we can directly encounter reality and not content ourselves with its mere reflection.

Knowledge is a Barrier to Understanding

The great discoveries of science are the result of understanding rather than thought. Scientists' tools are not just their intellects and laboratories; their whole beings down to their depths are hard at work. Intellect prepares the soil of the mind and sows the seeds there. Until the seeds sprout, intellect can do no more. To try would only be floundering in a void. Then, at unexpected moments, the seeds send shoots up into the intelligence. These moments usually come because the scientist has "hatched" them. He or she has "sat" on the problem while awake, asleep, eating, walking, until *suddenly a solution!* The new discovery breaks the old knowledge, and the intellect is forced to destroy today's structures to build tomorrow's. Old knowledge is the obstacle to new understanding; Buddhism calls it "the barrier built of knowledge." Like those who are awakened, great scientists have undergone great internal changes. If they are able to achieve profound realizations, it is because their powers of observation, concentration, and awareness are deeply developed.

Understanding is not an accumulation of knowledge. To the contrary, it is the result of the struggle to become free of knowledge. Understanding shatters old knowledge to make room for the new that accords better with reality. When Copernicus discovered that the Earth goes around the sun, most of the astronomical knowledge of the time had to be discarded, including the ideas of above and below. Today, physics is struggling valiantly to free itself from the ideas of identity and cause/effect that underlie classical science. Science, like the Tao (Way), urges us to get rid of all preconceived notions.

When Shakyamuni Buddha put forth the notion of "not self," he upset many concepts about life and the universe. He blasted our most firm and widespread conviction—that of a permanent self. Those who understand "not self" know that its function is to overthrow "self," not to replace it with a new concept of reality. The notion of "not self" is a method, not a goal. If it becomes a concept, it must be destroyed along with all other concepts.

Unable to Describe It

Understanding, in humans, is translated into concepts, thoughts, and words. Understanding is not an aggregate of bits of knowledge. It is a direct and immediate penetration. In the realm of sentiment, it is feeling. In the realm of intellect, it is perception. It is an intuition rather than the culmination of reasoning. Every now and again it is fully present in us, and we find we cannot express it in words, thoughts, or concepts. "Unable to describe *it*," that is our situation at such moments. Insights like this are spoken of in Buddhism as "impossible to reason about, to discuss, or to incorporate into doctrines or systems of thought."

Who Knows?

We boast of the knowledge that we, as humans, have achieved. These are the treasures of our species, transmitted since the beginning of time when we were "inorganic," on the edge of becoming "organic." When we discuss "knowing," we immediately think of humans with our large brains, forgetting that knowing is present in all species, even those we consider inanimate. Certainly, bees, spiders, and wasps, are highly skilled— they build beautiful structures. Looking at a bee hive, a wasp's nest, or a spider's web, we admit their know-how, but we say, "These species do not know how to think. They cannot do mathematics. They cannot plan and design projects. They don't have intelligence. All they have is instinct." Still, it was not we humans who gave them nests and webs, it was the little "brainless" creatures themselves who designed and built those marvelous architectures that we so admire. If they do not *know*, who does? They know. Their species in its evolution has acquired this knowledge.

When we look at plants, we also see miracles of knowing. The apple tree *knows* how to make roots, branches, leaves, flowers, and fruit. You say that the apple tree, having no intelligence, has no other choice. But your ribs, your glands, your backbone, have you created them with your intelligence? It is the work of "knowing," which embraces all, including our ability to think.

Knowing in the Blue Sky

Let us try to move away from our notions of self and use a kind of language in which the subject is absent. For example, we say, "It is raining." "It" is the subject, but that really does not tell us anything. We may say, "The rain is falling." "Rain" is the subject and "is falling" the verb. But this sentence does not make much sense either, because when it is raining there must be water falling or it is not rain. So we can say, "Raining in London," or "Raining in Chicago," without using a subject, and the reality is clearly expressed.

Let us use the word "know" in this way. "Knowing in the person." "Knowing in the bee." "Knowing in the apple tree." It sounds strange because we are used to using a subject when we speak. The word "knowing" here can be either a subject or a verb, as in "Raining in London" or "Raining in Chicago." If "Raining in London" means there is rain in London, then "Knowing in the person" means there is knowledge in the person, nothing is obscured! To my mind, understanding is present everywhere, always unfolding. Knowing in Fred, knowing in Rachel, knowing in a bee, knowing in an apple tree, knowing in nothingness, knowing in the Milky Way. If we can say, "Raining in Chicago," there is no reason we cannot say, "Knowing in the blue sky."[9] While conducting a week-long retreat on the practice of not-self, a Zen master might propose to the retreatants that they use only this language, without subjects. I am sure this method would bear excellent results.

There is Knowing in the Wind

Let us amuse ourselves for a moment with a dance, so that we can better understand "knowing." Suppose I say, "I know that it's windy." "I" refers more to my mind than my body, so this sentence really means, "My mind knows that it is windy." Mind is the knower, so really we are saying, "The knower knows that it is windy." "The knower" is the subject, "knows" is the verb, and "it is windy" is the object. But it is funny to say, "The knower knows," isn't it? We imagine that the knower is an entity which exists independently of its object and which resides in our brain making brief excursions into the "outside world" to see what is happening out there. Just as we use a ruler to measure something, we fit our mind to a preconceived model, one that was created by our mind itself. Therefore, what we call "mind" is not pure and true mind. It is enmeshed in concepts.

When we say, "I know the wind is blowing," we don't think that there is something blowing something else. "Wind" goes with "blowing." If there is no blowing, there is no wind. It is the same with knowing. Mind is the knower; the knower is mind. We are talking about knowing in relation to the wind. "To know" is to know something. Knowing is inseparable from the wind. Wind and knowing are one. We can say, "Wind," and that is enough. The presence of wind indicates the presence of knowing, and the presence of the action of blowing. If we reduce the sentence "I know the wind is blowing" to simply "Wind," we can avoid grammatical mistakes and approach reality. In daily life, we have grown used to a way of thinking and expressing ourselves that is based on the idea that everything is independent of everything else. This way of thinking and speaking makes it difficult to penetrate non-dualistic, non-discriminatory reality, a reality which cannot be contained in concepts.

Each Action Its Own Subject

The wind blows. The rain falls. The river flows. In sentences like these we can see clearly that the subject and the verb are one and the same. There is no wind without "blowing," no rain without "falling," no river without "flowing." If we look closely, we can see that the subject of the act is in the action, that the act itself is exactly its own subject.

The most universal verb is the verb *to be*: I am, you are, the mountain is, a river is. The verb "to be" does not express the dynamic living state of the universe. To express that we must say "become." These two verbs can also be used as nouns: "being," "becoming." But being what? Becoming what? "Becoming" means "evolving ceaselessly" and is as universal as the verb "to be." It is not possible to express the "being" of a phenomenon and its "becoming" as if the two were independent. In the case of wind, "blowing" is the being *and* the becoming. For rain, its being *and* becoming are "falling." For the river, its being *and* becoming are "flowing."

We say that "rain falls," but "fall" is not the most precise term. Snow, leaves, and even radiation also fall. If we say "to rain," that would be a more precise description for the activity of the subject "rain." We can say, "The rain rains," to describe this activity, using "rain" as both subject and verb. Or we can just say, "Raining," or even, "Rain." In the same way we can say, "The painter paints," "The reader reads," "The meditator meditates." Following this pattern of usage we can also say, "The king kings," "The mountain mountains," "The cloud clouds." The reason for the existence of the king is to be king, to act king. The reason for the existence of the mountain is to be, to act, to do mountain. "Acting-being" king means doing what a king does—reigning over the people, giving royal audiences, and a thousand other things. So, as in the case of "rain rains," we can simply say, "The king kings." Then the first word is the subject and the second the verb, a verb which is not universal, a verb which is used just for kings. Thus each subject becomes a verb, and the verb is the being of the subject. To our ears, "The painter paints," sounds better than "The king kings;" but in fact there is no difference between them. Many, many years ago, Confucius used this kind of language. He said, "King kings, subject subjects, parent parents, child childs." That is, "The king is-does king," "The subject is-does subject," and so on. We can add further explanations, such as, "The king must do his duty as a king," or "A king must serve sincerely as king," but in the end these additions and embellishments add nothing. When we have seen that each action is its own subject, we can begin to comprehend the immense application of the word "knowing."

Inanimate Objects, Do You Have a Soul?

We are so used to thinking of "knowing" in terms of feelings and perceptions that we label inorganic objects "inanimate, insensitive, devoid of intelligence." But these things are only inanimate from our point of view. A rock is composed of countless molecules, which are in turn composed of countless atomic and subatomic particles, which are all held together by electro-magnetic and nuclear forces. Atoms are not lifeless bits of solid, inert matter. They are vast empty spaces in which infinitely small particles (protons, electrons, neutrons, and so forth) are in perpetual movement at enormous speeds. Why do they act this way? Can we still say that a rock is "inert, inanimate, insensitive?" The poet Lamartine once asked, "Inanimate objects, do you have a soul?"[10] If we define soul according to our ideas and beliefs, no doubt they haven't, or at least, they do not manifest it. But in the sense of a dynamic, living reality, they surely do!

The Known Manifests Itself in Countless Ways

"Knowing" reveals itself in many ways. "Knowing" can be active whenever there is hearing, seeing, feeling, comparing, remembering, imagining, reflecting, worrying, hoping, and so forth. In the Vijñanavadin school of Buddhism, which specialized in the study of "consciousnesses," many more fields of activity were attributed to knowing. For instance, in *alayavijñana*, or "store-house consciousness," the fields of activity of "knowing" are "maintaining, conserving, and manifesting." According to the Vijñanavadins, all sensation, perception, thought, and knowledge arise from this basic store-house consciousness. *Manyana* is one of the ways of knowing based on this consciousness and its function is to grasp onto the object and take it as a "self." *Manovijñana* serves as the headquarters for all sensations, perceptions, and thoughts, and makes creation, imagination, as well as dissection of reality possible. *Amala* is the consciousness that shines like a pure white light on the store-house consciousness.[11]

In any phenomena, whether psychological, physiological, or physical, there is dynamic movement, life. We can say that this movement, this life, is the universal manifestation, the most commonly recognized action of knowing. We must not regard "knowing" as something from the outside which comes to breathe life into the universe. It is the life of the universe itself. The dance and the dancer are one.

Tasting Yourself at the Foot of an Apple Tree

You know, I haven't been saying all this just to provide amusement, juggling words and understanding for your entertainment. These are tools which we can use to shatter and demolish our habitual and troublesome ways of thinking, old habits forged by our everyday lives. These are chisels and crowbars and axes to dismantle our furniture or split trees into logs for the fire. To split a log, you must insert a wedge into a crack and hammer at it until the log gradually splits in two. In the same way, reading this may put a wedge in you, depending on your interest, and your meditation practice. If what I have been saying is not clear for you, it may be because you are not yet used to seeing in this upside-down way. It may be the first time you have been encouraged to examine reality with a non-discriminatory spirit. Or it may be that my dancing is still too clumsy. It doesn't matter. We will try to find another way. If we cannot enter through one particular door, there are many others to try. In Buddhism it is said there are 84,000 doors to enter into the Dharma. I think we have to create even more. The point is to "see into" reality, not to understand what I am saying. My words can only be hints of an evocative dance, a pointing finger. You must see with your own eyes, eyes opened in full awareness.

I hope you are not going to transform my words into concepts, new concepts that can be stored inside you. I don't want to give you anything. I only want to dance for you, like the bee. If you see something, you must realize that you yourself have seen it. It is in you, not in my dance. Please go and sit next to a sleeping child. Look at the child. Or go into your yard and sit at the foot of an apple tree. Or go into the kitchen and make yourself a cup of tea. Whatever you do, do it in full attentiveness, in full awareness. Do not lose yourself in forgetfulness. Please don't think at all about becoming one with the child, the tree, the tea. There is no need to think at all. Taste yourself with the child, taste yourself with the tree, taste yourself with the tea while a smile blossoms on your lips.

The Universe in a Speck of Dust

Mind and Object Are One

The other afternoon, when I returned to my hermitage, I closed all the doors and windows because it was so windy. This morning, my window is open and I can see the cool, green forest. The sun is shining and a bird is singing beautifully. Little Thuy has already left for school. I must stop writing for a moment so I can look at the trees stretching across the hillside. I am aware of their presence and my own presence. It is not always necessary to close our sense-doors in order to be concentrated. Beginning meditators, to make concentrating on their breath or another object easier, may find it beneficial to close their sight and sound windows, but concentration is also possible with these windows open. Sense objects do not exist just outside the body. Even while we are not seeing, hearing, smelling, or tasting, we cannot ignore the feelings inside our bodies. When you have a toothache, or a cramp in your leg, you feel the pain. When all your organs are healthy, you feel a sense of well-being. Buddhism speaks of three kinds of feelings: pleasant, unpleasant, and neutral. But really, so-called neutral feelings can be quite pleasant, if we are aware.

The feelings inside the body are an uninterrupted stream, whether we are aware of them or not, so to "close all our sense-doors" is actually impossible. Even if we were somehow able to barricade them, the mind and consciousness would continue to work, and we would have images, concepts, and thoughts arising from memory. Some people think that to meditate is to separate ourselves from the world of thoughts and feelings and return to a kind of pure state where the mind contemplates itself and becomes "true mind."[12] It is a lovely idea, but it is basically misleading. Since mind is not separate from the world of thoughts and feelings, how can it leave and retire into itself? When I look at the trees in front of me, my mind does not go outside of me into the forest, nor does it open a door to let the trees in. My mind fixes on the trees, but they are not a distinct object. My mind and the trees are one. The trees are only one of the miraculous manifestations of the mind.

> Forest.
> Thousands of tree-bodies and mine.
> Leaves are waving,

Ears hear the stream's call,
Eyes see into the sky of mind,
A half-smile unfolds on every leaf.
There is a forest here
Because I am here.
But mind has followed the forest
And clothed itself in green.

The sage enters samadhi, and he or she does not know there is an "outside world" to keep out or an "inside world" to penetrate. The world reveals it-self, even when the eyes are closed. The world is neither inner nor outer. It is vital and complete in any object of contemplation—the breath, the tip of the nose, a kung-an, or anything else, as tiny as a speck of dust or as huge as a mountain. Whatever the object, it is not fragmented from ultimate reality. In fact, it contains the vast totality of reality.

Small Is Not Inside, Big Is Not Outside

I invite you to meditate with me. Please sit in a position that you find relaxing, so that you are comfortable, and place your attention on your breathing, letting it become very gentle, very light. After a few moments, move your attention to the feelings in your body. If you feel any pain or dis-comfort, or if you feel anything pleasurable, bring your attention there and enjoy that feeling with all of your awakened consciousness. After a little

while, notice the functioning of your different organs—your heart, lungs, liver, kidneys, digestive
system, and so forth. Normally these organs function without difficulty and do not attract your attention unless they are in pain. Notice the blood
flowing like a river through the countryside,
nourishing the fields with fresh water.

You know that this river of blood nourishes all
the cells of your body and that your organs, composed of cells, enrich (digestive system), purify
(liver, lungs), and propel (heart) the blood. All the
body's organs, including the nervous system and
glands, rely on each other for existence. Lungs are
necessary for blood, so lungs belong to blood. Blood
is necessary to lungs, so blood belongs to lungs. In
the same way we can say lungs belong to heart,
liver belongs to lungs, and so forth, and we see that
every organ in the body implies the existence of all
the others. This is called, "the interdependence of
all things," or "interbeing" in the *Avatamsaka Sutra*.
Cause and effect are no longer perceived as linear,
but as a net, not a two-dimensional one, but a system of countless nets interwoven in all directions
in multi-dimensional space. Not only do the organs contain in themselves the existence of all the
other organs, but each cell contains in itself all the
other cells. One is present in all and all are present
in each one. This is expressed clearly in the
Avatamsaka Sutra as, "One is all, all is one."

When we fully grasp this, we are freed from the
pitfall of thinking of "one" and "many," a habit

that has held us trapped for so long. When I say, "One cell contains in itself all the other cells," do not misunderstand me and think that there is some way that one cell's capacity can be stretched to fit all the others inside of it. I mean that the presence of one cell implies the presence of all the others, since they cannot exist independently, separate of the others. A Vietnamese Zen master once said, "If this speck of dust did not exist, the entire universe could not exist."[13] Looking at a speck of dust, an awakened person sees the universe. Beginners in meditation, although they do not see this as clearly as an apple in their hand, are able to understand it with observation and reflection. The *Avatamsaka Sutra* contains phrases that can terrify and confuse readers who have not meditated on the principle of interdependence. "In every speck of dust I see innumerable Buddha worlds, in each of these worlds countless Buddhas shining, their precious auras shining." "Putting one world in all worlds, putting all worlds in one world." "Innumerable Sumeru Mountains can be hung on the end of a hair." In the phenomenal world, things seem to exist as separate entities which have a specific place: "This" is on the outside of "that." When we deeply penetrate the principle of interdependence, we see that this sense of separateness is false. Each object is composed of and contains all others. In the light of meditation on interdependence, the concept of "one/many" collapses, and takes with it "large/small," "inside/outside," and all the others. The poet Nguyen Cong Tru, upon realizing this, exclaimed:

> In this world and in the worlds beyond,
> Buddha is incomparable!
> Small is not inside.
> Big is not outside.[14]

The Sun My Heart

Since we now realize that "One is all, all is one" in our bodies, let us go another step and meditate on the presence of the entire universe in ourselves. We know that if our heart stops beating, the flow of our life will stop, and so we cherish our heart very much. Yet we do not often take the time to notice that there are other things, outside of our bodies, that are also essential for our survival. Look at the immense light we call the sun. If it stops shining, the flow of our life will also stop, and so the sun is our second heart, our heart outside of our body. This immense "heart" gives all life on earth the warmth necessary for existence. Plants live thanks to the sun. Their leaves absorb the sun's energy, along with carbon dioxide from the air, to produce food for the tree, the flower, the plankton. And thanks to plants, we and other animals can live. All of us—people, animals, and plants—"consume" the sun, directly and indirectly. We cannot begin to describe all the effects of the sun, that great heart outside of our body. In fact, our body is not limited to what lies inside the boundary of our skin. Our body is much greater, much more immense. If the layer of air around our earth disappears even for an instant, "our" life will end. There is no phenomenon in the universe that does not intimately concern us, from a pebble resting at the bottom of the ocean, to the movement of a galaxy millions of light years away. The poet Walt Whitman said, "I believe a leaf of grass is no less than the journey-work of the stars...." These words are not philosophy. They come from the depths of his soul. He said, "I am large, I contain multitudes."[15]

Interbeing and Interpenetration

The meditation that I just suggested might also be called "Interbeing Endlessly Interwoven," that is, meditation on the manifestation of all phenomena as interdependent. This meditation can help free us from the concepts of "unity/diversity," or "one/all." This meditation can dissolve the concept of "me," because the concept of self is built on the opposition of unity and diversity. When we think of a speck of dust, a flower, or a human being, our thinking cannot break loose from the idea of unity, of one, of calculation. We see a line between one and many, between one and not one. In daily life we need this just as a train needs a track.

But if we truly realize the interdependent nature of the dust, the flower, and the human being, we see that unity cannot exist without diversity. Unity and diversity interpenetrate each other freely. Unity is diversity. This is the principle of interbeing and interpenetration of the *Avatamsaka Sutra*.

Interbeing means "This is that," and "That is this." Interpenetration means "This is in that," and "That is in this." When we meditate deeply on interbeing and interpenetration, we see that the idea of "one/many" is only a mental construct which we use to contain reality, much as we use a bucket to hold water. Once we have escaped the confinement of this construct, we are like a train breaking free of its rails to fly freely in space. Just as when we realize that we are standing on a spherical planet which is rotating around its own axis and around the sun, our concepts of above and below disintegrate, so when we realize the interdependent nature of all things, we are freed from the idea of "one/many."

The image of a Indra's jeweled net is used in the *Avatamsaka Sutra* to illustrate the infinite variety of interactions and intersections of all things. The net is woven of an infinite variety of brilliant gems, each with countless facets. Each gem reflects in itself every other gem in the net, and its image is reflected in each other gem. In this vision, each gem contains all the other gems.

We can also use an example from geometry. Imagine a circle with its center point "C". The circle is composed of all the points equidistant from C. The circle is there because all the points are there. If even one point is missing, the circle immediately disappears. It is like a house of cards. Remove one card and all the rest collapse. Each card depends on all the others, and without each one there is no house. The presence of one point of the circle depends on the presence of all the other points. Here too we see that "One is all, all is one." Every point of the circle is of equal importance. Every card in the house of cards is of equal importance. Each is vital to the existence of the whole and therefore to the existence of all the other parts. This is interdependence.

To envision the interwoven nature of relationships, which illustrate the character of interbeing and interpenetration, we can picture a sphere which is composed of all the points on its surface and all the points within its volume. There are extremely many points, yet without each of them the sphere does not exist. Now let us imagine connecting each point with all the other points. First we connect point A to each of the other points. Then we connect point B with each of the others, including A, and so on until all the points are connected. As you can see we have woven an extremely dense net intertwining all the points.

"The Bodhisattva sees the interdependent nature of all things, sees in one dharma all dharmas, sees in all dharmas one dharma, sees the multiplicity in the one and the one in the multiplicity,

sees the one in the immeasurable and the immeasurable in the one. Birth and existence of all dharmas is of a changing nature and thus unreal and
cannot touch the enlightened ones." As I mentioned earlier, in contemporary physics there is the
"bootstrap" idea which is very close to the idea of
interbeing and interpenetration. "Bootstrap" renounces the idea of basic elements of matter. The
universe is a network of interdependent phenomena in which each phenomenon is formed by the
coordination of all other phenomena. The universe is a dynamic fabric of interdependent events
in which none is the fundamental entity. What we
call particles are only mutual relationships among
the particles themselves.[16]

Someone may ask, "Although I agree that each
phenomenon depends on all other phenomena for
its birth and existence, where does the *all*, the complete body which includes all phenomena, come
from?" Would you please give him an answer?

Eyes Opening in Samadhi

Meditation is not imitation, but creation. Meditators who only imitate their instructors cannot go
far. The same is true of cooking, or anything. A
good cook is someone with a creative spirit. You
can enter the Meditation on the Interdependence
of All Phenomena through many different doors—
observing your internal organs: blood, heart, in-

testines, lungs, liver, kidneys; or thousands of other means, including thoughts, feelings, images, poetry, dreams, or a river, a star, a leaf, and so on.

A good practitioner uses meditation throughout daily life, not wasting a single opportunity, a single event, to see deeply the nature of dependent co-arising. All day long practice is carried out in perfect concentration. With eyes open or closed, the nature of meditation is no other than samadhi. You can discard the idea that you must close your eyes to look inside and open them to look outside. A thought is no more an inner object than a mountain an outer one. Both are objects of knowledge. Neither is inner or outer. Great concentration is achieved when you are fully present, in profound communion with living reality. At these times the distinction between subject and object disappears and you penetrate living reality with ease, are one with it, because you have set aside all tools for measuring knowledge, knowledge which Buddhism calls "erroneous knowledge."[17]

Seeing and Loving Always Go Together

There are times while watching our children play that we think about the future. We know that life is filled with worries, fears, hopes, and disappointments, and we worry for them and anxiously think about the struggles before them. It is at that very moment that we *enter* into our children. It is easy to find our way into them because we know they are of our own blood.

Meditation is the same. As we meditate on the interdependent nature of all things, we can penetrate reality easily, and see the fears, anguish, hopes, and despair of all beings. Watching a green caterpillar on a leaf, we understand the importance of the caterpillar, not just from our self-centered point of view as a human, but from the penetration based on the interdependence of all things. Realizing the preciousness of the life of every being, we dare not deprive the caterpillar of its life. If some day we have to kill a caterpillar, we will feel as if we are killing ourselves, that something of ourselves dies with the caterpillar.

In ancient times, people hunted to feed themselves and their families. They did this in order to live. They did not kill just for amusement. Today some people hunt for pleasure. The interdependence of all beings is not a philosophical game removed from spiritual and practical life. In bringing to light the interdependence of all phenomena, the meditator comes to see that the lives of all beings are one, and he or she is overcome with compassion for all. When you feel this love you know that your meditation is bearing fruit. Seeing and loving always go together. Seeing and loving are one. Shallow understanding accompanies shallow compassion. Great understanding goes with great compassion.

Heartbreak

Have you ever watched a wildlife show on public television, where predators hunt other animals for food? The tiger hunts a deer or a snake swallows a frog. These shows are filled with suspense. We hope that the deer will escape the tiger's claws, and the frog will be saved from the snake's fangs. It is painful to watch the tiger tear apart the deer and the frog disappear into the snake's mouth. This kind of program is not invented—it is real life. We long for the well-being of the frog and the deer, but rarely do we consider that the tiger and the snake must also eat in order to live. We humans eat chickens, pigs, shrimp, fish, and cows, and, like the tiger and the snake, even deer and frogs. Yet because it is painful to watch, we take the side of the prey and hope it will escape.

In these situations, as meditators, we must remain very clear. We cannot take either side, because we exist in both. Some people can remain unmoved or even enjoy the sight of a tiger tearing apart its prey, but most of us, feeling its agony, take the side of the victim. If a scene like this were occurring in front of us, we would try to find a way to save the deer and the frog. But we have to be careful not to do this just to avoid our own anguish. We must also feel the pain of the tiger or snake deprived of food, and have compassion for them. All beings have to struggle to survive. The more deeply we penetrate into life, the more we see its miracles and the more we see its heart-breaking and terrifying events. Have you seen the life of a spider? Have you lived through a war? Have you seen torture, prison, and killing? Have you seen a pirate rape a young girl on the high seas?

Reconciliation Originates in the Heart of Compassion

Millions of people follow sports. If you love to watch soccer, you probably root for one team and identify with them. You watch the games with despair and elation. Perhaps you give a little kick to help the ball along. If you do not take sides, the fun is missing. In wars we pick sides, usually the side which is being threatened. Peace movements are born of this feeling. We get angry, we shout, but rarely do we rise above all this to look at a conflict the way a mother would who is watching her two children fighting. She seeks only their reconciliation. Real efforts for reconciliation must arise from this heart of compassion which arises from meditating on the nature of interbeing and interpenetration of all beings.

In our lives, we may be lucky enough to meet someone whose love extends to animals and plants. We may also know people who, although they themselves live in a safe situation, realize that famine, disease, and oppression are destroying millions of people on earth and look for ways to help those who suffer. They cannot forget them, even amidst the pressures of their own lives. At least to some extent, these people have realized the interdependent nature of life. They know that the survival of the underdeveloped countries cannot be separated from the survival of the materially wealthy, technically advanced countries. Poverty and oppression bring war. In our times, every war involves all countries. The fate of each country is linked to the fate of all others.

Little Room for Compassion

In a civilization where technology is crucial for success, there is little room for compassion. But when we meditate deeply on life, we come to identify even with ants and caterpillars. If we become farmers, we may fail because we will probably refuse to use insecticides to kill pests. And if we do not have the heart to kill an animal, how can we point a gun at another human being? If we become officials in the Department of Defense, we may encourage people to become conscientious objectors. If we become Governors, we may oppose building nuclear power plants in our states, and so we will be ousted from the system. Many of us share these kinds of feelings. We are ill at ease with our society, and in a variety of ways we express our opposition.

David Bohm, a physics professor at the University of London, said, "If we want society to change, a few superficial and individual changes, or changes in the economic system are not enough. A complete change in consciousness is necessary. We don't know yet how this change is to be realised, but I am certain that it is absolutely vital."[18] This change of consciousness, as we have seen, can be achieved by realizing the interdependent nature of reality, a realization that each of us can experience in a unique way. This kind of realization is not the result of any ideology or system of thought, but is the fruit of the direct experience of reality in its multiple relationships. It requires the dropping of habitual thinking which fragments reality, a reality that is actually indissoluble.

Fearless in Life and Death

Continue to practice the meditation on interdependence for awhile and you will notice a change in yourself. Your perspective will widen, and you will find that you look at all living beings with compassion. The grudges and hatreds that you thought were impenetrable will begin to erode, and you will find yourself caring for each and every being. Most important, you will no longer be afraid of life and death.

Perhaps you have heard of Erwin Schrödinger, who discovered wave mechanics. After reflecting on the self, life and death, the universe, and unity and multiplicity, he wrote,

> Thus you can throw yourself flat on the ground, stretched out upon Mother Earth, with the certain conviction that you are one with her and she with you. You are as firmly established, as invulnerable as she, indeed a thousand times firmer and more invulnerable. As surely as she will engulf you tomorrow, so surely will she bring you forth anew to new striving and suffering. And not merely 'some day': now, today, every day she is bringing you forth, not *once* but thousands upon thousands of times, just as every day she engulfs you a thousand times over. For eternally and always there is only *now*, one and the same now; the present is the only thing that has no end.[19]

If a view like Schrödinger's is well rooted in our daily lives, we will be immovable before life and death.

Past, Present, and Future on the Tip of a Hair

Schrödinger's observation about time encourages us to take another step in our meditation on interdependence. Our conceptions of inner and outer, one and many, begin to fall away when we look at the nature of interbeing and interpenetration of all things. But these ideas will not drop away completely as long as we believe that absolute space and absolute time are necessary for the appearance of all phenomena. In the early days of the Dharma-laksana ("Meditation on Phenomena") School of Buddhism, space was viewed as an absolute reality outside the realm of birth and death. When the Madhyamika ("Meditation on Noumena," or essential nature) School began to develop, time and space were described as false conceptions of reality which depend on one another for existence. Since the principle of interbeing and interpenetration in the *Avatamsaka Sutra* refuses to accept the concepts of inner/outer, big/small, one/many as real, it also refuses the concept of space as an absolute reality. With respect to time, the conceptual distinction between past, present, and future is also destroyed. The *Avatamsaka Sutra* says that past and future can be put into the present, present and past into future, present and future into past, and finally all eternity into one *ksana*, the shortest possible moment. To summarize, time, like space, is stamped with the seal of interdependence, and one instant contains three times: past, present, and future.

> The past in the present and future
> The future in the present and past
> Three times and several aeons in an instant
> Not long, not short—that is liberation.
>
> I can penetrate the future
> putting all eternity into one instant.

The *Avatamsaka Sutra* continues, "Not only does a speck of dust contain in itself 'infinite' space, it also contains 'endless' time; in one *ksana* we find both 'infinite' time and 'endless' space."[20]

> Past present and future on the tip of a hair
> And innumerable Buddha worlds as well.

*Entering the World of Interdependence
with the Theory of Relativity*

The *Avatamsaka Sutra* says that time and space contain each other, depend on one another for existence, and are not separable by knowledge. The Relativity Theory of Albert Einstein, born 2000 years later, confirms the inseparable relationship of time and space. Time is considered the fourth dimension of the four dimensional space-time continuum.[21] This theory refutes the hypothesis that space is an absolute and immutable framework inside of which the universe is evolving. The idea of absolute and universal time is simultaneously destroyed. It proclaims that space is simply the positional ordering of relationships of things among themselves in a given reference frame, and time is nothing more than the chronological ordering of events in a given reference frame.

Time, according to the theory, can only be local and not universal. This is why the concept "now" can only be applied to "here" and not to other places in the universe. Likewise, "here" can only be applied to this instant, "now," and not to either past or future. This is because time and space can only exist together. They cannot exist independently of one another. This theory allows us to use scientific discoveries about the relative nature of space and time to break down our ideas based on "infinite" space and "endless" time, such ideas as finite and infinite, inside and outside, before and after. If we look up at the sky and wonder what exists beyond the outermost edge of the universe, we still do not understand relativity and still have not shed the idea of an absolute space that exists independent of things. And if we ask where the universe is heading, it is because we still believe in eternal, universal time. The Theory of Relativitiy contributes to the progress of both science and philosophy. It is a pity that Einstein did not take this superb spaceship even further on the voyage into the world of reality.

A Raft to Cross the River

With all new scientific discoveries comes the destruction of some old ideas of reality. One merit of the Theory of Relativity is that it overturned the classical ideas of time and space through its elaboration of the space-time continuum. According to the theory, everything has a four-dimensional structure and is located in curved four-dimensional space-time. Dropping the Euclidean three-dimensional straight line model of the universe, Einstein imagined a universe composed of curved lines in a four-dimensional space-time continuum. In 1917 he proposed this model in which space is seen as a three-dimensional facet of a four-dimensional hyperspace, with time as an axis. If we try to imagine this for a sphere, we will no longer see a sphere; instead we will see a hypercylinder in which each minute is a separate sphere, much like the sequence of separate image-frames of a film. Einstein's universe is at the same time finite and infinite, because it is composed of curved space-time lines and not separate straight lines that belong either to time or to space. An ant walking on an orange can always go straight ahead, never reaching the end, because it is walking on a curved path. But the ant stays on the orange; that is its limit. Einstein's model generalized straight lines and reconciled finite and infinite.

Yet if endless time and infinite space are only forms of perception, the curved four-dimensional space-time continuum, although closer to reality, is still just another form of perception. If space cannot be conceived without the presence of "things," the four dimensions of space-time are no more than mental creations in relation to the ideas of "thing" and "movement." The space-time curve must be thought of as only an idea which replaces those of three-dimensional space, endless time, and straight lines. It must be left behind, the same way we leave behind the raft after we have crossed the river.

The Ability to Abandon and the Capacity to Discover

Reality is transformed by our looking at it, because we enter it with our baggage of concepts. Modern physicists know this. Some of them have readily abandoned concepts that have long formed the basis of science—ideas such as cause and effect, and past, present, and future. But it is not easy to abandon concepts. We think that penetrating reality without arming ourselves with ideas is like going into battle empty handed. The armor of a scientist is his or her acquired knowledge and system of thought, and it is most difficult to leave that behind. I believe that the scientists with the greatest ability to abandon that "armor" are the ones who have the greatest capacity to make discoveries.

Religious seekers have always been reminded that they must let go of all their concepts in order to directly experience reality, from the concepts of self and other, to those of birth and death, permanence and impermanence, existence and nonexistence. If reality is described as inconceivable, the tool to directly experience reality must be a mind pure of all concepts.

Cutting the Net of Birth & Death

Mind Creates the Form of Reality

Yesterday afternoon, little Thuy surprised her teacher. After lunch, she took a broom and swept the classroom floor without anyone asking her to. No child in the village had ever done that before. Later in the afternoon, after class, Thuy's teacher followed her up the hill to our cottage to tell me about it. I told her that all poor children in my country would have done the same thing. They take care of housework by themselves without being asked by the adults.

Today is a French holiday and Thuy is off from school. She and I took a walk this morning, and together we collected pine cones. She told me that the earth gives birth to pine cones so we can use them to start fires to keep warm in winter, but I told her that pine cones are there to give birth to baby pine trees, not for lighting fires. Rather than being disappointed by my explanation, her eyes got even brighter.

Do you remember our conversation about the concepts of space and time in the *Avatamsaka Sutra* and in the Theory of Relativity? Once we abandon the concepts of absolute space and absolute time, many related concepts that have long formed our patterns of thinking begin to break down. Bootstrap theorists recognize that all atomic particles, such as electrons, cannot exist independently of one another. They are actually "interconnections" among particles, and these "particles" are in turn "interconnections" among other particles. No particle has an independent nature. This is very close to interdependence, interbeing, and interpenetration.

The Theory of Relativity has had a significant influence on our understanding of nuclear particles. In relativity, mass and energy are the same, just as we discovered that rain can be the subject and the verb of a sentence at the same time. When we know that mass is only a form of energy, we come to the realization that "interconnections" among particles are themselves dynamic realities of four-dimensional space-time. For today's scientists, a nuclear particle, just like "a speck of dust" or "the tip of a hair" in the *Avatamsaka Sutra*, combines both space and time. These particles can be considered a "speck" of time, just as the shortest possible moment (*ksana*) in the *Avatamsaka Sutra* is said to contain not only past, present, and future, but also matter and space. A particle can no longer be thought of as a three-dimensional object (like a marble or a speck of dust) situated in space. It has become more abstract to our minds. Electrons, for example, can be called "dynamic four-dimensional bodies in space-time" or "waves of probability." We must keep in mind that words such as "particle," "body," and "wave" no longer have the same meanings as in ordinary language. Contemporary physics has struggled to go beyond the world of concepts, and as a result, particles are now regarded as abstract mathematical quantities (from the point of view of ordinary, discriminative knowledge).

Some scientists proclaim that the properties of nuclear particles are nothing but creations of their own minds, that in reality particles have no properties independent of the minds of those observing them. This implies that in the world of particles, the mind which perceives reality in fact creates it.

Observer and Participant

For physicists today, the object of mind and the mind itself cannot be separated. Scientists can no longer observe anything with complete objectivity. Their minds cannot be separated from the objects. John Wheeler has suggested that we replace the term "observer" with the term "participant." For there to be an "observer," there must be a strict boundary between subject and object, but with a "participant," the distinction between subject and object blurs and even disappears, and direct experience is possible. This notion of a participant/observer is very close to meditation practice. When we meditate on our body, according to the *Satipatthana Sutta* we meditate on "the body *in* the body" (emphasis added). This means that we do not consider our body as a separate object, independent of our mind which is observing it. Meditation is not measuring or reflecting on the object of the mind, but directly perceiving it. This is called "perception without discrimination" (*nirvikalpajñana*).

The habit of distinguishing the mind from its object is so deeply ingrained in us that only gradually, with meditation, can we eliminate it. The *Satipatthana Sutta* presents four objects of meditation: the body, feelings, mind, and objects of mind. This kind of meditation was practiced by the disciples of the Buddha during his lifetime. Classifying reality this way is to help our meditation, not to help us in the analysis of these things. In the *Sutta*, all material phenomena are regarded as "objects of mind." Of course we can observe that body, feelings, and even mind can also be categorized as "objects of mind." The fact that all phenomena, including material ones, are considered "objects of mind" in the *Sutta* clearly shows that since the earliest times, Buddhism opposed discriminating between mind and its objects.

Mountains are Again Mountains,
Rivers are Again Rivers

Elementary-particle physicists, when they return home from a day's work in their laboratories, often have the feeling that ordinary objects, such as a chair or a piece of fruit, have lost the substantiality they seemed to have previously. After entering the world of elementary particles, these scientists cannot find anything essential in the world of matter except their own minds. Alfred Kastler said, "Matter can only be considered from its two complementary aspects, which are waves and particles. Objects or things that had always been thought of as constituents of nature must be renounced."[22]

Although a chair or an orange may no longer be "matter" for us, we must still sit on the chair and eat the orange. We are composed of the same essence as they are, even if it is just a mathematical formula which we ourselves can contrive. Meditators realize that all phenomena interpenetrate and inter-are with all other phenomena, so in their everyday lives they look at a chair or an orange differently from most people. When they look at mountains and rivers, they see that "rivers are no longer rivers and mountains are no longer mountains." Mountains "have entered" rivers, and rivers "have entered" mountains (interpenetration). Mountains become rivers, and rivers become mountains (interbeing). However, when they want to go for a swim, they have to go into the river and not climb the mountain. When they return to everyday life, "mountains are again mountains, rivers are again rivers."

Neither Form Nor Emptiness

A scientist who realizes the nature of interdependence among particles is likely to be influenced in the way he or she perceives reality even in everyday life. Because of this, some kind of transformation may occur in his or her spiritual life as well. Meditators who realize the interpenetration and interbeing of things also undergo a change in themselves. Former concepts of "one's self" and "objects" dissolve and they see themselves in everything and all things in themselves. This transformation is the primary goal of meditation. This is why "awareness of being" is maintained throughout the day and not just during periods of meditation. A meditator is aware when he or she is walking, standing, lying down, and so forth. There are certainly scientists who also do this, reflecting on their topic of research all day long, through their whole beings, even as they eat or bathe.

The notion of inter-origination (*paratantra*) is very close to living reality. It annihilates dualistic concepts, one/many, inside/outside, time/space, mind/matter, and so forth, which the mind uses to confine, divide, and shape reality. The notion of inter-origination can be used not only to destroy habits of cutting up reality, but also to bring about a direct experience of reality. As a tool, however, it should not be considered a form of reality in itself.

Paratantra is the very nature of living reality, the absence of an essential self. Just as a triangle exists only because three lines intersect each another, you cannot say any thing exists in itself. Because they have no independent identity, all phenomena are described as empty (*sunya*). This does not mean that phenomena are absent, only that they are empty of an essential self, of a permanent identity independent of other phenomena. In the same way, in bootstrap physics the word "particles" does not mean three-dimensional specks which exist independently of one another.

The word "emptiness" here is different from the everyday term. It transcends the usual concepts of emptiness and form. To be empty is not to be non-existent. It is to be devoid of a permanent identity. To avoid confusion, Buddhist scholars often use the term "true emptiness" to refer to this kind of emptiness. Zen Master Hue Sinh, who lived in the 11th century during the Ly dynasty, said that we cannot use the words empty and form to describe objects because reality is beyond these two concepts:

> Dharmas are the same as non-dharmas,
> Neither existing nor not existing.
> He who fully understands this
> Realizes that all beings are Buddha.

The Udumbara Flower is Still Blooming

There is a practice called Meditation on True Emptiness, in which the practitioner lets go of habitual ways of thinking about being and non-being by realizing that these concepts were formed by incorrectly perceiving things as independent and permanent. When an apple tree produces flowers, we don't see apples yet, and so we might say, "There are flowers but no apples on this tree." We say this because we do not see the latent presence of the apples in the flowers. Time will gradually reveal the apples.

When we look at a chair, we see the wood, but we fail to observe the tree, the forest, the carpenter, or our own mind. When we meditate on it, we can see the entire universe in all its inter-woven and interdependent relations in the chair. The presence of the wood reveals the presence of the tree. The presence of the leaf reveals the presence of the sun. The presence of the apple blossom reveals the presence of the apple. Meditators can see the one in the many, and the many in the one. Even before they see the chair, they can see its presence in the heart of living reality. The chair is not separate. It exists only in its interdependent relations with everything else in the universe. It *is* because all other things *are*. If it *is not*, then all other things *are not* either.

Every time we use the word "chair" or the concept "chair" forms in our mind, reality is severed in half. There is "chair" and there is everything which is "not-chair." This kind of separation is both violent and absurd. The sword of conceptualization functions this way because we do not realize that the chair is made entirely from non-chair elements. Since all non-chair elements are present in the chair, how can we separate them? An awakened individual vividly sees the non-chair elements when looking at the chair, and realizes that the chair has no boundaries, no beginning, and no end.

When you were small, you may have played with a kaleidoscope. So many wonderful images are formed by bits of colored glass between two lenses and three mirrors. Each time you move your fingers slightly, a new and equally beautiful image appears. We could say that each image has a beginning and an end, but we know that the true nature of it, lenses and colored glass, does not come into being or end with each new configuration. These thousands or millions of patterns are not subject to the notion of "beginning and end." In the same way, we follow our breathing and meditate on the beginningless and endless nature of ourselves and the world. Doing so, we can see that liberation from birth and death is already within reach.

To deny the existence of a chair is to deny the presence of the whole universe. A chair which exists cannot become non-existent, even if we chop it up into small pieces or burn it. If we could succeed in destroying one chair, we could destroy the entire universe. The concept of "beginning and end" is closely linked with the concept of "being and non-being." For example, from what moment in time can we say that a particular bicycle has come into existence and from what moment is it no longer existent? If we say that it begins to exist the moment the last part is assembled, does that mean we cannot say, "This bicycle needs just one more part," the prior moment? And when it is broken and cannot be ridden, why do we call it "a broken bicycle?" If we meditate on the moment the bicycle *is* and the moment it *is no longer,* we will notice that the bicycle cannot be placed in the categories "being and non-being" or "beginning and end."

Did the Indian poet Rabindranath Tagore exist before his birth or not? Does he exist after his death or has he ceased to exist? If you accept the principle from the *Avatamsaka Sutra* of "interpenetration" or the principle from bootstrap physics of "interbeing," you cannot say that there has ever been a time when "Tagore *is not,*" even the times before his birth or after his death. If Tagore is not, the entire universe cannot be, nor can you or I exist. It is not because of his "birth" that Tagore exists, nor because of his "death" that he does not exist.

Late one afternoon I was standing on Vulture Peak in the Indian state of Bihar when I saw a very beautiful sunset, and suddenly I found that Shakyamuni Buddha was still sitting there:

The great mendicant of old is still there on
    Vulture Peak
contemplating the beautiful sunset.
Gotama, how strange!
Who said that the Udumbara flower
    blooms only once every 3,000 years?
That sound of the rising tide,
you cannot help hearing it
if you have an attentive ear.

I have heard several friends express regret that they did not live at the time of the Buddha. I think that even if they passed him on the street, they would not recognize him. Not only Tagore and Shakyamuni Buddha, but all of us are without beginning and without end. I am here because you are there. If anyone of us does not exist, no one else can exist either. Reality cannot be confined by concepts of being, non-being, birth, and death. The term "true emptiness" can be used to describe reality and to destroy all ideas which imprison and divide us and which artificially create a reality. Without a mind free from preconceived ideas, we cannot penetrate reality. Scientists are coming to realize that they cannot use ordinary language to describe non-conceptual insights. Scientific language is beginning to have the symbolic nature of poetry. Today such words as "charm" and "color" are being used to describe properties of particles that have no conceptual counterpart in the "macro-realm." Some day reality will reveal itself beyond all conceptualizations and measurements.

The Tathagata Neither Arrives Nor Departs

This non-conceptualizable reality, or true emptiness, is also called "suchness" (*bhutatathata*). Suchness, sometimes translated "thusness," means "it is so." It cannot be conceived or described through words and concepts but must be directly experienced. Suppose there is a tangerine on the table and someone asks you, "What does it taste like?" Rather than give an answer, you have to section the tangerine and invite the questioner to have a taste. Doing this, you allow him or her to enter the suchness of the tangerine without any verbal or conceptual description.

To remind his disciples of the unconditioned, beginningless and endless nature of reality, Buddha asked them to address him as the Tathagata. This is not an honorific title. Tathagata means "one who thus comes" or "one who thus goes." It means he arises from suchness, abides in suchness, and returns to suchness, to non-conceptualizable reality. Who or what does not arise from suchness? You and I, a caterpillar, a speck of dust all arise from suchness, all abide in suchness, and some day will return to suchness. Actually, the words "arise from," "abide in," and "return to" have no real meaning. One can never leave suchness. In the

Anuradha Sutra, the Buddha replied to a question which was troubling many monks: "What happens to the Tathagata after death? Does he continue to exist? Does he cease to exist? Does he both continue and cease to exist? Does he neither continue nor cease to exist?"

The Buddha asked Anuradha, "What do you think? Can the Tathagata be recognized through form?"

"No, master."

"Can the Tathagata be found outside of form?"

"No, master."

"Can the Tathagata be recognized through feeling, perception, mental formations, or consciousness?"

"No, master."

"Anuradha, you cannot find the Tathagata even in this life, why do you want to solve the problem of whether I will continue to exist or cease to exist, or both continue and cease to exist, or neither continue nor cease to exist after death?"[23]

Robert Oppenheimer, the physicist known as the father of the first atomic bomb, had a chance to read this section of the *Anuradha Sutra.* He understood it based on his observations of particles, which cannot be confined by concepts of space, time, being, or not-being. He wrote:

> To what appeared to be the simplest questions, we will tend to give either no answer or an answer which will at first sight be reminiscent more of a strange catechism than of the straightforward affirmatives of

physical science. If we ask, for instance, whether the position of the electron remains the same, we must say "no;" if we ask whether the electron's position changes with time, we must say "no;" if we ask whether the electron is at rest, we must say "no;" if we ask whether it is in motion, we must say "no."[24]

As you can see, the language of science has already begun to approach the language of Buddhism. After reading the above quote from the *Anuradha Sutra*, Oppenheimer said that until this century scientists would not have been able to understand the Buddha's replies of 2,500 years ago.

The Net of Birth and Death Can be Torn Asunder

There is another meditation which can be used in place of the one on true emptiness. It is called the meditation on the miraculousness of existence. "Existence" means being in the present. "The miraculousness of existence" means to be aware that the universe is contained in each thing, and that the universe could not exist if it did not contain each thing. This awareness of interconnectedness, interpenetration, and interbeing makes it impossible for us to say something "is" or "is not," so we call it "miraculous existence."

Even though Oppenheimer replied "No" four times to the questions about the nature of electrons, he did not mean that electrons are nonexistent. Even though the Buddha said, "You cannot find the Tathagata even in this life," he did not mean that the Tathagata is nonexistent. The *Great Prajña Paramita Sutra* uses the word "not-empty" (*asunya*) to describe this state. "Not-empty" is the same as "the miraculousness of existence." "True emptiness" and "the miraculousness of existence" can keep us from falling into the trap of discriminating between being and non-being.

Both electrons and Tathagata are beyond the concepts of being and non-being. The nature of true emptiness and the miraculousness of existence of the electrons and the Tathagata save us from the traps of being and non-being and lead us directly into the world of non-conceptualization. How can we practice the meditation on the miraculousness of existence? Anyone who understands the theory of relativity knows that space is intimately connected with both time and matter. For such persons, space has a larger meaning than for persons who still believe that space exists independently of time and matter. When we look at a bee, we may like to see it first through the eyes of a physicist who understands relativity, and then go even beyond that to see true emptiness and the miraculousness of existence in it. If you attempt to do this regularly, with your whole being, I am sure that it will free you from entanglement in the net of birth and death. In Zen circles, the problem of birth and death has always been regarded as the most urgent. Zen Master Hakuin calligraphed the character for Death quite large and then added in smaller strokes: "Anyone who sees to the depths of this word is a true hero."[25]

I used to think that liberation from birth and death was a remote goal. While I was teaching at the Van Hanh Buddhist University in Saigon, I looked at the statues of emaciated Arahats, and I thought it must be necessary to deplete our strength that much, to reduce our desires until total exhaustion overtakes us, to realize this liberation. But later, while I was practicing at Phuong Boi, in central Vietnam, I realized that liberation from birth and death is not an abstract or long-term project. Birth and death are only concepts. To be free from these concepts is to be free from birth and death. It is attainable.

But liberation from birth and death cannot come from intellectual comprehension alone. When you see the interdependent nature of everything in the universe, when you understand the meaning of true emptiness and the miraculousness of existence, you have sown the seeds of liberation in the field of your consciousness. For these seeds to grow we need to practice meditation. Through the practice of meditation, we may become strong enough to break through the concept of birth and death, which is really just one of the many, many concepts we create.

A physicist who is able to see the interpenetration and interbeing of elementary particles without going beyond his or her intellect has, from the viewpoint of Buddhist liberation, attained just a decorative façade. Someone who studies Buddhism without practicing meditation has also accumulated knowledge only as decoration. We hold our own fates in our own hands. We have the capacity to practice until all concepts about birth and death, and being and non-being, are uprooted.

The images which I have offered—the sun, an orange, a chair, a caterpillar, a bicycle, electrons, and so forth—can be objects which bring us to a direct experience of reality. Meditate on the sun as your second heart, the heart of your "outer-self." Meditate on the sun in every cell of your body. Meditate to see the sun in plants, in each nourishing morsel of the vegetables you eat. Gradually you will see "the body of ultimate reality" (*Dharmakaya*) and recognize your own "true nature." Then birth and death can no longer touch you, and you will have attained success. Tuê Trung, a 14th century Vietnamese Zen master, wrote:

> Birth and death,
> You have been crushing me.
> Now you can no longer touch me.

Please meditate deeply on these two sentences until you can see Tuê Trung in each cell of your body.

A Leaf Can Lead Us Directly
into Non-Conceptual Reality

The Lin-chi school of Zen in China developed the
use of kung-ans (Japanese: *koans*) as tools for awakening. By making the meditator keep one subject
in mind, kung-ans aid in creating strong
concentration. Here are a few examples of kung-
ans that are presented as questions:

> What was your true face before your parents
>   brought you into the world?
> What is the sound of one hand clapping?
> Everything returns to the one. Where does
>   the one return?

Using the form of questions demands our attention. Some kung-ans, such as the following, are not
presented as questions, but still have the same
questioning effect:

> A dog does not have the nature of awaken-
>   ing.
> Nothing is sacred.
> Te-shan's hair is white, Tche-hai's is black.

Questioning, therefore, is an important element in
the practice of meditation using a kung-an. The
goal of kung-an practice is to shatter concepts and
conceptualizing. Although not their intention,
kung-ans sometimes confine the meditator in his

thoughts and conceptualizations for too long. Often it is only when the practitioner arrives at an impasse and is completely exhausted from conceptual thinking that he or she is ready to drop concepts and return to himself or herself. I think this is a weakness of Zen kung-an practice.

In meditation on "interbeing" or on "the miraculousness of existence," a practitioner can take any phenomenon as the object of meditation, but he or she must be able to maintain it for some time, in mindfulness. She may choose the sun, a leaf, a caterpillar. Such meditation is not so enigmatic as kung-an meditation, but if the practitioner is determined to keep the sunlight of her awareness on it hour after hour, she will succeed. This kind of meditation keeps the practitioner from wasting a lot of time straining her intellect looking for solutions to questions that cannot be solved through the intellect. The sun, a leaf, or a caterpillar can take the practitioner directly into the world of nonconceptual reality—a living, direct experience.

Unobstructed Mind and Unobstructed Object

Another important meditation, called "Mind and Object Contain One Another," aims at ending all discrimination between the mind and its objects. When we look at the blue sky, the white clouds, and the sea, we are prone to seeing them as three separate phenomena. But if we look more care-

fully, we can see that the three are of the same nature and cannot exist independently of one another. If you say, "I was afraid of the snake I just
encountered," you treat the snake as physical and
fear as psychological. The meditation on "Mind
and Object Contain One Another" is a means of
overcoming that kind of separation.

Leibniz, a German mathematician, proposed
that not only colors, light, and temperature, but
also forms, content, and movement of everything
in the universe may be nothing but properties
which the mind projects onto reality. In light of
quantum theory, no one today can continue to
think, as Descartes did, that mind and object are
two distinct realities which exist independently
and separately from one another.

To say it simply, in the sentence, "I was afraid of
the snake," we recognize an "I," a snake, and fear.
Fear, a psychological phenomenon, is not only inextricably tied to the physical phenomena "I" and
snake, it is inextricably woven into the web of the
entire universe and has the same nature as the
universe. The concept "fear" includes the concept
"snake" and the concept of the person who is afraid
of being bitten by the snake. If we try to be objective, we may find ourselves unsure about what
exactly is the nature of a snake or the nature of a
person, but fear is a direct experience we can recognize and identify.

In the meditation on interdependence, we can
see that each moment of consciousness includes

the whole universe. This moment might be a memory, a perception, a feeling, a hope. From the point of view of space, we can call it a "particle" of consciousness. From the point of view of time, we can call it a "speck" of time (*ksana*). An instant of consciousness embraces all past, present, and future, and the entire universe.

When we speak of mind, we usually think of psychological phenomena, such as feelings, thoughts, or perceptions. When we speak of objects of mind, we think of physical phenomena, such as mountains, trees, or animals. Speaking this way, we see the phenomenal aspects of mind and its objects, but we don't see their nature. We have observed that these two kinds of phenomena, mind and objects of mind, rely on one another for their existence and are therefore interdependent. But we do not see that they themselves have the same nature. This nature is sometimes called "mind" and sometimes called "suchness" (*tathata*) or God. Whatever we call it, we cannot measure this nature using concepts. It is boundless and all inclusive, without limitations or obstacles. From the point of view of unity, it is called *Dharmakaya*. From the point of view of duality, it is called "mind without obstacle" encountering "world without obstacle." The *Avatamsaka Sutra* calls it unobstructed mind and unobstructed object. The mind and the world contain each other so completely and perfectly that we call this "perfect unity of mind and object."

The Great and Perfect Mirror

In 1956, in a lecture on Mind and Matter at Trinity College in Cambridge, the physicist Erwin Schrödinger asked whether consciousness should be singular or plural. He concluded that from the outside, there seem to be many minds but that in reality there is only one.[26] Schrödinger had been influenced by Vedanta philosophy. He was very interested in what he called "the arithmetical paradox" of mind. As we have seen, the separation of one and many is a measurement made by perception. As long as we are prisoners of that separation, we are prisoners of the arithmetical paradox. We can only be free when we see the interbeing and interpenetration of everything. Reality is neither one nor many.

The Vijñanavadins described "perfect unity of mind and object" as "a mirror in which all phenomena are reflected." Without phenomena, there can be no reflections, and without reflections, there can be no mirror. The image used to describe mind is "a large, round mirror which nothing can cover and nothing can hide." All phenomena are said to be stored in a "store-house" (alaya). The contents and the proprietor (subject of knowledge) in this store are one. In the teachings of the Vijñanavadins, alaya contains the seeds (bija) of all physical, physiological, and psychological phenomena. At the same time it functions as the ground from which the subjects and objects of knowledge arise.

Alaya is not bounded by space or limited by time. In fact, even space and time arise from *alaya*.[27]

Crucial to the Vijñanavada teaching is understanding the object of perception. They are of three types: pure objects or reality in itself (*svabhava*), representations or conceptualized visible objects (*samanya-laksana*), and pure images or conceptualized objects that remain in memory and may reappear in the mind when the correct conditions are present.

Manyana and Vijñapti

From the *alaya* arise two kinds of consciousness, *manyana* and *vijñapti*. *Vijñapti* causes all feelings, perceptions, concepts, and thoughts to appear. It is based in the sense organs, the nervous system, and the brain. The object of *vijñapti* is reality in itself (*svabhava*) and is possible only when feelings and perceptions are pure and direct. When seen through the veil of conceptualization, the same object can be only an image of reality (*samanya laksana*) or a pure image such as a dream while asleep or a daydream. Although the object of a pure sensation is reality in itself, when this reality is seen through concepts and thoughts, it is already distorted. Reality in itself is a stream of life, always moving. Images of reality produced by concepts are concrete structures framed by the concepts of space-

time, birth-death, production-destruction, exis-
tence-nonexistence, one-many.

Manyana is a kind of intuition, the sense that
there is a separate self which can exist independently of the rest of the world. This intuition is
produced by habit and ignorance. Its illusory nature
has been constructed by *vijñapti*, and it, in turn,
becomes a basis for *vijñapti*. The object of this intuition is a distorted fragment of *alaya* which it considers to be a self, comprised of a body and a soul. It
of course is never reality in itself, but just a representation of reality. In its role as a self as well as
consciousness of the self, *manyana* is regarded as
the basic obstacle to penetrating reality. Contemplation performed by *vijñapti* can remove the erroneous perceptions brought about by *manyana*.

Within *vijñapti*, there are six consciousnesses:
consciousness of seeing, hearing, smelling, tasting,
touching, and thinking. The mind-consciousness
(*manovijñana*) has the broadest field of activity. It
can be active in conjunction with the other senses,
for example awareness of seeing. It can also be active on its own, such as in conceptualizing, reflecting, imagining, and dreaming. Following the
five consciousnesses of the senses, mind-consciousness is called the sixth consciousness.
Manyana (or *manas*) and *alaya* are the seventh and
eighth consciousnesses.

To See Reality with the Eyes of Understanding

As already mentioned, it is only in the case of pure sensation that the object of consciousness is reality-in-itself. The senses are only of relative value in penetrating reality. That is why, although the content of any sensation is reality-in-itself, what is sensed is never reality in its entirety. Science has shown, for example, that human eyes can perceive only a minute portion of the electromagnetic spectrum. Radium and cosmic rays are among the many waves which are of too high a frequency for us to see. We cannot see radio waves. When we see light and and hear sounds, we perceive only waves within certain frequencies. Infra-red rays are invisible to us, as they have longer wave lengths than are visible to us. Since x-rays have shorter wave lengths than those of visible light, we cannot see them either. Everything in the universe would appear quite different if we could see x-rays! Nor can we hear the high-pitched sounds to which the ears of dogs and other animals are sensitive. Among animals on the earth, many can perceive much more of reality than we humans can.

Therefore, the perfect ultimate reality of the universe can only be observed with eyes of great understanding, but these eyes can only open when the concepts which compose the *manyana* and attachment to wrong views are uprooted. Only then can the *alaya* reveal itself as a great, perfect mirror reflecting the whole universe.

Is Alaya One or Many?

If we were to ask, "Does everyone have his or her own *alaya*, or do we all share a common *alaya*?," it would show that we have not yet realized the true nature of interbeing and interpenetration. We are still bewildered by what Schrödinger called the "arithmetical paradox." We may then ask, "If we do not each have separate *alayas*, why do we have separate, individual memories?"

Can we say that one child learns his lesson and another knows it by heart? Waves break on the water's surface, and although they cannot exist apart from the water, they have their own form and their own place. Many streams may flow into a river, but all of them are one with the river. On the surface of the sea of phenomena, we see many waves glistening, but for each wave to be formed, for each to be destroyed, it must be dependent on every other wave. The memories of each of us are not just our own personal treasures. They are living realities that are related to all other living realities. They undergo ceaseless transformation, as do our bodies. Each thing is reality, but reality is not subject to ideas of "one" or "many."

Let the Sun of Awareness Shine on the Dharmakaya

These teachings from the Vijñanavada school are given to us to help our meditation practice, not as

Descriptions of Reality. We should not forget that the phenomena which we call the sixth and seventh consciousnesses, reality-in-itself, representations of reality, do not exist independently of one another or of space-time. A representation of an object which appears in a dream is also a living reality in which the whole universe is present. We often think that an image of a fairy in a dream has no reality since it is without material basis, but what about the images on our TV screens? Are they real? Can we grasp their substance or find their material basis? Still, they are real. The entire universe is present in them. The presence of an illusion includes everything in the universe. The illusion can exist only because everything else exists. Its existence has the same marvelous nature as a particle. In modern science, a particle is no longer seen as solid or concretely defined.

When the sixth *vijñana*, mind-consciousness, remains in deep concentration, it does not create illusory objects. At such times, a living and direct experience of ultimate reality is possible. To be conscious always means to be conscious of something. Therefore we should not think that we can bring our consciousness to a "pure" state in which there are no objects. A consciousness without an object is a consciousness which is not manifested. It is latent in the *alaya*, just as a wave is latent in calm water. There is a state of concentration which can be attained during meditation, called "concentration without perception," in which consciousness is no longer active. In dreamless sleep, consciousness also remains in this latent state in the *alaya*.

During meditation, we focus all our attention on one object, and concentration can arise. This meditation is not passive or dull; in fact we must be very alert. We maintain concentration on the object, which is the mind itself, just as the sun continues to shine on freshly fallen snow or vegetation. We can also synchronize our breathing with our attention to the object, and this may improve our concentration. If we use a leaf as the object of our concentration, we can see, through the leaf, the perfect oneness of mind and universe. If we meditate on the presence of the sun throughout our body, we can experience that Dharmakaya has no beginning and no end. Meditating on interbeing and interpenetration of reality is a means to destroy concepts, and using such means, we can arrive at a direct experience of ultimate reality in mind and body simultaneously. In the Vijñanavada school, this is called *vijñaptimatrata*.

From Interdependence (Paratantra) to Perfect Reality (Nispañña)

The practice of meditation on the three-fold nature of things (*tri-svabhava*) is similar to meditation on the principle of multi-interiorigin. In both cases, we begin by meditating on the interdependent relationship of all things (*paratantra*) in order to realize that the image of reality we have in our mind is erroneous because it is built within the framework of birth/death, one/many, space/time, and other concepts, i.e. it is based on illusion. By looking deeply into reality in the light of interdependence, we gradually free ourselves from the net of clinging to "myself" as a separate self and all dharmas as separate "own-beings." Even if in the *alaya* many deep roots of illusion (*anusaya*) still exist, they can be uprooted and destroyed, and perfect liberation achieved each moment which is fully lived in the light of interdependence. Just as the raft is no longer needed after we reach the other shore, when we live in the present moment in harmony with all beings, we do not need the concept of interdependence. We can dwell peacefully in the true nature of consciousness. This is called ultimate reality. It is the world of suchness (*tathata*), the world of perfect oneness of mind and object.

Conditioned Reality and Ultimate Reality Cannot Be Separated

There is no need for us to attain the world of suchness, because suchness *is* available at all times. The *Avatamsaka Sutra* calls it the "Dharma Realm of Truth," the world of true nature. The world of mountains and rivers, plants and animals, where each thing seems to have its own place, is called

the "Dharma Realm of Phenomena." But these
two worlds are not separate. They are one, exactly
like water and waves. That is why they are also re-
ferred to as the "Dharma Realm of Unobstructed
Interpenetration of Truth and Phenomena." Interpenetration in this world of phenomena, where
one phenomenon is all phenomena and where all
are one is called the "Dharma Realm of Unobstructed Interpenetration of Every Phenomenon."
These are called the Four Dharma Realms, mentioned frequently in the *Avatamsaka Sutra*. Zen
Master Fa Cang of Tang Dynasty China, one of the
great scholars in this field wrote a text which describes the methods of meditation which can help
us destroy wrong views and return to the source,
prior to their origination, which means having a
clear, perfect view of the world of suchness.[28]

David Bohm has expounded a theory on what
he calls "the implicate order and the explicate order," which is very close to the notion of the
Dharma Realm of the Unobstructed Interpenetration of All Phenomena. Bohm has said that all realities which are thought to exist independently of
one another belong to the explicate order, an order
in which one thing seems to exist outside of another. However, if we see deeply, everything is
linked to everything else in the whole universe,
and from one particle we can see the whole universe, which is included in it and out of which it is
created. This leads us to the world of the implicate
order in which "time and space no longer decide

whether things are dependent on or independent of one another." According to Bohm, present day science must start from the wholeness of the implicate order to be able to see the real nature of each phenomenon. At a conference in Córdoba, he said, "The electron is always the whole."[29] This view is very close to the "one in the all" of the *Avatamsaka Sutra*. If Bohm is willing to go even further in his research and practice meditation which involves both mind and body, he may well arrive at some unexpected result and cause a major breakthrough in physics.

Look Deeply at Your Hand

Happiness Arises from Awareness of Being

The sky was clear and it was quite warm this morning. Little Thuy left for school after eating the fried rice I made for her, and I went into the garden to transplant some lettuce. When I came in to wash my hands, I saw that my guest was already awake and washing his face. I boiled water and made a pot of tea. With two cups on the table in the courtyard, I sat and waited for him to come outside.

We drank tea in the warm sunshine. My friend asked me how we can see the results of meditation, and I told him that peace and happiness are the guides for measuring the fruit of practice. If we do not become calmer and happier, something is wrong with our practice.

Sometimes people say that without a teacher, meditation can cause confusion and imbalance, but it is not always possible to find a highly developed teacher. Such people are rare, although it is often possible to find teachers who have not yet fully realized the Way. If you are not able to study with a realized teacher, the most intelligent way to practice is to rely primarily on the teacher in yourself.

Proceed slowly and carefully. For example, it is not necessary to practice the Four Formless Meditations. Never force your body or your mind. Be kind to yourself. Live your daily life simply, with awareness. If you are mindful, you have everything; you are everything! Please have a look at *The Miracle of Mindfulness* and *The Sutra on the Full Awareness of Breathing*. They are filled with practical suggestions concerning the practice. Read the sections on the Four Dharma Realms, the Eight Consciousnesses, and the Three Natures. Reading books with practical suggestions are useful not just before practicing sitting meditation but anytime. A minute of meditation is a minute of peace and happiness. If meditation is not pleasant for you, you are not practicing correctly.

Meditation brings happiness. This happiness comes, first of all, from the fact that you are master of yourself, no longer caught up in forgetfulness. If you follow your breathing and allow a half-smile to blossom, mindful of your feelings and thoughts, the movements of your body will naturally become more gentle and relaxed, harmony will be there, and true happiness will arise. Keeping our mind present in each moment is the foundation of meditation practice. When we achieve this, we live our lives fully and deeply, seeing things that others, in forgetfulness, do not.

Providing Conditions Conducive to Living in Mindfulness

In *The Miracle of Mindfulness*, I proposed more than 30 exercises of mindfulness, including a suggestion for how to arrange one day of mindfulness each week. If you read it, you will see clear instructions. This book has been translated into 35 languages. It is a small book, but it is very practical and easy to read. In fact, I still follow its instruction myself. You can read it many times, because each time you read it you will have a chance to examine your own practice and from your own experience discover things not in the book. More than ten years have passed since it was published, and I still receive many letters from readers all over the world expressing their gratitude, telling how this book has brought great changes in their lives. A surgeon in New York told me that he always maintains mindfulness while performing operations. (I think to myself that this surgeon will never forget his surgical instruments in his patients' bodies.)

The first few months of your practice may lack continuity, since it is natural to forget to practice mindfulness sometimes. But you can always start again. If you have a practicing companion, you are very lucky. Friends who practice together often remind each other to practice mindfulness, and they can share experiences and progress. Mindfulness can be nurtured in you by many different means. An autumn leaf that you pick up in your backyard can be taped to your bathroom mirror, and every morning when you see it, the leaf will remind you to smile and return to mindfulness. While you wash your face and brush your teeth, you will be relaxed and in mindfulness. A bell from a nearby church or clock-tower, or even the telephone can also bring you back to mindfulness. I recommend you let the phone ring two or three times before answering, while you breathe in and out and take the time to return to your true self.

My Love, Who Are You?

Some day, if you need a topic for meditation, choose one that you care about, one that you find very interesting, so that it will command your attention. It can be the sun, a caterpillar, a dew drop, time, your face and your eyes before you were born. Every phenomenon, concrete or abstract, physical, physiological, psychological, or metaphysical, can be the subject of your meditation. After you choose a topic, plant it in the depths of your spiritual life. An egg needs to be incubated by its mother hen in order to become a baby chick. In the same way, the topic you sow must be nurtured. Your "self," or the "self" of the person you like the most, or the "self" of the person you hate the most can be the subject of your practice. Any subject can bring about awakening if it is sown deeply into the ground of your being. But if it is only entrusted to your intellect, it is unlikely to bear fruit.

Have you meditated on the subject "Who am I?" Who were you before you were born? At the time when there was not the slightest trace of your physical existence, did you exist or not? How can you become something from nothing? If on the day I was conceived my parents had other appointments and were not able to see each other, then who am I now? If that day the egg of my mother was not penetrated by that sperm of my father, but by another sperm of his, then who am I now? Would I be a brother or a sister of mine? If that day, my mother did not marry my father or my father did not marry my mother, but married someone else, then who am I today? Each healthy living cell in your body controls its own activity, but does this mean that each cell has its own self? In the biological classification system, species make up smaller subdivisions of genus. Does each species represent a "self?" If such questions are asked with your deepest conviction and intelligence, and if you plant them deeply into your spiritual life with your whole being, one day an unexpected discovery will arise.

Have you ever looked into the eyes of your loved one and asked deeply, "Who are you, my love?" For either of you to answer, you cannot be satisfied by the usual responses. "My love, who are you who comes to me and takes my suffering as your suffering, my happiness as your happiness, my life and death as your life and death? Who are you whose 'self' has become my 'self?' My love, why aren't you a dew drop, a butterfly, a bird, a pine tree?" Don't be satisfied with mere poetic images. You must ask and answer these questions with your whole mind and heart, with your whole being. Some day, you will even have to question the person you hate the most in this same way: "Who are you who brings me such pain, who makes me feel so much anger and hatred? Are you part of the chain of cause and effect, the fire which forges me on the path?" In other words, "Are you me myself?" You have to become that person. You have to be one with him or her, to worry about what he or she worries about, to suffer his or her suffering, to appreciate what he or she appreciates. That person and you cannot be "two." Your "self" cannot be separate from their self. You are that person, the same as you are your love, and the same as you are yourself.

Continue practicing until you see yourself in the most cruel and inhumane political leader, in the most devastatingly tortured prisoner, in the wealthiest man, and in the child starving, all skin and bones. Practice until you recognize your presence in everyone else on the bus, in the subway, in the concentration camp, working in the fields, in a leaf, in a caterpillar, in a dew drop, in a ray of sun-shine. Meditate until you see yourself in a speck of dust and in the most distant galaxy.

Standard for Orientation

As you continue practicing, the flower of insight will blossom in you, along with the flowers of compassion, tolerance, happiness, and letting go. You can let go, because you do not need to keep anything for yourself. You are no longer a fragile and small "self" that needs to be preserved by all possible means. Since the happiness of others is also your happiness, you are now filled with joy, and you have no jealousy or selfishness. Free from attachment to wrong views and prejudices, you are filled with tolerance. The door of your compassion is wide open, and you also suffer the sufferings of all living beings. As a result, you do whatever you can to relieve these sufferings. These four virtues are called the Four Immeasurables: lovingkind-ness, compassion, sympathetic joy, and non-at-tachment. They are the fruits of the meditation on the principle of the interdependent co-arising of things. The development of these Four Im-measurables in you shows that you are proceeding in the right direction and are also capable of guiding others in their practice.

A Love Letter

Where are you now, my good friend? Are you out in the field, in the forest, on the mountain, in a military camp, in a factory, at your desk, in a hospital, in prison? Regardless of where you are, let us breathe in and out together, and let the Sun of Awareness enter. Let us begin with this breath and this awareness. Whether life is an illusion, a dream, or a wondrous reality depends on our insight and our mindfulness. Awakening is a miracle. The darkness in a totally dark room will disappear the moment the light is switched on. In the same way, life will reveal itself as a miraculous reality the second the Sun of Awareness begins to shine.

I have a poet friend who was put into a "re-education" camp in Vietnam, in a remote jungle area. During his four years there, he practiced meditation and was able to live in peace. Upon release, he was lucid, like a sharp sword. He knew that he had not lost anything during those four years. On the contrary, he knew he had "re-educated" himself in meditation.

As I write these lines, I am writing a love letter. I hope these words will be read by you, my known and unknown brothers and sisters, who are living in circumstances regarded as hopeless and tragic, that you may renew your energies and courage.

If You Want Peace, Peace is With You Immediately

Fifteen years ago, I wrote four Chinese characters on a paper lamp shade. These four characters can be translated as, "If you want peace, peace is with you immediately." A few years later, in Singapore, I had the chance to practice these words.

Several of us organized a program to help the Indochinese refugees in the Gulf of Siam. The program was called *Mau Chay Ruot Mem* ("When blood is shed, we all suffer"). At that time, the world did not know about the "boat people," and the governments of Thailand, Malaysia, and Singapore would not allow them to land. So we hired two large ships, the Leapdal and the Roland, to pick up refugees on the open sea, and two small ships, the Saigon 200 and the Blackmark, to communicate between them and to transport food and supplies. We planned to fill the two large ships with refugees and take them to Australia and Guam. We had to do our work secretly, since the situation of the boat people was something most of the world's governments did not want to acknowledge at that time, and we knew they would give us a hard time if they found out.

Unfortunately, after nearly 800 refugees had been rescued from small boats at sea, the government of Singapore discovered our program. At 2:00 one morning, the Singapore police were ordered to surround the house where I was staying. One officer blocked the front and another the back, while four others rushed in and confiscated my travel documents. They ordered me to leave the country within 24 hours.

With 800 people aboard our two large ships, we had to find a way for them to travel safely to Australia or Guam. The Saigon 200 and the Blackmark were not allowed to leave port to take food and water to the refugees on the Leapdal and the Roland. The Roland had enough fuel to reach Australia if we could get food to them. Then its engine broke down. The day was very windy and the sea quite rough, and we worried about the ship's safety, even drifting off shore, but the Malaysian government would not allow it to enter Malaysian water. I tried to get permission to enter a neighboring country, to continue the rescue operation, but the governments of Thailand, Malaysia, and Indonesia would not grant me an entry visa. Even though I was on land, I found myself drifting on the sea and my life was one with the lives of the 800 refugees on board.

In that situation, I decided that I must practice the meditation topic: "If you want peace, peace is with you immediately," and I was surprised to find myself quite calm, not afraid or worried about anything. I was not just careless—this was truly a peaceful state of mind. And in that state of mind, I was able to overcome this difficult situation. As long as I live, I will never forget those seconds of sitting meditation, those breaths, those mindful footsteps during that 24-hour period.

There were more problems than it seemed possible to solve in just 24 hours. Even in a whole lifetime, many of us complain that there is not enough time. How could so much be done in a mere 24 hours? Success came when I faced the problem directly. I vowed that if I could not have peace at that moment, I would never be able to have peace. If I could not be peaceful in the midst of danger, then the kind of peace I might have in simpler times would not mean anything. Without finding peace in the midst of difficulty, I would never know real peace. Practicing this topic, "If you want peace, peace is with you immediately," I was able to resolve many problems, one after another, when that was what was needed.

Effect Follows Cause More Quickly than a Bolt of Lightning

Peace can exist only in the present moment. It is ridiculous to say, "Wait until I finish this, then I will be free to live in peace." What is "this?" A diploma, a job, a house, the payment of a debt? If you think that way, peace will never come. There is always another "this" that will follow the present one. If you are not living in peace at this moment, you will never be able to. If you truly want to be at peace, you must be at peace right now. Otherwise, there is only "the hope of peace some day."

My poet-friend did not wait to be released from the re-education camp to live in peace. He did not know that he would only be there four years. (Many stay ten years or longer.) He practiced meditation on a topic similar to, "If you want peace, peace is with you immediately." We need to sit down and find a method of practice that works for us so we can live in peace and happiness. Peace does not come only after many long days of practice. What is most important is your wish, your determination. If your determination is strong, the effect will follow the cause more quickly than a bolt of lightning. You can nurture peace through your breathing, your footsteps, or your smile, through seeing, hearing, or feeling, until you are one with peace.

Everything Depends on Your Peace

If the earth were your body, you could feel the many areas where there is suffering. War, suppression, and famine wreak destruction in so many places. Many children have become blind from malnutrition. Their hands search through mounds of trash for things they can trade for a few ounces of food. Many adults are dying slowly and hopelessly in prisons. Others are killed for trying to oppose the violence. We have enough nuclear weapons to destroy dozens of Earths, but we continue to manufacture more.

Aware of all of this, how can we withdraw to a forest or even to our own rooms to sit in meditation? The peace we seek cannot be our personal possession. We need to find an inner peace which makes it possible for us to become one with those who suffer, and to do something to help our brothers and sisters, which is to say, ourselves. I know many young people who are aware of the real situation of the world and who are filled with compassion. They refuse to hide themselves in artificial peace, and they engage in the world in order to change the society. They know what they want, yet after a period of involvement they become discouraged. Why? It is because they lack deep, inner peace, the kind of peace they can take with them into their life of action. Our strength is not in weapons, money, or power. Our strength is in our peace, the peace within us. This peace makes us indestructible. We must have peace while taking care of those we love and those we want to protect.

I have recognized this peace in many, many people. Most of their time and effort is spent protecting the weak, watering the trees of love and understanding everywhere. They belong to various religious and cultural backgrounds. I do not know how each of them came to their inner peace, but I have seen it in them. If you are attentive, I am sure you will see it too. This peace is not a barricade which separates you from the world. On the contrary, this kind of peace brings you into the world and empowers you to undertake whatever you

want to do to try to help—struggling for social justice, lessening the disparity between the rich and
the poor, stopping the arms race, fighting against
discrimination, and sowing more seeds of understanding, reconciliation, and compassion. In any
struggle, you need determination and patience.
This determination will dissipate if you lack peace.
Those who lead a life of social action especially
need to practice mindfulness during each moment
of daily life.

A Bodhisattva Looks at All Beings
with the Eyes of Compassion

Peace and compassion go hand in hand with understanding and non-discrimination. We choose
one thing over another when we discriminate.
With the eyes of compassion, we can look at all of
living reality at once. A compassionate person sees
himself or herself in every being. With the ability
to view reality from many viewpoints, we can
overcome all viewpoints and act compassionately
in each situation. This is the highest meaning of
the word "reconciliation."

Reconciliation does not mean to sign an agree-
ment with duplicity and cruelty. Reconciliation
opposes all forms of ambition, without taking
sides. Most of us want to take sides in each encounter or conflict. We distinguish right from
wrong based on partial evidence gathered directly

or by propaganda or hearsay. We need indignation in order to act, but indignation alone is not enough, even righteous, legitimate indignation. Our world does not lack people willing to throw themselves into action. What we need are people who are capable of loving, of not taking sides so that they can embrace the whole of reality as a mother hen embraces all her chicks, with two fully spread wings.

The practice of meditation on interdependent co-arising is one way to arrive at this realization. When it is attained, discrimination vanishes and reality is no longer sliced by the sword of conceptualization. The boundaries between good and evil are obliterated, and means and ends are recognized as the same. We have to continue practicing until we can see a child's body of skin and bones in Uganda or Ethiopia as our own, until the hunger and pain in the bodies of all living species are our own. Then we will have realized non-discrimination, real love. According to the *Lotus Sutra*, looking at all living beings with the eyes of compassion is a capacity of Avalokitesvara Bodhisattva. When we see someone who can look at all beings with the eyes of compassion, we know that Avalokitesvara Bodhisattva is present in them. When we meditate on the First Noble Truth, the truth of suffering, Avalokitesvara Bodhisattva is present in us. When we ask a favor of Avalokitesvara Bodhisattva, he appears even before we ask.

"Look into Your Hand, My Child"

I have a friend who is an artist. He has been away from home for nearly 40 years. He told me that every time he misses his mother, all he has to do is look at his hand and he feels better. His mother, a traditional Vietnamese woman, could read only a few Chinese characters and has never studied Western philosophy or science. Before he left Vietnam, she held his hand and told him, "Whenever you miss me, look into your hand my child. You will see me immediately." How penetrating these simple, sincere words! For nearly 40 years, he has looked into his hand many times.

The presence of his mother is not just genetic. Her spirit, her hopes, and her life are also present in him. I know that my friend practices meditation, but I do not know whether he has chosen the subject, "Looking into your Hand" as a kung-an. This subject can take him far in his practice. From his hand, he can penetrate deeply into the reality of beginningless and endless time. He will be able to see that thousands of generations before him and thousands of generations after him are all him. From time immemorial until the present moment, his life has never been interrupted and his hand is still there, a beginningless and endless reality. He can recognize his "true face" 500 million years ago and 500 million years from now. He exists not only in the evolutionary tree branching along the axis of time, but also in the network of interdependent relations. As a result, each cell in his body is just as free from birth and death as he is. In this case, the subject "Looking into your Hand" can produce a deeper effect than the subject "The Sound of One Hand" proposed by Zen Master Hakuin.

When my niece came to visit me from America last summer, I gave her "Looking into your Hand" as a Zen subject for her to cherish. I told her that every pebble, every leaf, every caterpillar on the hill by the hermitage is present in her hand.

"Why Do You Cry, Sister?"

A few years ago, a pro-government group in Ho Chi Minh City spread a rumor that I had passed away from a heart attack. This news caused much confusion inside the country. A Buddhist nun wrote me that the news arrived at her community while she was teaching a class of novices, and the atmosphere in the class sank and one nun passed out. I have been in exile for more than 20 years because of my involvement in the peace movement, and I do not know this young nun or the present generation of Buddhist monks and nuns in Vietnam. But life and death is only a fiction, and not very deep; why do you cry, sister? You are studying Buddhism, doing what I am doing. So if you exist, I also exist. What does not exist cannot come into existence and what exists cannot cease to be. Have you realized that, sister? If we cannot bring a speck of dust from "existence" to "non-existence," how can we do that to a human? On earth, many people have been killed struggling for peace, for human rights, for freedom and social justice, but no one can destroy them. They still exist. Sister, do you think that Jesus Christ, Mahatma Gandhi, Lambrakis, Dr. Martin Luther King, Jr. are "dead people?" No, they are still here. We are they. We carry them in each cell of our bodies. If you ever hear such news again, please smile. Your serene smile will prove that you have attained great understanding and courage. Buddhism and all of humankind expect this of you.

All is in the Word "Know"

A friend of mine who is a research scientist is now guiding many Ph.D. candidates on their theses. He wants to do everything in a scientific way, but he is also a poet and as a result he often is not very "scientific." Last winter, he went through a tremendous spiritual crisis. Hearing of this, I sent him a drawing of a wave riding on silky-smooth water. Beneath the drawing I wrote, "As always, the wave lives the life of a wave, and at the same time, the life of water. When you breathe, you breathe for all of us."

As I wrote that sentence, I swam with him to help him get across that time of difficulty, and fortunately, it helped us both. Most people view themselves as waves and forget that they are also water. They are used to living in birth-and-death, and they forget about no-birth-and-no-death. A wave also lives the life of water, and we also live the life of no-birth-no-death. We only need to know that we are living the life of no-birth-no-death. All is in the word "know." To know is to realize. Realization is mindfulness. All the work of meditation is aimed at awakening us in order to know one and only one thing: birth and death can never touch us in any way whatsoever.

Notes

Chapter One, Sunshine and Green Leaves

[1] "Prajña," from Thich Nhat Hanh, *Footprints on the Sand* (San Jose: La Boi Press).

[2] In the teaching of Vijñanavada, *smrti* is accompanied by *samadhi* and *prajña*, and forgetfulness is accompanied by dispersion and wrong views. Dispersion and wrong views are the opposites of *samadhi* and *prajña*. *Smrti, samadhi,* and *prajña* are three among the five wholesome mental formations. Forgetfulness, dispersion, and wrong views are three among the 26 unwholesome mental formations.

[3] Fritjof Capra, *The Tao of Physics: An Exploration of the Parallels Between Modern Physics and Eastern Mysticism* (Boston: Shambhala New Science Library, Second Edition, 1985). See also Thomas Cleary, trans., *The Flower Ornament Scripture: A Translation of the Avatamsaka Sutra,* 3 volumes (Boston: Shambhala, 1984-87).

[4] See, e.g., Dogen, *Moon in a Dewdrop,* ed. by Kazuaki Tanahashi (Berkeley: North Point, 1985), p. 314.

[5] Although in the Copenhagen interpretation of quantum theory, observer and observed are inseparable, most scientists do not practice this preaching.

[6] See Nyanaponika Thera, *The Heart of Buddhist Meditation* (New York: Weiser, 1962).

[7] "The terms *objective* and *subjective* only designate limited events. Through quantum mechanics we know that no totally objective phenomenon can exist, that is to say, independent of the observer's mind. Correlatively, all subjective phenom-

ena present an objective fact." Brian D. Josephson, *Science et Conscience* (Paris: Stock, 1980).

Chapter Two, The Dance of the Bees

[8] K. von Frisch, *Tanzsprache und Orientierung der Bienen* (Berlin, 1965).

[9] See David Bohm, *Wholeness and the Implicate Order* (London: Routledge & Kegan Paul, 1980), chapter 2, on the "rheo-mode."

[10] Alphonse de Lamartine, *Méditations poétiques* (1820).

[11] *Alaya*, the 8th consciousness, has the function of "maintaining" the maintainer, the object that is maintained, and the object taken as a self by the 7th consciousness, *manyana*. *Alaya* also has the function of maintaining all seeds (*bija*), i.e. the essence, or energy, of all things; as well as the function of concocting, i.e. transforming and making ripe all karmas so that new physical, psychological, and physiological phenomena arise. *Manyana* is a psychological attempt to cling to a part of *Alaya* as its self. *Amala* is pure white consciousness— the name of *Alaya* after it is freed from *manyana*. All of this is more fully explained in Chapter 4.

Chapter Three, The Universe in a Speck of Dust

[12] Many believe that entering the Four Dhyanas and the Four Formless States Samadhi is to enter a state where mind no longer has its object. In fact, mind always has an object—if not, it is not mind. In the Four Formless States, the object of the mind is limitless space, limitless consciousness, the absence of perception, and the state of neither perception nor non-perception. Samadhi is a state of mind in which the dis-

tinction of subject and object of consciousness no longer exists, i.e. the *nimittabhaga* (object) is not objectivized by the *darsanabhaga* (subject). Both object and subject are parts of consciousness, they cannot exist separately. They have the same ground of being: the *svabhavabhaga* (the self-nature of consciousness).

[13] Dao Hanh, Dhyana Master, Ly Dynasty, end of the 11th century.

[14] Nguyen Cong Tru was born in 1778 in the Vietnamese village of Uy Vieu, in Ha Tinh Province, and he died in 1859.

15 Walt Whitman, "Song of Myself." "Do I contradict myself?/Very well then, I contradict myself/I am large, I contain multitudes."

[16] "It is a question here, on the contrary, of pushing to the limit the conception of particles as a network of related interconnections. The philosophy of *bootstrap* renounces not only the idea of elementary "building blocks" of matter, but any fundamental entity of any kind: laws, equations or principles. In it the universe is a dynamic tissue of interdependent events. No property of any part of it has the role of foundation; all is the result of the properties of the other parts, and it is the global coherence of their mutual relationships which determines the structure of the whole tissue." Fritjof Capra, "The Tao of Physics," in Josephson, ed., *Science et Conscience* (Paris, 1980), *op. cit.*

[17] *vikalpa.*

[18] David Bohm, "Imagination and the Implicate Order," in Josephson, *op. cit.*, p. 453.

[19] Edwin Schrödinger, *My View of the World* (London: Cambridge University Press, 1964), p. 22.

[20] The terms endless (*vo ang*) and infinite (*vo tan*) are in single quotes because I am using them provisionally.

[21] Those of you who are not familiar with the Theory of Relativity may not understand the notion of the "four-dimensional continuum." Before Einstein, the German mathematician Minkowski had already said that time and space separated from each other are fictitious ghosts; only when together can they represent reality. The Theory of Relativity says that all moving things (all pieces of rock on earth are moving together with Earth also) can only assert themselves in time and space at the same time. For example, if a plane takes off from Paris to go to New Delhi, the flight controller on the ground not only has to know the longitude x, the latitude y, and the altitude z, but he also has to know the time t in order to know the exact position of the plane throughout the flight. Time t is thus the fourth dimension.

Time, space, mass, and movement exist in interrelationship with each other, and the greater the density of the mass, the more curved the space surrounding that mass will be. Light emitted from celestial bodies, when passing by huge masses like the sun, will follow a curved line, because in the vicinity of the sun, space is more curved. Light and energy also have masses, because matter and energy are one, according to the famous formula $e=mc^2$, in which e is energy, m is mass, and c is the speed of light. The presence of matter brings about the curved nature of space; therefore in relativity, the absolute straight line of Euclidian mathematics is no longer possible.

Chapter Four, Cutting the Net of Birth and Death

[22] Alfred Kastler, *Cette étrange matiére* (Paris: Stock, 1976).

[23] *Anuradha Sutra, (Samyutta Nikaya,* XLIV, 2).

[24] J. Robert Oppenheimer, *Science and the Common Understanding* (New York: Simon and Schuster, 1954), p. 40.

[25] Literally, "Death, if anyone sees to the depth, is called a hero." See Isshu Miura and Ruth Fuller Sasaki, *The Zen Koan* (New York: Harcourt, Brace, Jovanovich, 1965).

[26] Erwin Schrödinger, *What is Life? & Mind and Matter*, (London: Cambridge University Press, 1967), pp. 138 ff.

[27] Interestingly, in the latest unification theories, superstrings are supposed to give rise to space and time themselves.

[28] Fa Cang, *Wang Jin Hai Yuan Guan* ("Ending Illusions and Going Back to Your Own Source"), no. 1876, Revised Chinese Tripitaka.

[29] David Bohm, *Wholeness and the Implicate Order* (London: Routledge & Kegan Paul, 1980).

Touching Peace

Practicing the Art of Mindful Living

Edited by Arnold Kotler

Drawings by Mayumi Oda

Contents

Life Is a Miracle

*I*n Vietnam when I was a young monk, each village
temple had a big bell, like those in Christian
churches in Europe and America. Whenever the bell
was invited to sound, all the villagers would stop
what they were doing and pause for a few moments
to breathe in and out in mindfulness. At Plum Village, the community where I live in France, we do
the same. Every time we hear the bell, we go back to
ourselves and enjoy our breathing. When we breathe
in, we say, silently, "Listen, listen," and when we
breathe out, we say, "This wonderful sound brings
me back to my true home."

Our true home is in the present moment. To live in
the present moment is a miracle. The miracle is not to
walk on water. The miracle is to walk on the green
Earth in the present moment, to appreciate the peace
and beauty that are available now. Peace is all around
us—in the world and in nature—and within us—in
our bodies and our spirits. Once we learn to touch

this peace, we will be healed and transformed. It is not a matter of faith; it is a matter of practice. We need only to find ways to bring our body and mind back to the present moment so we can touch what is refreshing, healing, and wondrous.

Last year in New York City, I rode in a taxi, and I saw that the driver was not at all happy. He was not in the present moment. There was no peace or joy in him, no capacity of being alive while doing the work of driving, and he expressed it in the way he drove. Many of us do the same. We rush about, but we are not at one with what we are doing; we are not at peace. Our body is here, but our mind is somewhere else—in the past or the future, possessed by anger, frustration, hopes, or dreams. We are not really alive; we are like ghosts. If our beautiful child were to come up to us and offer us a smile, we would miss him completely, and he would miss us. What a pity!

In *The Stranger*, Albert Camus described a man who was going to be executed in a few days. Sitting alone in his cell, he noticed a small patch of blue sky through the skylight, and suddenly he felt deeply in touch with life, deeply in the present moment. He vowed to live his remaining days in mindfulness, in full appreciation of each moment, and he did so for several days. Then, just three hours before the time of his execution, a priest came into the cell to receive a confession and administer the last rites. But the man wanted only to be alone. He tried many ways to get the priest to leave, and when he finally succeeded, he said to himself that that priest lived like a dead man.

"Il vit comme un mort." He saw that the one who was trying to save him was less alive than he, the one who was about to be executed.

Many of us, although alive, are not really alive, because we are not able to touch life in the present moment. We are like dead people, as Camus says. I would like to share with you a few simple exercises we can practice that can help us reunify our body and mind and get back in touch with life in the present moment. The first is called conscious breathing, and human beings like us have been practicing this for more than three thousand years. As we breathe in, we know we are breathing in, and as we breathe out, we know we are breathing out. As we do this, we observe many elements of happiness inside us and around us. We can really enjoy touching our breathing and our being alive.

Life is found only in the present moment. I think we should have a holiday to celebrate this fact. We have holidays for so many important occasions— Christmas, New Year's, Mother's Day, Father's Day, even Earth Day—why not celebrate a day when we can live happily in the present moment all day long. I would like to declare today "Today's Day," a day dedicated to touching the Earth, touching the sky, touching the trees, and touching the peace that is available in the present moment.

Ten years ago, I planted three beautiful Himalayan cedars outside my hermitage, and now, whenever I walk by one of them, I bow, touch its bark with my cheek, and hug it. As I breathe in and out mindfully, I look up at its branches and beautiful leaves. I receive a lot of peace and sustenance from hugging trees. Touching a tree gives both you and the tree great pleasure. Trees are beautiful, refreshing, and solid. When you want to hug a tree, it will never refuse. You can rely on trees. I have even taught my students the practice of tree-hugging.

At Plum Village, we have a beautiful linden tree that provides shade and joy to hundreds of people every summer. A few years ago during a big storm, many of its branches were broken off, and the tree almost died. When I saw the linden tree after the storm, I wanted to cry. I felt the need to touch it, but I did not get much pleasure from that touching. I saw that the tree was suffering, and I resolved to find ways to help it. Fortunately, our friend Scott Mayer is a doctor for trees, and he took such good care of the linden tree that now it is even stronger and more beautiful than before. Plum Village would not be the same without that tree. Whenever I can, I touch its bark and feel it deeply.

In the same way that we touch trees, we can touch ourselves and others, with compassion. Sometimes, when we try to hammer a nail into a piece of wood, instead of pounding the nail, we pound our finger. Right away we put down the hammer and take care of our wounded finger. We do everything possible to help it, giving first aid and also compassion and concern. We may need a doctor or nurse to help, but we also need compassion and joy for the wound to heal quickly. Whenever we have some pain, it is wonderful to touch it with compassion. Even if the pain is inside—in our liver, our heart, or our lungs—we can touch it with mindfulness.

Our right hand has touched our left hand many times, but it may not have done so with compassion. Let us practice together. Breathing in and out three times, touch your left hand with your right hand and, at the same time, with your compassion. Do you notice that while your left hand is receiving comfort and love, your right hand is also receiving comfort and love? This practice is for both parties, not just one. When we see someone suffering, if we touch her with compassion, she will receive our comfort and love, and we will also receive comfort and love. We can do the same when we ourselves are suffering. Touching in this way, everyone benefits.

The best way to touch is with mindfulness. You know, it is possible to touch without mindfulness. When you wash your face in the morning, you might touch your eyes without being aware that you are touching them. You might be thinking about other things. But if you wash your face in mindfulness, aware that you have eyes that can see, that the water comes from distant sources to make washing your face possible, your washing will be much deeper. As you touch your eyes, you can say, "Breathing in, I am aware of my eyes. Breathing out, I smile to my eyes."

Our eyes are refreshing, healing, and peaceful elements that are available to us. We pay so much attention to what is wrong, why not notice what is wonderful and refreshing? We rarely take the time to appreciate our eyes. When we touch our eyes with our hands and our mindfulness, we notice that our eyes are precious jewels that are fundamental for our happiness. Those who have lost their sight feel that if they could see as well as we do, they would be in paradise. We only need to open our eyes, and we see every kind of form and color—the blue sky, the beautiful hills, the trees, the clouds, the rivers, the children, the butterflies. Just sitting here and enjoying these colors and shapes, we can be extremely happy. Seeing is a miracle, a condition for our happiness, yet most of the time we take it for granted. We don't act as if we are in paradise. When we practice breathing in and becoming aware of our eyes, breathing out and smiling to our eyes, we touch real peace and joy.

We can do the same with our heart. "Breathing in, I am aware of my heart. Breathing out, I smile to my heart." If we practice this a few times, we will realize that our heart has been working hard, day and night, for many years to keep us alive. Our heart pumps thousands of gallons of blood every day, without stopping. Even while we sleep, our heart continues its work to bring us peace and well-being. Our heart is an element of peace and joy, but we don't touch or appreciate it. We only touch the things that make us suffer, and because of that, we give our heart a hard time by our worries and strong emotions, and by what we eat and drink. Doing so, we undermine our own peace and joy. When we practice breathing in and becoming aware of our heart, breathing out and smiling to our heart, we become enlightened. We see our heart so clearly. When we smile to our heart, we are massaging it with our compassion. When we know what to eat and what not to eat, what to drink and what not to drink, what worries and despair we should avoid, we will keep our heart safe.

The same practice can be applied to other organs in our body, for instance our liver. "Breathing in, I know that my liver has been working hard to keep me well. Breathing out, I vow not to harm my liver by drinking too much alcohol." This is love meditation. Our eyes are us. Our heart is us. Our liver is us. If we cannot love our own heart and our own liver, how can we love another person? To practice love is, first of all, to practice love directed toward ourselves—taking care of our body, taking care of our heart, taking care of our liver. We are touching ourselves with love and compassion.

When we have a toothache, we know that not having a toothache is a wonderful thing. "Breathing in, I am aware of my non-toothache. Breathing out, I smile at my non-toothache." We can touch our non-toothache with our mindfulness, and even with our hands. When we have asthma and can hardly breathe, we realize that breathing freely is a wonderful thing. Even when we have just a stuffed nose, we know that breathing freely is a wonderful thing.

Every day we touch what is wrong, and, as a result, we are becoming less and less healthy. That is why we have to learn to practice touching what is not wrong—inside us and around us. When we get in touch with our eyes, our heart, our liver, our breathing, and our non-toothache and really enjoy them, we see that the conditions for peace and happiness are already present. When we walk mindfully and touch the Earth with our feet, when we drink tea with friends and touch the tea and our friendship, we get healed, and we can bring this healing to society. The more we have suffered in the past, the stronger a healer we can become. We can learn to transform our suffering into the kind of insight that will help our friends and society.

We do not have to die to enter the Kingdom of Heaven. In fact we have to be fully alive. When we breathe in and out and hug a beautiful tree, we are in Heaven. When we take one conscious breath, aware of our eyes, our heart, our liver, and our non-tooth-ache, we are transported to Paradise right away. Peace is available. We only have to touch it. When we are truly alive, we can see that the tree is part of Heaven, and we are also part of Heaven. The whole universe is conspiring to reveal this to us, but we are so out of touch that we invest our resources in cutting down the trees. If we want to enter Heaven on Earth, we need only one conscious step and one conscious breath. When we touch peace, everything becomes real. We become ourselves, fully alive in the present moment, and the tree, our child, and everything else reveal themselves to us in their full splendor.

"The miracle is to walk on Earth." This statement was made by Zen Master Lin Chi. The miracle is not to walk on thin air or water, but to walk on Earth.

The Earth is so beautiful. We are beautiful also. We can allow ourselves to walk mindfully, touching the Earth, our wonderful mother, with each step. We don't need to wish our friends, "Peace be with you." Peace is already with them. We only need to help them cultivate the habit of touching peace in each moment.

We Are All Flowers

*I*n the Zen tradition, poetry and meditation always
go together. Poetry is made of images and music,
and images make the practice easy. Here is an exercise to help us in the practice of mindfulness that
many friends have found inspiring and effective:

> Breathing in, I know I am breathing in.
> Breathing out, I know I am breathing out.
> *In/Out.*
>
> Breathing in, I see myself as a flower.
> Breathing out, I feel fresh.
> *Flower/Fresh.*
>
> Breathing in, I see myself as a mountain.
> Breathing out, I feel solid.
> *Mountain/Solid.*

Breathing in, I see myself as still water.
Breathing out, I reflect things as they are.
Water/Reflecting.

Breathing in, I see myself as space.
Breathing out, I feel free.
Space/Free.

All of us, children and adults, are beautiful flowers. Our eyelids are exactly like rose petals, especially when our eyes are closed. Our ears are like morning glories listening to the sounds of the birds. Our lips form a beautiful flower every time we smile. And our two hands are a lotus flower with five petals. The practice is to keep our "flowerness" alive and present, not just for our own benefit but for the happiness of everyone.

You know that if you leave a flower out of water for several hours, the stem will dry out. When you put it back, it may be too late; it may not be able to absorb the water. To save the flower, you have to cut the stem again, if possible while it is submerged so the water can flow into the cells right away. You can even cut the sides of the stem a little, to help the water flow in laterally. Within a short time, your flower will bloom again.

Each of us is a flower, but sometimes our flowerness is tired and needs to be revived. We human flowers need air. If we breathe in and out deeply and consciously, we will bloom right away. We can breathe while sitting, standing, lying down, or walking and, after just a few minutes, we will be fresh enough to share our flowerness with others. Our friends need us to be a flower. When they are sad, if they see us looking happy, they will remember to return to their own flowerness and smile again. We support each other. If we know how to revive our flowerness when it is not very fresh, we provide a real community service.

Meditation is to bring peace, joy, and harmony to ourselves and others. "Stopping" is the basic practice of meditation. To keep our flowerness fresh, we have to learn how to stop our worries, anxieties, agitation, and sadness so that we can find peace and happiness, and smile again. When things are not going well, it is good to stop in order to prevent the unpleasant, destructive energies from continuing. Stopping does not mean repressing; it means, first of all, calming. If we want the ocean to be calm, we don't throw away its water. Without the water, nothing is left. When we notice the presence of anger, fear, and agitation in us, we don't need to throw them away. We only have to breathe in and out consciously, and that alone is enough to calm the storm. We do not need to wait for a storm to begin to practice. When we are not suffering, conscious breathing will make us feel wonderful, and it is the best way to prepare ourselves to deal with troubles when they come.

Breathing is the best way to stop—to stop unhappiness, agitation, fear, and anger. You can practice while sitting, lying down, walking, standing, or in any position. It is especially pleasant to practice outdoors, where the air is so refreshing. You can lie down or sit on the grass or walk slowly and breathe in and out, focusing your attention on each breath. Without thinking of anything else, you say, silently, *"Breathing in, I know I am breathing in. Breathing out, I know I am breathing out."* If you want, you can just say *"In"* as you breathe in, and *"Out"* as you breathe out. We know that those who have asthma only want to breathe freely, and we remember how enjoyable breathing can be. Breathing nourishes us, and it can bring us a lot of happiness. Please practice "In/Out" as many times as you wish—five times, ten times, twenty times, or more. It is essential for the practice of stopping, calming, and returning to our true home in the present moment.

Then, when you feel ready, try the second verse, *"Breathing in, I see myself as a flower. Breathing out, I feel fresh."* When you breathe in, say *"Flower"* and when you breathe out, say *"Fresh."* Even though we were born as flowers, after a lifetime of worries and anxiety, we may not be fresh anymore. We may have not taken good enough care of our flowerness. Practicing this verse, we water our flower. If we do it well, every cell in our body will smile, and in just five or ten seconds, the time it takes to breathe in and out, we will restore our flowerness. We continue until our flowerness becomes solid.

When we see someone who is very fresh, we like to sit close to him. He knows how to preserve himself as a flower. With mindful breathing, we can also be fresh. Young people who have not suffered much are

still beautiful flowers, the kind of flowers that can be
a source of joy for anyone at any time. Just by breathing in and out and smiling, we too have a flower to
offer, and the more we practice breathing and smiling, the more beautiful our flower will become. A
flower does not have to do anything to be of service,
it only has to be a flower. That is enough. A human
being, if she is a true human being, is enough to
make the whole world rejoice. So please practice
breathing in and out and recover your flowerness.
You do it for all of us. Your freshness and your joy
bring us peace.

*"Breathing in, I see myself as a mountain. Breathing
out, I feel solid. Mountain/Solid."* This is best practiced
sitting on a cushion on the floor, if possible in the lotus or half-lotus position. These are very stable positions, and the stability of your body helps bring
about the stability of your mind. It is helpful to
choose a cushion that is the right thickness to support
you. To sit in the lotus position, place one foot (for
the half-lotus) or both feet (for the full-lotus) on the
opposite thighs. If this is too difficult, you can sit in
any comfortable position, but try to keep your back
straight and your hands gently folded on your lap. If
you prefer to sit in a chair, your feet should be flat on
the floor and your hands on your lap. Or if you want
to lie on your back, keep your legs straight and your
arms at your sides.

Picture a tree in a storm. At the top of the tree, the
small branches and leaves are swaying violently in
the wind. The tree looks vulnerable, quite fragile—it

seems it can break at any time. But if you look at the
trunk, you will see that the tree is solid; and if you
look down to its root structure, you will know that
the tree is deeply and firmly rooted in the soil. The
tree is quite strong. It can resist the storm. We are also
a kind of tree. Our trunk, our center, is just below our
navel. The zones of our thinking and our emotions
are at the levels of our head and chest. When we are
taken hold of by a strong emotion, like despair, fear,
anger, or jealousy, we should do our best to leave the
zone of the storm and go down to the valley to practice breathing in and out. If we stay in the winds of
the storm, it may be too dangerous. We can go for refuge into the trunk, breathing in and out, aware of the
rising and falling of our abdomen.

Many people do not know how to handle emotions. When a strong feeling takes hold of them, they
cannot bear it, and they may even contemplate suicide. This is because they are caught in the heart of
the storm, where they feel helpless. They feel that all
of life is this one emotion—fear, despair, anger, or
jealousy—and that the only way to end their suffering is to end their life.

We have to practice conscious breathing so that we
can learn how to cope when difficult moments come
and strong emotions take hold of us. "Breathing in, I
see myself as a mountain. Breathing out, I feel solid.
Mountain/Solid." If you are attentive to the rise and
fall of your abdomen, you can help it rise a little
more as you breathe in, and you can bring it in a little
closer as you breathe out. Practicing like this for a

few minutes, you will see that you are stronger than you thought. You are much more than your emotion. An emotion comes, stays for a while, and goes—that is its nature. Why should we die because of an emotion? It will always pass, sooner or later. Go down to the trunk and hold on to it firmly, breathing in and out. After a few minutes, your emotion will subside, and you can practice walking meditation, sitting meditation, or drinking tea in mindfulness.

Don't wait for conditions to become adverse to begin. If you practice breathing in "Mountain," breathing out "Solid" daily, it will become a habit in less than three weeks. Then, when strong emotions come up, it will be easy for you just to observe them until they pass. If you practice while lying down before going to sleep, you will go peacefully into your sleep. There is a mountain in you. Please get in touch with it. You are more solid and resilient than you think.

Meditation is not to avoid problems or run away from difficulties. We do not practice to escape. We practice to have enough strength to confront problems effectively. To do this, we must be calm, fresh, and solid. That is why we need to practice the art of stopping. When we learn to stop, we become more calm, and our mind becomes clearer, like clear water after the particles of mud have settled. Sitting quietly, just breathing in and out, we develop strength, concentration, and clarity. So sit like a mountain. No wind can blow the mountain down. If you can sit for half an hour, enjoy sitting for half an hour. If you can

sit for a few minutes, enjoy sitting for a few minutes.
That is already good.

"*Breathing in, I see myself as still water. Breathing out,
I reflect things as they are. Water/Reflecting.*" Near the
mountain, there is a lake with clear, still water reflecting the mountain and the sky with pristine clarity.
You can do the same. If you are calm and still
enough, you can reflect the mountain, the blue sky,
and the moon exactly as they are. You reflect whatever you see exactly as it is, without distorting anything.

Have you ever seen yourself in a mirror that dis-
torts the image? Your face is long, your eyes are
huge, and your legs are really short. Don't be like
that mirror. It is better to be like the still water on the
mountain lake. We often do not reflect things clearly,
and we suffer because of our wrong perceptions. In
Being Peace, I used this example: Suppose you are
walking in the twilight and see a snake. You scream
and run into the house to get your friends, and all of
you run outside with a flashlight. But when you
shine your light on the snake, you discover that it
isn't a snake at all, just a piece of rope. This is a distorted perception.

When we see things or listen to other people, we
often don't see clearly or really listen. We see and
hear our projections and our prejudices. We are not
clear enough, and we have a wrong perception. Even
if our friend is giving us a compliment, we may argue with him because we distort what he says. If we
are not calm, if we only listen to our hopes or our an-

ger, we will not be able to receive the truth that is trying to reflect itself on our lake. We need to make our
water still if we want to receive reality as it is. If you
feel agitated, don't do or say anything. Just breathe in
and out until you are calm enough. Then ask your
friend to repeat what he has said. This will avoid a
lot of damage. Stillness is the foundation of understanding and insight. Stillness is strength.

The practice of stopping and calming contains in it
the practice of insight. Not only the mountain, but
everything—the trees, the wind, the birds, everything
inside and around us—wants to reflect itself in us.
We don't have to go anywhere to obtain the truth. We
only need to be still and things will reveal themselves
in the still water of our heart.

The refreshing moon of the Buddha
is traveling in the sky of utmost emptiness.
If the pond of the mind is still,
the beautiful moon will reflect itself in it.

*"Breathing in, I see myself as space. Breathing out, I
feel free. Space/Free."* When you arrange flowers, it is
good to leave space around each flower so it can reveal itself in its full beauty and freshness. You don't
need a lot of flowers—two or three are enough. We
human beings also need space to be happy. We practice stopping and calming in order to offer space to
ourselves, inside and outside, and also to those we
love. We need to let go of our projects, preoccupa-

tions, worries, and regrets, and create space around us. Space is freedom.

One day the Buddha was sitting with about thirty monks in a forest near the city of Vaisali. It was early afternoon and they were about to have a dharma discussion, when a farmer came along, looking very upset. He said that all twelve of his cows had run away, and he wanted to know if the Buddha or the monks had seen them. He added that he also had two acres of sesame plants that had been eaten up by insects, and he said, "Monks, I think I am going to die. I am the unhappiest person in the world."

The Buddha replied, "Sir, we have not seen your cows. Please try looking in the other direction." After the man left, the Buddha turned to his monks and said, "Friends, you are very lucky. You don't have any cows." Our practice is to let go of our cows. If we have too many cows, inside us or around us, we should let them go. Without space, there is no way we can be happy. We take care of so many things, we worry about so many things, we have so many projects, and we think they are all crucial for our happiness; but that is not correct. The more cows we release, the happier we will be.

"The refreshing moon of the Buddha is traveling in the sky of utmost emptiness" is the image of someone who has space and freedom, inside and outside. We can do everything—walking, drinking tea, talking—in a way that reclaims our liberty. We don't have to do things under pressure. We can limit ourselves to a few projects and do them with joy and serenity. We can resist being carried away by our cows. Our freedom and happiness are too important to sacrifice for the sake of these things.

We must stop destroying our body and soul for the idea of happiness in the future. We have to learn to live happily in the present moment, to touch the peace and joy that are available now. If someone were to ask us, "Has the best moment of your life arrived yet?" we may say that it will come very soon. But if we continue to live in the same way, it may never arrive. We have to transform this moment into the most wonderful moment, and we can do that by stopping—stopping running to the future, stopping worrying about the past, stopping accumulating so many cows. You are a free person; you are alive. Open your eyes and enjoy the sunshine, the beautiful sky, and the wonderful children all around you. Breathing in and out consciously helps you become your best—calm, fresh, solid, clear, and free, able to enjoy the present moment as the best moment of your life.

Transforming Our Compost

When we look deeply at a flower, we can see that it is made entirely of non-flower elements, like sunshine, rain, soil, compost, air, and time. If we continue to look deeply, we will also notice that the flower is on her way to becoming compost. If we don't notice this, we will be shocked when the flower begins to decompose. When we look deeply at the compost, we see that it is also on its way to becoming flowers, and we realize that flowers and compost "inter-are." They need each other. A good organic gardener does not discriminate against compost, because he knows how to transform it into marigolds, roses, and many other kinds of flowers.

When we look deeply into ourselves, we see both flowers and garbage. Each of us has anger, hatred, depression, racial discrimination, and many other kinds of garbage in us, but there is no need for us to be afraid. In the way that a gardener knows how to transform compost into flowers, we can learn the art

of transforming anger, depression, and racial discrimination into love and understanding. This is the
work of meditation.

According to Buddhist psychology, our consciousness is divided into two parts, like a house with two
floors. On the ground floor there is a living room,
and we call this "mind consciousness." Below the
ground level, there is a basement, and we call this
"store consciousness." In the store consciousness, everything we have ever done, experienced, or perceived is stored in the form of a seed, or a film. Our
basement is an archive of every imaginable kind of
film stored on a video cassette. Upstairs in the living
room, we sit in a chair and watch these films as they
are brought up from the basement.

Certain movies, such as *Anger*, *Fear*, or *Despair*,
seem to have the ability to come up from the basement all by themselves. They open the door to the
living room and pop themselves into our video cassette recorder whether we choose them or not. When
that happens, we feel stuck, and we have no choice
but to watch them. Fortunately, each film has a limited length, and when it is over, it returns to the basement. But each time it is viewed by us, it establishes a
better position on the archive shelf, and we know it
will return soon. Sometimes a stimulus from outside,
like someone saying something that hurts our feelings, triggers the showing of a film on our TV screen.
We spend so much of our time watching these films,
and many of them are destroying us. Learning how
to stop them is important for our well-being.

Traditional texts describe consciousness as a field, a plot of land where every kind of seed can be planted—seeds of suffering, happiness, joy, sorrow, fear, anger, and hope. Store consciousness is also described as a storehouse filled with all our seeds. When a seed manifests in our mind consciousness, it always returns to the storehouse stronger. The quality of our life depends on the quality of the seeds in our store consciousness.

We may be in the habit of manifesting seeds of anger, sorrow, and fear in our mind consciousness; seeds of joy, happiness, and peace may not sprout up much. To practice mindfulness means to recognize each seed as it comes up from the storehouse and to practice watering the most wholesome seeds whenever possible, to help them grow stronger. During each moment that we are aware of something peaceful and beautiful, we water seeds of peace and beauty in us, and beautiful flowers bloom in our consciousness. The length of time we water a seed determines the strength of that seed. For example, if we stand in front of a tree, breathe consciously, and enjoy it for five minutes, seeds of happiness will be watered in us for five minutes, and those seeds will grow stronger. During the same five minutes, other seeds, like fear and pain, will not be watered. We have to practice this way every day. Any seed that manifests in our mind consciousness always returns to our store consciousness stronger. If we water our wholesome seeds carefully, we can trust that our store consciousness will do the work of healing.

Our bodies have a healing power. Every time we cut our finger, we wash the wound carefully and leave the work of healing to our body. In a few hours or a day, the cut is healed. Our consciousness also has a healing power. Suppose you see someone on the street you knew twenty years ago, and you cannot remember his name. The seed of him in your memory has become quite weak, since it has not had the chance to manifest in the upper level of your consciousness in such a long time. On your way home, you look throughout your basement to find the seed of his name, but you cannot find it. Finally you get a headache from looking so hard, so you stop looking and listen to a tape or a compact disc of beautiful music. Then you enjoy a delicious dinner and get a good night's sleep. In the morning, while you are brushing your teeth, his name just pops up. "Oh yes, that's his name." This means that during the night while your mind consciousness ceased the search, the store consciousness continued to work, and in the morning it brought you the results.

Healing has many avenues. When we feel anger, distress, or despair, we only need to breathe in and out consciously and recognize the feeling of anger, distress, or despair, and then we can leave the work of healing to our consciousness. But it is not only by touching our pain that we can heal. In fact, if we are not ready to do that, touching it may only make it worse. We have to strengthen ourselves first, and the easiest way to do this is by touching joy and peace. There are many wonderful things, but because we

have focused our attention on what is wrong, we
have not been able to touch what is *not* wrong. If we
make some effort to breathe in and out and touch
what is not wrong, the healing will be easier. Many of
us have so much pain that it is difficult for us to
touch a flower or hold the hand of a child. But we
must make some effort so that we can develop the
habit of touching what is beautiful and wholesome.
This is the way we can assist our store consciousness
to do the work of healing. If we touch what is peaceful and healing in us and around us, we help our
store consciousness do the work of transformation.
We let ourselves be healed by the trees, the birds, and
the beautiful children. Otherwise, we will only repeat
our suffering.

One wonderful seed in our store consciousness—
the seed of mindfulness—when manifested, has the
capacity of being aware of what is happening in the
present moment. If we take one peaceful, happy step
and we know that we are taking a peaceful, happy
step, mindfulness is present. Mindfulness is an important agent for our transformation and healing, but
our seed of mindfulness has been buried under many
layers of forgetfulness and pain for a long time. We
are rarely aware that we have eyes that see clearly, a
heart and a liver that function well, and a non-toothache. We live in forgetfulness, looking for happiness
somewhere else, ignoring and crushing the precious
elements of happiness that are already in us and
around us. If we breathe in and out and see that the
tree is there, alive and beautiful, the seed of our

mindfulness will be watered, and it will grow stronger. When we first start to practice, our mindfulness will be weak, like a fifteen-watt light bulb. But as soon as we pay attention to our breathing, it begins to grow stronger, and after practicing like that for a few weeks, it becomes as bright as a one-hundred-watt bulb. With the light of mindfulness shining, we touch many wonderful elements within and around us, and while doing so, we water the seeds of peace, joy, and happiness in us, and at the same time, we refrain from watering the seeds of unhappiness.

When we start out, the seeds of unhappiness in us are quite strong, because we have been watering them every day. Our seeds of anger have been watered by our spouse and our children. Because they themselves suffer, they only know how to water our seeds of suffering. When those seeds of unhappiness are strong, even if we do not invite them up from the basement, they will push the door open and barge into the living room. When they enter, it is not at all pleasant. We may try to suppress them and keep them in the basement, but because we have watered them so much, they are strong enough to just show up in the upper level of our consciousness even without an invitation.

Many of us feel the need to do something all the time—listen to a walkman, watch TV, read a book or a magazine, pick up the telephone. We want to keep ourselves busy in our living room so we can avoid dealing with the worries and anxieties that are in our basement. But if we look deeply into the nature of the

guests we are inviting into the living room, we will
see that many carry the same toxins as are present in
the negative seeds we are trying so hard to avoid.
Even as we prevent these negative seeds from coming up, we are watering them and making them
stronger. Some of us even do social and environmental work to avoid looking at our real problems.

For us to be happy, we need to water the seed of
mindfulness that is in us. Mindfulness is the seed of
enlightenment, awareness, understanding, care, compassion, liberation, transformation, and healing. If we
practice mindfulness, we get in touch with the refreshing and joyful aspects of life in us and around
us, the things we are not able to touch when we live
in forgetfulness. Mindfulness makes things like our
eyes, our heart, our non-toothache, the beautiful
moon, and the trees deeper and more beautiful. If we
touch these wonderful things with mindfulness, they
will reveal their full splendor. When we touch our
pain with mindfulness, we will begin to transform it.
When a baby is crying in the living room, his mother
goes in right away to hold him tenderly in her arms.
Because mother is made of love and tenderness,
when she does that, love and tenderness penetrate
the baby and, in only a few minutes, the baby will
probably stop crying. Mindfulness is the mother who
cares for your pain every time it begins to cry.

While the pain is in the basement, you can enjoy
many refreshing and healing elements of life by producing mindfulness. Then, when the pain wants to
come upstairs, you can turn off your walkman, close

your book, open the living room door, and invite your pain to come up. You can smile to it and embrace it with your mindfulness, which has become strong. If fear, for example, wishes to come up, don't ignore it. Greet it warmly with your mindfulness. "Fear, my old friend, I recognize you." If you are afraid of your fear, it may overwhelm you. But if you invite it up calmly and smile at it in mindfulness, it will lose some of its strength. After you have practiced watering the seeds of mindfulness for a few weeks, you will be strong enough to invite your fear to come up any time, and you will be able to embrace it with your mindfulness. It may not be entirely pleasant, but with mindfulness you are safe.

If you embrace a minor pain with mindfulness, it will be transformed in a few minutes. Just breathe in and out, and smile at it. But when you have a block of pain that is stronger, more time is needed. Practice sitting and walking meditation while you embrace your pain in mindfulness, and, sooner or later, it will be transformed. If you have increased the quality of your mindfulness through the practice, the transformation will be quicker. When mindfulness embraces pain, it begins to penetrate and transform it, like sunshine penetrating a flower bud and helping it blossom. When mindfulness touches something beautiful, it reveals its beauty. When it touches something painful, it transforms and heals it.

Another way to accelerate the transformation is called looking deeply. When we look deeply at a flower, we see the non-flower elements that help it to

be—the clouds, the Earth, the gardener, the soil.
When we look deeply at our pain, we see that our
suffering is not ours alone. Many seeds of suffering
have been handed down to us by our ancestors, our
parents, and our society. We have to recognize these
seeds. One boy who practices at Plum Village told me
this story. When he was eleven, he was very angry at
his father. Every time he fell down and hurt himself,
his father would get angry and shout at him. The boy
vowed that when he grew up, he would be different.
But a few years ago, his little sister was playing with
other children and she fell off a swing and scraped
her knee. It was bleeding, and the boy became very
angry. He wanted to shout at her, "How stupid! Why
did you do that?" But he caught himself. Because he
had been practicing mindfulness, he knew how to
recognize his anger as anger, and he did not act on it.

A number of adults who were present were taking
good care of his sister, washing her wound and putting a bandage on it, so he walked away slowly and
practiced looking deeply. Suddenly he saw that he
was exactly like his father, and he realized that if he
did not do something about his anger, he would
transmit it to his children. It was a remarkable insight
for an eleven-year-old boy. At the same time, he saw
that his father may have been a victim just like him.
The seeds of his father's anger might have been
transmitted by his grandparents. Because of the practice of looking deeply in mindfulness, he was able to
transform his anger into insight. Then he went to his

father, and told him that because he now understood
him, he was able to really love him.

When we are irritated and we say something unkind to our child, we water the seeds of suffering in
him. When he reacts, he waters the seeds of suffering
in us. Living this way escalates and strengthens the
suffering. In mindfulness, calmly breathing in and
out, we can practice looking deeply at the types of
suffering we have in ourselves. When we do so, we
also begin to understand our ancestors, our culture,
and our society. The moment we see this, we can go
back and serve our people with loving kindness and
compassion, and without blame. Because of our insight, we are capable of practicing real peace and reconciliation. When you remove the conflict between
yourself and others, you also remove the conflict
within yourself. One arrow can save two birds at the
same time—if you strike the branch, both birds will
fly away. First, take care of yourself. Reconcile the
conflicting elements within yourself by being mindful and practicing loving kindness. Then reconcile
with your own people by understanding and loving
them, even if they themselves lack understanding.

The seeds of suffering are always trying to
emerge. If we try to suppress them, we create a lack
of circulation in our psyche and we feel sick. Practicing mindfulness helps us get strong enough to open
the door to our living room and let the pain come up.
Every time our pain is immersed in mindfulness, it
will lose some of its strength, and later, when it returns to the store consciousness, it will be weaker.

When it comes up again, if our mindfulness is there to welcome it like a mother greeting her baby, the pain will be lessened and will go back down to the basement even weaker. In this way, we create good circulation in our psyche, and we begin to feel much better. If the blood is circulating well in our body, we experience well-being. If the energy of our mental formations is circulating well between our store consciousness and mind consciousness, we also have the feeling of well-being. We do not need to be afraid of our pain if our mindfulness is there to embrace it and transform it.

Our consciousness is the totality of our seeds, the totality of our films. If the good seeds are strong, we will have more happiness. Meditation helps the seed of mindfulness grow and develop as the light within us. If we practice mindful living, we will know how to water the seeds of joy and transform the seeds of sorrow and suffering so that understanding, compassion, and loving kindness will flower in us.

We Have Arrived

*O*ne day I was sitting on a bus in India with a friend who was organizing my visit there. My friend belonged to the caste that has been discriminated against for thousands of years. I was enjoying the view out the window, when I noticed that he was quite tense. I knew he was worried about making my time enjoyable, so I said, "Please relax. I am already enjoying my visit. Everything is fine." There was really no need for him to worry. He sat back and smiled, but, in just a few moments, he was tense again. When I looked at him, I saw the struggle that has been going on for four or five thousand years, within him as a person, and with the entire caste. Now, organizing my visit, he continued to struggle. He couldn't relax for one second.

We all have the tendency to struggle in our bodies and our minds. We believe that happiness is possible only in the future. That is why the practice "I have arrived" is very important. The realization that we have already arrived, that we don't have to travel any further, that we are already here, can give us peace and joy. The conditions for our happiness are already sufficient. We only need to allow ourselves to be in the present moment, and we will be able to touch them.

Sitting on the bus, my friend still did not allow himself to be in the present moment. He was worrying about how to make me comfortable while I was already comfortable. So I suggested that he allow himself to be, but it was not easy for him, because the habit energy had been there for a long time. Even after our bus arrived at the station and we got off, my friend still could not enjoy himself. My entire visit to India went very well, and his organizing was a complete success, but I am afraid that to this day, he is still unable to relax. We are under the influence of previous generations of our ancestors and our society. The practice of stopping and looking deeply is to stop the habit energy sustained by our negative seeds. When we are able to stop, we do it for all of them, and we end the vicious circle that is called *samsara*.

We have to live in a way that liberates the ancestors and future generations who are inside of us. Joy, peace, freedom, and harmony are not individual matters. If we do not liberate our ancestors, we will be in bondage all our lives, and we will transmit that to our children and grandchildren. Now is the time to do it. To liberate them means to liberate ourselves. This is the teaching of interbeing. As long as our ancestors in us are still suffering, we cannot really be happy. If we take one step mindfully, freely, happily touching the Earth, we do it for all previous and future generations. They all arrive with us at the same moment, and all of us find peace at the same time.

Inside each of us is a baby we have to protect. That baby is all future generations, and the best way to take care of her is to practice the art of mindful living. Even before our child is conceived, she is already there. If we take care of her now, we will be ready when the doctor tells us that she is in our womb. In the *Avatamsaka Sutra*, there is a story about Mahamaya, the mother of the Buddha, and a young man named Sudhana, who vowed to attain enlightenment. Mahamaya had been living a mindful, peaceful life, and her joyful presence was a delight to everyone. When she learned she was pregnant, she was ready. Sudhana's teacher, Manjusri Bodhisattva, had asked him to study with others in order to develop his understanding, so Sudhana set off on pilgrimage. During his travels he met fifty-three teachers, including intellectuals, workers, children, monks, nuns, laypersons, Buddhists, and non-Buddhists. This means that we can learn from everyone. Among the fifty-three was Mahamaya.

Sudhana discovered that it is not easy to get an appointment with the mother of the Buddha. He was advised to meditate in deep concentration if he really wanted to see her. So he sat down, crossed his legs, and practiced conscious breathing, and, suddenly, a huge lotus flower with one hundred million petals sprang forth from the Earth right in front of him. In a flash, he found himself sitting on one of the petals, which was also a huge lotus flower with one hundred million petals. Directly in front of him was Mahamaya. She was sitting on another lotus with one hundred million petals, and the petal she was sitting on was also, in itself, a huge lotus with one hundred million petals. Sudhana smiled with joy as he bowed to the mother of the Buddha.

Mahamaya could see in Sudhana that he was seeking enlightenment, and she said to him, "My deepest congratulations, young man. I am delighted to see you. I am the mother of all the buddhas in the cosmos—past, present, and future." Then she told him, "Young man, when I became pregnant with Siddhartha, the Buddha Shakyamuni, hundreds of millions of buddhas and bodhisattvas from every quarter of the universe came to pay their respects to my son. I could not refuse, and all of them entered my womb at the same time. And you know, there was more than enough room for all of them!"

At that moment, Sudhana vowed to realize enlightenment so he could wake up all living beings, and, immediately, he felt all the buddhas in the universe reaching out their arms to pat him on the head in congratulation, and their hands did not collide! When someone vows to be a bodhisattva, the effect can be felt throughout the universe. This vow is enough to change the world, and all the buddhas know this, so they pat you on the head and smile in congratulation.

In the same sutra, we read that when Diamond
Matrix attained the highest of the ten stages of a
bodhisattva, he gave a discourse about his experience
in the practice. Many other bodhisattvas came to hear
him, and after the talk, millions more bodhisattvas
named Diamond Matrix appeared from all quarters
of the universe and told him, "Congratulations! We
are also named Diamond Matrix, and we have been
giving the exact same discourse throughout the universe."

These images illustrate the principle of interbeing—the one is the many, and the many are the one.
To take good care of your baby is to take good care of
everything. In the *Avatamsaka Sutra*, the *dharmadhatu* is described as a world of light and interbeing.
The moon is in me. My beloved is in me. Those who
make me suffer are also in me. Our world of discrimination and misery is called the *lokadhatu*. It is a
world where things exist outside of each other—I am
outside of you, and Saddam Hussein is outside of
George Bush. But in the dharmadhatu, President
Hussein is in President Bush, and there is no hatred
or blaming. In the dharmadhatu, we are in the wonder of interbeing. Life and death inter-are. No one is
afraid to die, because dying means being born as
something else at the same time. When a cloud dies,
it becomes rain. To nourish ourselves, we have to
step into the dharmadhatu.

In fact, the dharmadhatu is not different from the
lokadhatu. With one mindful step, touching the Earth
in full awareness, we enter the dharmadhatu and are

surrounded by light. We are everything else, there is no discrimination. Everything we do for ourselves is for others, everything we do for others is for us. Practicing mindfulness is to take the best care of the baby in our womb and to give birth to that baby in every moment of our life. Every moment we are awake, a baby buddha is born. When we practice peace and are able to smile, our peace can influence the whole universe. Each of us is pregnant with a buddha in us. Everyone has buddha-nature. Everyone is a buddha-to-be. We have to take good care of our baby buddha.

After he grew up and had been practicing meditation for a number of years, looking deeply into his body, feelings, perceptions, mental formations, and consciousness, one day Siddhartha, the buddha-to-be, felt that he was about to have a breakthrough. Meditating under a beautiful pippala tree, he had the sense that some time that night he would realize full enlightenment and become a buddha. Suddenly, Mara appeared. Mara sometimes appears as doubt, sometimes as anger, darkness, jealousy, craving, or despair. When we feel doubtful or skeptical, he is there. When we feel angry, irritated, or lacking in self-confidence, that is Mara. Siddhartha had been visited by Mara many times before, and he knew that the best way to treat him was to be very gentle.

That day Mara came in the form of skepticism. He said, "Who do you think you are? You think you can attain great enlightenment? Don't you realize how much darkness, despair, and confusion there are in the world? How can you hope to dissipate all of it?"

Siddhartha smiled, expressing great confidence. Mara continued, "I know you have practiced, but have you practiced enough? Who will witness that you have practiced long and hard enough? Who will testify that you can gain enlightenment?" Mara demanded that someone confirm that Siddhartha was going to become a buddha, a fully awakened person. At that moment, Siddhartha touched the Earth with his right hand, very deeply, with all his mindfulness, and said, "The Earth will testify for me." Suddenly, the Earth trembled and appeared as a goddess, offering him flowers, leaves, fruits, and perfumes. After that, Earth looked directly at Mara, and Mara just disappeared.

Even after the Buddha attained enlightenment, Mara continued to visit him. One time, after he had been teaching for a year and a half, he returned to his home town, Kapilavastu, to share his insight with his own family and people. One day, sitting alone, he was absorbed in the thought that there must be a nonviolent way to run a country that would avoid the kinds of suffering brought about by prisons, tortures, executions, and war and bring real happiness to people. Suddenly Mara appeared and said, "Lord Buddha, why don't you become a politician? You can apply your wisdom, knowledge, and skills as a politician." The Buddha looked directly at Mara and smiled, "Mara, my old friend, I know you well," and Mara just disappeared. The Buddha did not want to be a politician. He only wanted to be a monk, and he knew that it was Mara who was trying to tempt him

to become a politician. All he did was recognize Mara
and smile at him. When we recognize Mara as Mara,
everything is all right.

At times we ourselves touch the Earth, but not
deeply enough. When the Buddha touched the Earth
with his hand, he touched it with all his mindfulness.
At Plum Village, when we are visited by Mara—
when we feel irritated, lacking in self-confidence, angry, or unhappy—we practice walking meditation,
touching the Earth deeply with our feet. When we do
it mindfully and joyfully, Mara leaves us in less than
an hour.

The Earth, our mother, has brought us to life many
times, and each time she receives us back into her
arms. She knows everything about us, and that is
why the Buddha invoked her as a witness. She appeared as a goddess, offering flowers, leaves, fruits,
and perfumes to the Buddha. Then she just looked at
Mara and smiled, and Mara disappeared. Mara is not
much in the presence of the Earth. Every time you
are approached by Mara, if you come to the Earth
and ask for help by touching her deeply, the way the
Buddha did, you will be offered flowers, fruits, butterflies, and many other gifts of nature, and the Earth
will look at Mara in such a way that he will disappear.

We have so many reasons to be happy. The Earth
is filled with love for us, and patience. Whenever she
sees us suffering, she will protect us. With the Earth
as a refuge, we need not be afraid of anything, even
dying. Walking mindfully on the Earth, we are nour-

ished by the trees, the bushes, the flowers, and the sunshine. Touching the Earth is a very deep practice that can restore our peace and our joy. We are children of the Earth. We rely on the Earth, and the Earth relies on us. Whether the Earth is beautiful, fresh, and green, or arid and parched, depends on our way of walking. Please touch the Earth in mindfulness, with joy and concentration. The Earth will heal you, and you will heal the Earth.

One of the best ways to touch the Earth is by practicing walking meditation. We walk slowly, massaging the Earth and planting seeds of joy and happiness with each step, and following our breathing at the same time. We don't try to go anywhere. We arrive with every step. When we breathe in, we count the number of steps we take. If we take three steps, we say, silently, "In, in, in." When we breathe out, we do the same, "Out, out, out." If we take three steps as we breathe in and four steps as we breathe out, we say "Out, out, out, out." We listen to the needs of our lungs, and we breathe and walk accordingly. Walking up a hill, we will probably take fewer steps with each breath. As we walk, we bring our attention down into our feet. We breathe as if we were breathing from the soles of our feet. We don't stay in the zone of our thoughts and emotions.

After practicing "In, in, in," and "Out, out, out," five or ten times, you might like to practice "Flower, flower, flower," while breathing in, and "Fresh, fresh, fresh," while breathing out. You get flowerness and freshness from the Earth and from the air. You can hold the hand of a child as you walk. The child will receive your concentration and stability, and you will receive his or her innocence and freshness. At Plum Village, I proposed to the young people a simple *gatha* for walking meditation. I wanted them to respond to life, to society, to the Earth in a positive way, so I suggested they say, "*Oui, oui, oui,*" when they breathe in, and, "*Merci, merci, merci,*" when they breathe out. The children liked it very much.

After practicing "Flower/Fresh," you can switch to "Mountain/Solid." Practice each exercise as many times as you wish, enjoying your walking and not arriving anywhere, except the present moment. You can practice walking meditation between business meetings, walking from your car to the market, or on any other occasion. Allow enough time to walk. Instead of three minutes, give yourself eight or ten minutes. I always give myself an extra hour when I go to the airport so that I can practice walking meditation there. My friends want to keep me visiting right up to the last minute, but I always resist. I tell them that I need the time.

To strengthen the seeds of mindfulness in us, it is helpful if sometimes we practice in a park or some other beautiful, quiet place. We walk slowly, but not too slowly, as we don't want others to think we are too unusual. This is a kind of invisible practice. We can enjoy nature and our own serenity without making others uncomfortable. When we see something we want to touch with our mindfulness—the blue sky, the hills, a tree, or a bird—we just stop, but while we do so, we continue breathing in and out mindfully. If we don't continue to breathe consciously, sooner or later our thinking will settle back in, and the bird and the tree will disappear. Therefore, we always hold on to our breathing. At Plum Village, we practice walking meditation every time we go from one place to another, even for a short distance. Whenever I see someone walking mindfully, she is a bell of mindfulness for me. If I have lost my mindfulness and I see her, I return to my mindfulness right away. As a community, we can help each other a lot.

There is no need for us to struggle to arrive somewhere else. We know that our final destination is the cemetery. Why are we in a hurry to get there? Why not step in the direction of life, which is in the present moment? When we practice walking meditation for even a few days, we will will undergo a deep transformation, and we will learn how to enjoy peace in each moment of our life. We will smile, and countless bodhisattvas throughout the cosmos will smile back at us because our peace is so deep. Everything we think, feel, and do has an effect on our ancestors and all future generations and reverberates throughout the universe. Therefore, our smile helps everyone. This is the teaching of the *Avatamsaka Sutra*. To take good care of our baby, we only need to stop struggling. Peace is every step. We have already arrived.

The Happiness of One Person

T he practice of mindfulness is the practice of love itself. To encourage mindfulness in those who are about to live with another person, I have asked my students to help me start an Institute for the Happiness of One Person. We will have a one-year program and only one course, entitled "Looking Deeply." For a year, each student will practice looking deeply into himself in order to discover all the flowers and compost that are in him, not just of his own making but from his ancestors and society. At the end of the course, each student will receive a diploma that says he or she is qualified to be married. I think it is important for all young couples to practice in this way before embarking on the journey of mutual discovery that takes place in a marriage. If they do not come to know themselves well and take the time to untie their internal knots, the first year of their marriage will be difficult.

When we enter a relationship, we feel excitement, enthusiasm, and the willingness to explore. But we do not really understand ourselves or the other person very well yet. Living together twenty-four hours a day, we look, listen, and experience many things we have not seen or imagined before. When we fell in love, we constructed a beautiful image that we projected onto our partner, and now we are a little shocked as our illusions disappear and we discover the reality. Unless we know how to practice mindfulness together, looking deeply into ourselves and our partner, we may find it difficult to sustain our love through this period.

In Buddhist psychology, the word *samyojana* refers to internal formations, fetters, or knots. When someone says something unkind to us, for example, if we do not understand why he said it and we become irritated, a knot will be tied in us. The lack of understanding is the basis for every internal knot. If we practice mindfulness, we can learn the skill of recognizing a knot the moment it is tied in us and finding ways to untie it. Internal formations need our full attention as soon as they form, while they are still loosely tied, so that the work of untying them will be easy. If we do not untie our knots when they form, they will grow tighter and stronger. It is difficult for our mind to accept that it has negative feelings like anger, fear, and regret, so it finds ways to bury these in remote areas of our consciousness. We create elaborate defense mechanisms to deny their exist-

ence, but these problematic feelings are always trying
to surface.

The first step in dealing with unconscious internal
formations is to try to bring them into awareness. We
meditate, practicing conscious breathing to gain ac-
cess to them. They might reveal themselves as images, feelings, thoughts, words, or actions. We may
notice a feeling of anxiety and ask, "Why did I feel so
uncomfortable when she said that?" or "Why do I
keep doing that?" or "Why did I hate that character
in the movie so much?" Observing ourselves closely
can bring an internal formation into view. And as we
shine the light of our mindfulness on it, it begins to
reveal its face. We may feel some resistance to continuing to look at it, but if we have developed the capacity to sit still and observe our feelings, the source
of the knot will slowly reveal itself and give us an
idea how to untie it. Practicing like this, we come to
know our internal formations, and we make peace
with ourselves.

When we live with another person, it is important
to practice this way. To protect each other's happiness, we must learn to transform the internal formations we produce together as soon as they arise. One
woman told me that three days after her wedding,
she received several large internal formations from
her husband, and she kept them to herself for thirty
years. She was afraid that if she told him, there
would be a fight. How can we be happy like that,
with no real communication? When we are not mind-

ful in our daily life, we plant the seeds of suffering in the very person we love.

But when both partners are still light and not filled with too many knots, the practice is not difficult. Together we look at the misunderstanding that created the knot, and then we untie it. For example, if we hear our husband exaggerating to his friends about something he did, we may feel a knot being tied inside us in the form of some disrespect for him. But if we discuss it with him right away, the two of us can come to a clear understanding, and the knot will be untied easily.

If we practice the art of mindful living together, we can do this. We see that the other person, like us, has both flowers and compost inside, and we accept this. Our practice is to water the flowerness in her, and not bring her more garbage. We avoid blaming and arguing. When we try to grow flowers, if the flowers do not grow well, we do not blame or argue with them. We blame ourselves for not taking care of them well. Our partner is a flower. If we take care of her well, she will grow beautifully. If we take care of her poorly, she will wither. To help a flower grow well, we must understand her nature. How much water does she need? How much sunshine? We look deeply into ourselves to see our true nature, and we look into the other person to see her nature.

"Suchness" is a technical term that means true nature. Everything has its suchness; that is how we recognize it. An orange has its suchness; that is why we don't confuse it with a lemon. In my community, we cook with propane gas, and we know its suchness. We know that it can be very dangerous. If it leaks in the room while we are asleep and someone lights a match, it can kill us. But we also know that propane can help us cook a wonderful meal, and that is why we invite it into our house to live peacefully with us.

I would like to share a story about suchness. There was a patient in the mental hospital in Bien Hoa who seemed to be normal. He ate and talked like other people. But he believed that he was a kernel of corn, and every time he saw a chicken, he ran for his life. He did not know his suchness. When the nurse reported this to the doctor, the doctor told him, "Sir, you are not a kernel of corn, you are a human being. You have hair, eyes, a nose, and arms." He gave a kind of sermon like that, and finally he asked, "Now, sir, can you tell me what you are?"

The man replied, "Doctor, I am a human being. I am not a kernel of corn." The doctor was happy. He felt he had helped this patient a lot. But to be certain, he asked the man to repeat the sentence, "I am a human being, I am not a kernel of corn," four hundred times a day and to write it on a piece of paper three hundred more times each day. The man became devoted to doing it, and he stopped going out at all. He just stayed in his room repeating and writing exactly what the doctor had prescribed.

A month later, the doctor came to see him, and the nurse reported, "He is doing very well. He stays inside and practices the exercises you gave him very diligently."

The doctor asked, "Sir, how are things?"

"Very well, thank you, doctor."

"Can you tell me what you are?"

"Oh yes, doctor. I am a human being. I am not a kernel of corn."

The doctor was delighted. He said, "We will release you in a few days. Please come with me to my office." But while doctor, nurse, and patient were walking together to the office, a chicken walked by, and the man ran away so quickly that the doctor couldn't catch him. It was more than an hour later that the nurse brought him to the office.

The doctor was agitated. "You said you are a human being and not a kernel of corn. So why did you run away when you saw a chicken?"

The man said, "Of course I know that I am a human being and not a kernel of corn. But how can I be sure the chicken knows?"

Although he had been practicing very hard, he was not able to see his true nature, his suchness, and he did not understand the suchness of the chicken either. Each of us has our own suchness. If we want to live in peace and happiness with another person, we have to understand his or her suchness and our own. Once we see it, we will have no trouble living peacefully and happily together.

To meditate is to look deeply into the nature of things, including our own nature and the nature of the person in front of us. When we see the true nature of that person, we discover his or her difficulties, aspirations, suffering, and anxieties. We can sit down, hold our partner's hand, look deeply at him, and say, "Darling, do I understand you enough? Do I water your seeds of suffering? Do I water your seeds of joy? Please tell me how I can love you better." If we say this from the bottom of our heart, he may begin to cry, and that is a good sign. It means the door of communication may be opening again.

Loving speech is an important aspect of the practice. Every time the other person does something well, we should congratulate him or her to show our approval. This is especially true with children. We have to strengthen the self-esteem of our children. We have to appreciate and congratulate every good thing they say and do in order to help our children grow. We don't take things for granted. If the other person manifests some talent or capacity to love and create happiness, we must be aware of it and express our appreciation. This is the way to water the seeds of happiness. We should avoid saying destructive things like, "I doubt that you can do this." Instead, we say, "This is difficult, darling, but I have faith you can do it." This kind of talk makes the other person stronger.

When there is some problem, if we are calm enough, we can discuss it fully in a loving and nonviolent way. But if we are not calm enough, we should refrain from speaking. We can just breathe. If we need to, we can practice walking meditation in the fresh air, looking at the trees, the clouds, the river. Once we are calm and capable of using the language of loving kindness, we can talk together. If, during our conversation, the feeling of irritation comes up again, we can stop and just breathe. This is mindfulness.

All of us need to change and grow. When we marry, we can make a promise to change and grow together, sharing the fruits of our practice. When we as a couple are happy, when understanding and harmony are there, it is easy for us to extend our happiness and joy to many people. For those who have been married ten or twenty years, this kind of practice is also relevant. You can also enroll in our Institute and continue to develop the practice of living in mindfulness and learning from each other. You may think you already know everything about your spouse, but that is not true. Physicists study one electron for many years and still do not claim to understand everything about it. How can you think you know everything about one human being? Driving your car, paying attention only to your thoughts, you ignore her. If you continue to treat her that way, she will die slowly. She needs your attention, your gardening, your care.

When things become too difficult, we tend to think of divorce. Instead, I hope you will make an effort to preserve your marriage, to return to your spouse with more harmony and understanding. Many people have divorced three or four times, and they continue to make the same kinds of mistakes. If you can take the time to open the door of communication, the door of your heart, and share your sufferings and your dreams with one another, you do it not just for yourselves but for your children and for all of us.

In Plum Village, we practice a ceremony called Beginning Anew every week. At the Institute for the Happiness of One Person, we will also practice this. During the ceremony, everyone in the community sits in a circle with a vase of fresh flowers in the center. Each of us follows our breathing as we wait for the facilitator to begin. The ceremony has three stages: flower watering, expressing regrets, and expressing hurts and difficulties. This practice helps prevent feelings of hurt from building up over the weeks and helps make the situation safe for everyone in the family or the community.

We begin with flower watering. When one person is ready to speak, she joins her palms and the others join their palms to show that she has the right to speak. Then she stands, walks slowly to the flower, takes the vase in her hands, and returns to her seat. When she speaks, her words reflect the freshness and beauty of the flower that is in her hand. During flower watering, each speaker acknowledges the wholesome, wonderful qualities of the others. It is not flattery; we always speak the truth. Everyone has some strong points that can be seen with awareness. No one can interrupt the person holding the flower. She is allowed as much time as she needs to speak, and everyone else practices deep listening. When she finishes speaking, she stands up and slowly returns the vase to the center of the room.

In the second part of the ceremony, we express our regrets for what we have done to hurt others. It does not take more than one thoughtless phrase to hurt someone. The ceremony of Beginning Anew is an opportunity for us to recall some regret from earlier in the week and undo it. In the third part of the ceremony, we express ways in which others have hurt us. Loving speech is crucial. We want to heal the community, not harm it. We speak frankly, but we do not want to be destructive. Listening meditation is an important part of the practice. When we sit among a circle of friends who are all practicing deep listening, our speech becomes more beautiful and more constructive. We never blame or argue.

Compassionate listening is crucial. We listen with the willingness to relieve the suffering of the other person, not to judge or argue with her. We listen with all our attention. Even if we hear something that is not true, we continue to listen deeply so the other person can express her pain and release the tensions within herself. If we reply to her or correct her, the practice will not bear fruit. We just listen. If we need to tell the other person that her perception was not correct, we can do that a few days later, privately and calmly. Then, at the next Beginning Anew session, she may be the person who rectifies the error and we will not have to say anything.

We close the ceremony with a song or by holding hands with everyone in the circle and breathing for a minute. Sometimes we end with hugging meditation. Afterwards we always feel light and relieved, even if we have taken only a preliminary step towards healing. We now have confidence that, having begun, we can continue. The practice of Beginning Anew dates to the time of the Buddha. His communities of monks and nuns practiced this on the eve of every full moon and new moon.

Hugging meditation, on the other hand, is something I invented. The first time I learned hugging was in Atlanta in 1966. A woman poet took me to the airport and then asked, "Is it all right to hug a Buddhist monk?" In my country, we are not used to expressing ourselves that way in public, but I thought, "I am a Zen teacher. It should be no problem for me to do that." So I said, "Why not?" and she hugged me, but I was rather stiff. While on the plane, I decided that if I wanted to work with friends in the West, I would have to learn the culture of the West. That is why I invented hugging meditation.

Hugging meditation is a combination of East and West. According to the practice, you have to really hug the person you are hugging. You have to make him or her very real in your arms. You don't do it just for the sake of appearance, patting him on the back two or three times to pretend you are there. You are really there, so you do not have to do that. You breathe consciously while hugging, and you hug with all your body, spirit, and heart. "Breathing in, I know my dear one is in my arms, alive. Breathing out, he is so precious to me." While you hold him and breathe in and out three times, the person in your arms becomes real, and you become very real also. When you love someone, you want him to be happy. If he is not happy, there is no way you can be happy. Happiness is not an individual matter. True love requires deep understanding. In fact, love is another name for understanding. If you do not understand, you cannot love properly. Without understanding, your love will only cause the other person to suffer.

In Southeast Asia, many people are extremely fond of a big fruit with many thorns called durian. You might even say they are addicted to it. Its smell is extremely strong, and when some people finish eating the fruit, they put the skin under their bed so they can continue to smell it. To me, the smell of durian is horrendous.

One day when I was practicing chanting alone in my temple in Vietnam, there happened to be one durian on the altar that had been offered to the Buddha. I was trying to recite the *Lotus Sutra*, using a wooden drum and a large bowl-shaped bell for accompaniment, but I could not concentrate at all. I finally decided to turn the bell over and imprison the durian so I could chant the sutra. After I finished, I bowed to the Buddha and liberated the durian. If you were to say to me, "I love you so much I would like you to eat some of this durian," I would suffer. You love me, you want me to be happy, but you force me to eat durian. That is an example of love without understanding. Your intention is good, but you don't have the correct understanding.

In order to love properly, you have to understand. Understanding means to see the depth of the darkness, the pain, and the suffering of the other person. If you don't see that, the more you do for her, the more she will suffer. Creating happiness is an art. If during your childhood, you saw your mother or father create happiness in your family, you were able to learn from those things. But if your parents did not know how to create happiness in the family, you may not know how to do it. So in our Institute, we have to teach the art of making people happy. Living together is an art. Even with good will, you can make your partner quite unhappy. Art is the essence of life. We have to be artful in our speech and action. The substance of art is mindfulness.

When you first fall in love and you feel attached to the other person, that is not yet real love. Real love means loving kindness and compassion, the kind of love that does not have any conditions. You form a community of two in order to practice love—taking care of each other, helping your partner blossom, and making happiness something real in that small community. Through your love for each other, through learning the art of making one person happy, you learn to express your love for the whole of humanity and all beings. Please help us develop the curriculum for the Institute for the Happiness of One Person. Don't wait until we open the school. You can begin practicing right away.

Peace Treaty

*I*n Order That We May Live Long and Happily
Together, In Order That We May Continually Develop
and Deepen Our Love and Understanding, We the Un-
dersigned, Vow to Observe and Practice the Following:

I, the one who is angry, agree to:

1. Refrain from saying or doing anything that might
cause further damage or escalate the anger.

2. Not suppress my anger.

3. Practice breathing and taking refuge in the island of
myself.

4. Calmly, within twenty-four hours, tell the one who
has made me angry about my anger and suffering, either verbally or by delivering a Peace Note.

5. Ask for an appointment for later in the week (e.g.
Friday evening) to discuss this matter more thoroughly,
either verbally or by Peace Note.

6. *Not say: "I am not angry. It's okay. I am not suffer-ing. There is nothing to be angry about, at least not enough to make me angry."*

7. *Practice breathing and looking deeply into my daily life—while sitting, lying down, standing, and walk-ing—in order to see:*
    a. the ways I myself have been unskillful at times.
    b. how I have hurt the other person because of my own habit energy.
    c. how the strong seed of anger in me is the primary cause of my anger.
    d. how the other person's suffering, which waters the seed of my anger, is the secondary cause.
    e. how the other person is only seeking relief from his or her own suffering.
    f. that as long as the other person suffers, I cannot be truly happy.

8. *Apologize immediately, without waiting until the Friday evening, as soon as I realize my unskillfulness and lack of mindfulness.*

9. *Postpone the Friday meeting if I do not feel calm enough to meet with the other person.*

, *the one who has made the other angry, agree to:*

1. *Respect the other person's feelings, not ridicule him or her, and allow enough time for him or her to calm down.*

2. *Not press for an immediate discussion.*

3. *Confirm the other person's request for a meeting, either verbally or by note, and assure him or her that I will be there.*

4. *Practice breathing and taking refuge in the island of myself to see how:*
   a. I have seeds of unkindness and anger as well as the habit energy to make the other person unhappy.
   b. I have mistakenly thought that making the other person suffer would relieve my own suffering.
   c. by making him or her suffer, I make myself suffer.

5. *Apologize as soon as I realize my unskillfulness and lack of mindfulness, without making any attempt to justify myself and without waiting until the Friday meeting.*

We Vow, with Lord Buddha as Witness and the Mindful Presence of the Sangha, to Abide by These Articles and to Practice Wholeheartedly. We Invoke the Three Gems for Protection and to Grant Us Clarity and Confidence.

> *Signed,* _____
> *the* _____ *Day of* _____
> *in the Year* _____ *in* _____

When we get angry, we don't look like a beautiful flower. We look more like a bomb ready to explode. Hundreds of muscles in our face tense up. Because so much suffering arises when we become angry or upset, we at Plum Village recently drafted a "Peace Treaty" which couples and individuals can sign in the presence of the sangha to increase the likelihood that we will deal with our anger well. This is not just a piece of paper; it is a practice that can help us live long and happily together. The treaty has two parts—one for the person who is angry and one for the person who has caused the anger. When we get angry or when someone is angry at us, if we follow the terms of the Peace Treaty, we will know exactly what to do and what not to do.

According to the first article, we agree that when we are angry we will refrain from saying or doing anything that might cause further damage or escalate the anger. When we know we are angry, we impose on ourselves a kind of moratorium on speech and actions.

In the second article, we agree not to suppress our anger. At the proper time, we will express something, but not immediately. The minimum waiting period is the time of three conscious breaths. If we do not wait at least that long, it may not be safe to express our feelings about our anger.

In the third article, we agree to practice breathing on our anger and taking refuge in the island of ourselves. We know that anger is there. We do not suppress it and we do not deny it. We take care of it by

producing mindfulness of breathing and embracing
it in the loving arms of mindfulness. We sit quietly or
we walk, perhaps in nature. If we need a half hour,
we take a half hour. If we need three hours, we practice breathing for three hours.

The Buddha told his students, "My friends, do not
rely on anything outside of yourselves. Be an island
unto yourself, and take refuge in the island of yourself." During difficult moments when we do not
know what to do, this is a wonderful exercise to practice. If I were in an airplane about to crash, this is
what I would practice. If we practice well, our island
will have trees, birds, a beautiful stream, and land
that is very solid. The essence of a buddha is mindfulness. Mindful breathing is the living dharma, better than any book. The sangha is present in five
elements that comprise our "self": form, feeling, perception, mental formations, consciousness. When
these elements are in harmony, we have peace and
joy. When we practice conscious breathing and produce mindfulness in ourselves, the buddha is there. If
we go back and discover the buddha within us, we
will be safe.

According to the fourth article of the treaty, we
have up to twenty-four hours to calm ourselves.
Then we must tell the other person we are angry. We
do not have the right to keep our anger any longer
than that. If we do, it becomes poisonous, and it may
destroy us and the person we love. If we are used to
the practice, we may be ready to tell him in five or
ten minutes, but the maximum is twenty-four hours.

We can say, "My dear friend, what you said this morning made me very angry. I suffered very much and I want you to know it."

According to the fifth article, we end with this sentence, "I hope that by Friday evening both of us will have had a chance to look deeply into this matter." Then we make an appointment. Friday evening is a good time to defuse all the bombs, big or small, so that we will have the whole weekend for our enjoyment. If we feel it is not yet safe for us to speak to him, if we do not feel capable of doing it in a calm way and the deadline of twenty-four hours is approaching, we can use this "Peace Note":

Date:
Time:
Dear _____,

This morning (afternoon), you said (did) something that made me very angry. I suffered very much. I want you to know this. You said (did):

Please let us both look at what you said (did) and examine the matter together in a calm and open manner this Friday evening.

Yours, not very happy right now,

If we use this note, we have to make sure the other person receives it before the deadline. We cannot just say, "I put it on your desk and you didn't look at it, so it's your fault." This is for our own good, because the moment we know that the other person has received the note, we already feel some relief. It is best to tell him directly in a calm voice, but if we think we will not be able to do it calmly, we can fill out a peace note and hand it to him. But we have to make sure he gets it before the deadline.

The sixth article tells us not to pretend we aren't angry. We may have too much pride and do not want to admit our suffering. But we shouldn't say, "I am not angry. There's nothing to be angry about." We must refrain from hiding the truth. If we are angry, that is a fact. This is an important part of the Peace Treaty. Pride should not be an obstacle that destroys our relationship. We are committed to each other, we support each other, we are a brother or sister to each other. Why should we be so proud? My pain must be his pain. My suffering must be his suffering.

According to the seventh article, while we are practicing sitting, walking, breathing, looking deeply, and living our daily life mindfully, we should focus our attention on these points: (1) Recognize the ways we have not been mindful or skillful in the past. (2) See how we have hurt the other person in the past and acknowledge to ourselves, "I have the habit energy of getting angry and hurt very easily." (3) Recognize that the main cause of our anger is the strong seed of anger in our store consciousness that has the habit of manifesting itself. The other person is not the main cause of our suffering. We have friends who do not get angry so easily. The seed of anger is in them also, but apparently their seed of anger is not as strong as ours. (4) See that the other person is suffering also, and because of this, he behaved in an unskillful way, watering the seed of anger in us. We acknowledge that he was not the main cause of our suffering. He may have been the secondary cause, or perhaps he was misperceived by us to be the secondary cause—perhaps he did not mean to hurt us at all. (5) When some people get angry, they naïvely believe that if they say something strong to another person and make him suffer, they will feel some relief. This is not a wise thing to do, but many people do it. So we have to see that the other person may only be seeking some relief from his own suffering. (6) See that as long as he continues to suffer, we cannot be truly happy. When someone in a community is unhappy, the whole community is unhappy. For us to stop suffering, we have to help the other person stop suffering. We all have to find skillful ways to help that person. Only when he overcomes his suffering will happiness in the community be authentic.

The eighth article tells us that if, during the process of looking deeply we realize our unskillfulness and lack of mindfulness, we should apologize right away. We should not make the other person feel guilty any longer. There is no need to wait until Friday evening. If we find out that we got angry because we have the habit energy of responding too quickly or because of some misunderstanding, we have to go to the other person and say, "I'm sorry, I was unmindful. I got angry too easily and without any basis. Please forgive me." He will be relieved. It is best to stop the cycle of suffering as soon as possible.

The ninth article tells us that if, by Friday, we feel that we are not calm enough to talk about the matter, we should postpone the appointment for a few more days or another week. If we are not calm, it is not yet time to talk about it. We need to practice for a few more days.

In the second part of the Peace Treaty, there are the five articles concerning the one who has made the other person angry. According to the first article, when we see that the other person is angry, we should respect her feelings. We shouldn't say, "I haven't done anything, and you're angry." A feeling has a life span—a moment to be born, some time to stay, and then it will die down slowly. Even if we see that her anger is not founded at all, that she is completely wrong, we don't press her to stop being angry right away. We help her, or we leave her alone so that her anger can die down naturally.

According to the second article, after she has told us that she is suffering, we should not press for an immediate discussion. If we do, everything can be destroyed. We abide by the treaty and accept the Friday evening appointment. In the interim, we have a chance to look deeply at the situation. "What did I say? What did I do to make her angry?" While sitting, walking, and breathing, practice looking deeply. This is true meditation.

According to the third article, after we have received a peace note, we should respond right away that we will be there on Friday evening. This is important, because if she knows we have received it, she will get some relief.

The fourth article tells us to practice breathing, taking refuge in the island of ourselves, in order to see three things: (1) We have the seeds—the habit energy—of unkindness and anger. We have made the other person unhappy before. We acknowledge that even if now we do not see our fault in her suffering. We should not be too confident that we are not responsible this time. (2) We may have been suffering, and we thought that by saying something strong to her, we would get relief. This is the wrong kind of relief, and we have to recognize that seeking that kind of relief is unwise. We shouldn't hope to suffer less by making another person suffer. (3) We look deeply and we see that her suffering is our suffering. If we do something to help her stop suffering, we will also benefit.

The fifth article tells us that if we can apologize right away, we should not wait. We can pick up the telephone and call right away, without attempting to justify or explain anything we said or did. A straightforward apology can have a powerful effect. We just say, "I am very sorry. I was not mindful or understanding." There may be no need to wait for Friday.

The Peace Treaty is a mindfulness practice. Please study it deeply and prepare carefully for the occasion to sign it. The best way to sign it is in a meditation hall, with the witness and support of the sangha. At the end of a Day of Mindfulness, in the presence of the community, you vow to abide by the articles of the treaty and practice wholeheartedly according to it. Then you sign. Unless you are committed to practicing it, it is better not to sign. If you sign and practice according to the Peace Treaty, you and your partner will benefit, and all of us will also benefit from your skill in dealing with anger.

I hope you will support the practice of the Peace Treaty by writing articles and leading retreats and discussions on the nature of the treaty and how to carry out its practice. In this way, even those who have no experience in meditation can learn and benefit from it. I believe a Peace Treaty like this will become an important part of our practice in the future. You may like to add more articles to make it more relevant to your situation. Be harmonious and happy!

Love in Action

*I*n the *Maharatnakuta Sutra*, it says that when one bodhisattva gets angry at another bodhisattva, countless obstacles are set up everywhere in the universe. Is it possible for a bodhisattva to get angry? Of course it is. A bodhisattva doesn't have to be perfect. Anyone who is aware of what is happening and tries to wake up other people is a bodhisattva. We are all bodhisattvas, doing our best. Along the way, we may feel angry or frustrated from time to time. That is why we have to practice according to the Peace Treaty. When a bodhisattva gets angry at another bodhisattva, countless obstacles are set up everywhere in the universe. That is understandable. We know that when we have peace and joy in ourselves, our peace and joy vibrate throughout the cosmos. So when we have hatred and anger in ourselves, they too will rebound to all quarters.

When President Bush gave the order to attack Iraq, many of us suffered at the same time. I was at

Plum Village giving a lecture on the *Avatamsaka Sutra*, and in the middle of a sentence, I suddenly said, "I don't think I will go to America this spring. I really don't want to go there now." We all paused for a long moment to breathe, and then I resumed the lecture. That afternoon during a tea meditation, a number of students from North America told me that because I felt that way, I should go. They reminded me that friends in the U.S. had been working hard to organize retreats there, and they helped me see that many Americans also suffered when the President gave the order to attack. So I decided to go in order to support them and share their suffering.

I understood that President Bush is a bodhisattva trying in his way to serve his people. Early in the conflict he instituted an embargo, but because we did not encourage him enough, he became impatient and suddenly war was inevitable. When he ordered the ground attack and said, "God bless the United States of America," I knew that bodhisattva needed our help. Any leader needs our help and our understanding. We must use intelligent and loving language so he will listen to us. When we get angry, we cannot do that. I listened to my American friends in Plum Village quietly and serenely, and I accepted their advice to go to the United States.

If we get angry, countless obstacles will be set up, blocking our way. So, without anger, we have to find a way to tell the president that God cannot bless one country against another. He must learn to pray better than that. But we should not think that simply by electing another president, the situation will be transformed. If we want a better government, we have to begin by changing our own consciousness and our own way of life. Our society is ruled by greed and violence. The way to help our country and our president is by transforming the greed and violence in ourselves and working to transform society.

Look at the 500,000 men and women from America and the West and the 1,000,000 Iraqi soldiers who spent months waiting for the land offensive to begin. They had to practice killing day and night in order to prepare. During the day, they wore helmets, took up guns and bayonets, jumped and yelled as if they were not human beings, and plunged their bayonets into sandbags representing enemy soldiers. If they did not become less than human beings, they could not have done it. They had to become inhuman to learn to kill. They did that during the day, and during the night they did the same in their dreams— planting seeds of suffering, fear, and violence within their consciousness. This is the practice of war—one and a half million men and women practicing fear and violence for many months. They knew they had to do it in order to survive.

Then the war came. The actual killing was massive, and we called it a victory. When the 500,000 troops returned home, they were deeply wounded from practicing so much violence in reality and in their consciousness. For several generations, millions of their children and grandchildren will inherit those seeds of violence and suffering. How can we call that a victory? When the troops arrived home, they cried. They were alive. Their families and children also cried. Of course, they had the right to be happy, but the men and women who returned were not the same as the men and women who left. Their wounds will be with us for a long time.

We have to meditate together as a nation if we want to be able to love and understand our veterans, our president, and our government. Eighty percent of the American people supported the Gulf War and called it clean and moral. They do not understand the true nature of war. Anyone who has seen a war could not say that. The Gulf War was not clean or moral for the people of Iraq, or for the people of the United States. After a war, many people, especially young people, see violence as the way to solve problems. The next time there is a conflict somewhere in the world, they will be tempted to support another military solution, another quick war. This kind of thinking and acting damages the consciousness of those on the "winning side." If we want to protect life, we have to look deeply as individuals and as a nation into the true nature of war. When we see it, we have to reveal it to the whole country by projecting it onto a huge screen. We must learn together and do everything possible to prevent it from happening again. If we only protest, we will not be ready when the next war comes in five or ten years. To prevent the next war, we have to practice peace today. If we establish peace in our hearts and in our ways of looking at things, war will not come. The only way to stop a war is to have real peace. If we wait until another war is imminent to begin to practice, it will be too late.

The death of one Iraqi soldier means that one family is suffering, and more than 100,000 Iraqi soldiers and civilians were killed—we don't exactly know how many. After any war, the suffering continues on both sides for several generations. Look at the suffering of the Vietnam veterans in America and the suffering of the Vietnamese people. We have to practice mindfulness and not forget the suffering that is still going on on both sides. We need to be there for those who need us, to let them know that we share their suffering, that we suffer too. When someone feels understood, his suffering is diminished. Please don't forget this aspect of the practice.

We who have touched war have a duty to bring the truth about war to those who have not had a direct experience of it. We are the light at the tip of the candle. It is very hot, but it has the power of shining and illuminating. If we practice mindfulness, we will know how to look deeply into the nature of war, and, with our insight, wake people up so that together we can avoid repeating the same horrors again and again. We who were born from the war know what it is. The war is in us, but it is also in everyone. We all saw the video of the Los Angeles policemen beating Rodney King. When I saw those images, I identified with Rodney King, and I suffered a lot. You must have felt the same. We were all beaten at the same time. But when I looked more deeply, I saw that I am

also the five policemen. I could not separate myself
from the men who did the beating. They were manifesting the hatred and violence that pervades our
society.

Everything is ready to explode, and we are all co-
responsible. Not only does the one who is beaten suffer, but the ones who are doing the beating also suffer. If not, why would they do it? Only if you suffer
will you make other people suffer. If you are peaceful
and happy, you will not inflict suffering on other
people. The policemen also need our love and understanding. We have helped create them through our
forgetfulness, through the way we live our daily
lives. In my heart I feel no blame for anyone. Arrest-
ing and imprisoning the policemen will not help
them or solve the problem. The problem is much
deeper than that. Violence has become the substance
of our lives. The Vietnam veterans, the Persian Gulf
veterans, and the millions who absorb violence every
day are being trained to be exactly like those who did
the beating. We accept violence as a way of life, and
we water the seeds of violence in ourselves by watching violent TV programs and movies that are poisoning us and poisoning our society. If we do not transform all of this violence and misunderstanding, one
day it will be our own child who is beaten or killed,
or who is doing the beating. This is very much our
affair.

Please take the hand of your little boy or little girl
and walk slowly to the park. You may be surprised to
notice that while you are enjoying the sunshine, the

trees, and the birds, your child feels a little bored. Young people today get bored easily. They are used to television, Nintendo, war toys, loud music, and other kinds of excitement. As they get older, they ride in fast cars, or experiment with alcohol, drugs, sexuality, or other things that tax their bodies and minds. We adults too try to fill our loneliness with these kinds of things, and all of us suffer. We have to teach ourselves and our children how to appreciate the simple joys that are available. This may not be easy in our complex, distracted society, but it is essential for our survival. Sitting on the grass with your little boy or girl, point out the tiny yellow and blue flowers that grow among the grasses and contemplate these miracles together. Peace education begins on this occasion.

Diet for a Mindful Society

T o realize peace in our daily lives, we need some guidelines. Two thousand five hundred years ago, the Buddha offered five wonderful precepts to Anathapindika and his friends as a practice to help them live a peaceful and wholesome life. Since that time in many Asian countries, these guidelines have served as the ethical basis of a happy life. I would like to present them to you in a way that makes their applicability clear for our situation today. Violence, racial injustice, alcoholism, sexual abuse, environmental exploitation, and so many other problems compel us to find ways to stop the suffering that is rampant in ourselves and in society. I hope you will reflect on these five precepts and try to practice them, either in this form or in the way they are presented in your own tradition.

The First Precept

Aware of the suffering caused by the destruction of life, I vow to cultivate compassion and learn ways to protect the lives of people, animals, and plants. I am determined not to kill, not to let others kill, and not to condone any act of killing in the world, in my thinking and in my way of life.

The foundation of all precepts is mindfulness. With mindfulness, we see that lives everywhere are being destroyed, and we vow to cultivate compassion as a source of energy for the protection of people, animals, plants, and our entire planet. Just feeling compassion is not enough. We also have to develop understanding so we know what kind of action to take. We must make the effort to stop all wars.

The mind is the basis of our actions. To kill with the mind is more dangerous than to kill with the body. When you believe that you have the only way and that everyone who does not follow your way is your enemy, millions may be killed. So it is not just by killing with our hands that we break the first precept. If, in our thinking and our way of life, we allow killing to go on, this is also an offense. We must look deeply. When we buy something or consume something, we may be participating in an act of killing. This precept reflects our determination not to kill, either directly or indirectly, and also to prevent others from killing. Vowing to practice this precept, we commit ourselves to protecting our planet and becoming bodhisattvas energized to practice love and compassion.

The Second Precept

Aware of the suffering caused by exploitation, social injustice, stealing, and oppression, I vow to cultivate loving kindness and learn the ways of working for the well-being of people, animals, and plants. I vow to practice generosity by sharing my time, energy, and material resources with those who are in real need. I am determined not to steal and not to possess anything that should belong to others. I will respect the property of others, but I will prevent others from profiting from human suffering or the suffering of other species on Earth.

Stealing comes in many forms. Oppression is one form of stealing, and it causes much suffering both here and in the Third World. Countries are torn by poverty and oppression. We want to help hungry children help themselves, for example, but we are caught in a way of life that keeps us so busy that we do not have time. We do not need a lot of money to help them. Sometimes they only need one pill or one bowl of food, but because we cannot free ourselves from our own small problems and our lifestyles, we don't do anything.

This precept is also about awareness of suffering and cultivating loving kindness. We may have the capacity of being generous, but we must also develop specific ways to express our generosity. Time is more than money. Time is for bringing joy and happiness to other people and thus to ourselves. There are three kinds of gifts—the gift of material resources, the gift of helping people rely on themselves, and the gift of non-fear. Helping people not be destroyed by fear is the greatest gift of all. This precept teaches us the very deep practice of sharing time, energy, and material resources with those who are in real need and truly reflects the bodhisattva ideal of compassion.

The Third Precept

Aware of the suffering caused by sexual misconduct, I vow to cultivate responsibility and learn ways to protect the safety and integrity of individuals, couples, families, and society. I am determined not to engage in sexual relations without love and a long-term commitment. To preserve the happiness of myself and others, I am determined to respect my commitments and the commitments of others. I will do everything in my power to protect children from sexual abuse and to prevent couples and families from being broken by sexual misconduct.

We practice this precept to help ourselves and others avoid being wounded, and to restore peace and stability in ourselves, our families, and society. A sexual relationship is an act of communion that should be performed in mindfulness, with love, care, and respect. "Love" is a beautiful word, and we have to restore its meaning. When we say, "I love hamburgers," we spoil the word. We have to make the effort to heal words by using them properly and carefully. True love includes a sense of responsibility and accepting the other person as he or she is, with all strengths and weaknesses. If you like only the best things in a person, that is not love. You have to accept his or her weaknesses and bring your patience, understanding, and energy to help the person transform. This kind of love is safe.

We use the phrase "love sickness" to describe the kind of love that makes us sick. It is a kind of attachment, or addiction. Like a drug, it makes us feel wonderful, but once we are addicted, we cannot have peace. We cannot study, work, or sleep. We think only about the other person. This kind of love is possessive, even totalitarian. We want to own the object of our love, and we don't want anyone to prevent us from possessing him or her totally. It creates a kind of prison for our beloved one. He or she is deprived of the right to be himself or herself.

The feeling of loneliness is universal in our society, and it can push us into a relationship. We believe naïvely that having a sexual relationship will make us feel less lonely. But when there is no real communication between you and the other person, a sexual relationship will only widen the gap and cause both of you to suffer.

The phrase "long-term commitment" is not strong enough to express the depth of our love, but we need to say something so people will understand. To love our child deeply, we have to make a long-term commitment and help him or her through the journey of life as long as we are alive. When we have a good friend, we also make a long-term commitment. How much more so the person with whom we want to share our body and soul. It is important to make such a commitment in the context of a community—family or friends—to witness and support you. The feeling between the two of you may not be enough to sustain your happiness in times of adversity. Even if you do not accept the institution of marriage, it is still important to express your commitment in the presence of friends who love and support you. It will give you peace, stability, and a greater chance for real happiness.

This precept also applies to society. There are many ways our families and society are destroyed by sexual misconduct. Many people suffer every day because they were molested as children. When you practice this precept, you vow to protect children and also those who sexually abuse children. The ones who cause suffering must also become the objects of your love and protection. They are the product of an unstable society, and they need our help. Our society needs bodhisattvas who practice in this field to prevent suffering and the breaking up of relationships, families, and individual lives.

The Fourth Precept
Aware of the suffering caused by unmindful speech and the inability to listen to others, I vow to cultivate loving speech and deep listening in order to bring joy and happiness to others and relieve others of their suffering. Knowing that words can create happiness or suffering, I vow to learn to speak truthfully, with words that inspire self-confidence, joy, and hope. I am determined not to spread news that I do not know to be certain and not to criticize or condemn things of which I am not sure. I will refrain from uttering words that can cause division or discord, or that can

cause the family or the community to break. I will make all efforts to reconcile and resolve all conflicts, however small.

Loving speech is an act of generosity. When we are motivated by loving kindness, we can bring happiness to many others through our kind words. When we have a lot of pain, it is difficult to speak lovingly, so it is important to look deeply into the nature of our anger, despair, and suffering in order to be free of it. If we use words that inspire self-confidence and trust, especially with our children, they will flower.

In my tradition, whenever we want to inspire ourselves to practice the art of deep listening, we recite this verse:

> We invoke your name, Avalokitesvara. We aspire to learn your way of listening in order to help relieve the suffering in the world. You know how to listen in order to understand. We invoke your name in order to practice listening with all our attention and openheartedness. We will sit and listen without any prejudice. We will sit and listen without judging or reacting. We will sit and listen in order to understand. We will sit and listen so attentively that we will be able to hear what the other person is saying and also what is being left unsaid. We know that just by listening deeply, we already alleviate a great deal of pain and suffering in the other person.

Deep listening is the basis for reconciliation. To reconcile means to bring peace and happiness to

members of our family, society, and other nations. To
promote the work of reconciliation, we have to refrain from aligning ourselves with one party or another so that we understand both. This work takes
courage; we may be suppressed or even killed by
those we wish to help. After listening to both sides,
we can tell each side of the suffering of the other.
This alone will bring about greater understanding.
People are sorely needed to do this in many places in
the world, including South Africa, Eastern Europe,
the Middle East, and Southeast Asia. Our society
needs bodhisattvas who can bridge the huge gaps between religions, races, and peoples.

The Fifth Precept
*Aware of the suffering caused by unmindful consumption,
I vow to cultivate good health, both physical and mental,
for myself, my family, and my society by practicing mindful eating, drinking, and consuming. I vow to ingest only
items that preserve peace, well-being, and joy in my body,
in my consciousness, and in the collective body and consciousness of my family and society. I am determined not
to use alcohol or any other intoxicant or to ingest foods or
other items that contain toxins, such as certain TV programs, magazines, books, films, and conversations. I am
aware that to damage my body or my consciousness with
these poisons is to betray my ancestors, my parents, my
society, and future generations. I will work to transform
violence, fear, anger, and confusion in myself and in society by practicing a diet for myself and for society. I under-*

stand that a proper diet is crucial for self-transformation and for the transformation of society.

In the West, people have the impression that their body belongs to them, that they can do anything they want to their body. They feel they have the right to live their lives however they please. And the law supports them. This is individualism. But according to the teaching of interbeing, your body is not yours alone. Your body belongs to your ancestors, your parents, and future generations, and it also belongs to society and all other living beings. All of them have come together to bring about the presence of this body. Keeping your body healthy is an expression of gratitude to the whole cosmos—the trees, the clouds, everything. You practice this precept for everyone. If you are healthy, physically and mentally, all of us will benefit. We are what we consume and metabolize. We have to eat, drink, and consume, but unless we do it mindfully, we may destroy our bodies and our consciousness, expressing a lack of gratitude to our ancestors, parents, and future generations. Mindful consuming is the main subject of this precept.

It is important for each family to have at least one meal together every day. This meal should be an occasion to practice mindfulness, and to be aware of how fortunate we are to be together. After we sit down, we look at each person and, breathing in and out, smile to him or her for a few seconds. This practice can produce a miracle. It can make you real, and it can make the others at the table real also.

Then we practice meditation on the food. One person looks at one dish on the table and describes its content and history. Children and adults can learn from this and have a deeper look into the nature of the food. This may take only a few minutes, but it will help everyone enjoy the food much more. For example, someone says aloud, "This bread, made from wheat, Earth, sun, and rain, comes to us after much hard work. The wheat was grown organically by a farmer in Texas, and a considerable amount of fuel was used to transport the flour to a conscientious bakery in our home town. May we live in a way that is worthy of this food, and appreciate the positive and negative elements that are present in each bite."

Eating in silence, even for a few minutes, is a very important practice. It takes away all the distractions that can keep us from really touching the food. Our mindfulness may be fragile and it may be too difficult to carry on a conversation and really honor the food at the same time. So for the first five or ten minutes, it is wonderful to eat in silence. In my monastic tradition, we practice the Five Contemplations before eating. The second Contemplation is, "We vow to be worthy of this food." I think the best way to make ourselves worthy of this food is to eat it mindfully. The whole cosmos has come together to make this food available, and someone has spent an hour or more preparing the food. It would be a pity if we didn't eat it in mindfulness.

After the period of quiet, we can practice mindful talking, the kind of talking that can increase the hap-

piness in the family. We should never talk of things
that can separate us; we should never reproach someone during the meal. That would spoil everything.
Parents should refrain from discussing the mistakes
their children have made, and young people should
also only say things that will help bring about more
happiness and nourish the mindfulness in the family,
such as "Daddy, isn't this soup fantastic?" Speaking
this way waters the seeds of happiness in the whole
family. Life is an art. We should all be artists in order
to live a happy life. We will have time later to discuss
our business projects or what happened in school.
During dinnertime we feel grateful that we are together, we have food to eat, and we really enjoy the
food and the presence of each other.

It is important that we maintain a healthy diet.
There are so many wonderful things to eat and drink;
we have to refrain from consuming the things that
harm us. Alcohol causes a lot of suffering. So many
people have grown up receiving some form of abuse
from an alcoholic parent. The fruit and grain that
produce alcoholic beverages use farmland that could
be producing food for those who are hungry. And so
many traffic accidents involve someone who is intox-
icated. When we understand that we are practicing
not only for ourselves, we will stop drinking alcohol.
To stop drinking is a statement to our children and
our society that this is a substance not worthy of our
support. Even if we don't drink alcohol, we may get
killed by a drunken driver. In persuading one person
to refrain from drinking, we make the world a safer

place. Drinking wine is an element running deep in Western civilization, as is evident in the Eucharist and the Sabbath meal. I have spoken with priests and rabbis to see whether it might be possible to substitute grape juice or some other beverage for the wine, and they think it is possible.

Sometimes we don't need to consume as much as we do. Consuming itself can become a kind of addiction, because we feel so lonely. Loneliness is one of the afflictions of modern life. When we are lonely, we ingest food in our body and into our consciousness that can bring toxins into us. Just as we make every effort to maintain a proper diet for our body, we must also maintain a proper diet for our consciousness, refraining from ingesting toxic intellectual and spiritual food. When we watch TV, read magazines or books, or pick up the telephone, we only make our condition worse if our comsuming is not mindful. During one hour watching a film filled with violence, we water the seeds of violence, hatred, and fear in us. We do that, and we let our children do that. We need to have family meetings to discuss an intelligent policy for television watching. We may have to label our TV sets the same way we label our cigarette packs: "Warning: Watching TV can be hazardous to your health." Children see so many violent images on television. We need an intelligent policy concerning the use of television.

Of course there are many healthy and beautiful programs, and we should arrange our time so that the family will benefit from these. We don't have to

destroy our TV sets. We only have to use them with
mindfulness. We can ask television stations to broad-
cast healthier programs and encourage the boycott of
those who refuse. We can even support the manufacture of TV sets that only receive signals from stations
that produce healthy, educational programs. We need
to be protected because the toxins are overwhelming,
and they are destroying our society, our families,
and us.

The idea of a diet is the essence of this precept.
Our collective consciousness has so much violence,
fear, craving, and hatred in it, and it manifests in
wars and bombs. Bombs are a product of the fear in
our collective consciousness. Just to remove the
bombs is not enough. Even if we were able to transport all the bombs to the moon, we would not be
safe, because the roots of the war and the bombs are
still in our collective consciousness. We will not abol-
ish war with angry demonstrations. We have to
transform the toxins in our own consciousness and in
our collective consciousness. We have to practice a
diet for ourselves, our families, and our society, and
we have to work with artists, writers, filmmakers,
lawyers, psychotherapists, and others if we want to
stop the kind of consuming that is poisoning our collective consciousness.

The problem is very big. It is not just a question of
enjoying one glass of wine. If you stop drinking alcohol altogether or stop watching unwholesome films
and TV programs, you do it for the whole society.
When you see that we are in great danger, refraining

from the first glass of wine is a manifestation of your enlightenment. You are setting an example for your children, your friends, and all of us. On French television, they say, *"Une verre, ça va, deux verres, bonjour les dégâts."* "One glass is all right, but two glasses are destructive." They don't say that if there were no first glass, there could not be a second.

Please join me in writing down three things. First, what kind of toxins do you already have in your body, and what kind of toxins do you already have in your psyche, your consciousness? What makes you suffer now? If you need to practice sitting or walking meditation in order to look deeply enough, please do so. When you have done this, please sit quietly for a few moments, and then look into the bodies and souls of your children, your spouse, or others who are close to you, since all of you are practicing together. Recognizing these toxins and listing them on a sheet of paper is meditation—looking deeply in order to call things by their true names.

Second, please ask yourself, "What kind of poisons am I putting into my body and my consciousness every day?" What am I ingesting every day that is toxic to my body and my consciousness? What is my family ingesting? What are my city and my nation ingesting concerning violence, hatred, and fear? The beating of Rodney King is a manifestation of how much hatred, fear, and violence are in our society. What kinds of poisons do we ingest every day in our families, our cities, and our nation? This is a collective meditation.

Third, write down a prescription that arises from your insight. For example, "I vow that from today I will not ingest more of this, this, and this. I vow only to use this, this, and this to nourish my body and my consciousness." This is the foundation of practice—the practice of loving kindness to yourself. You cannot love someone else unless you love and take care of yourself. Practicing in this way is to practice peace, love, and insight. When you look deeply, you have insight, and your insight brings about compassion.

Before you begin to eat, breathe in and out and look at the table to see what is good for your body and what is not. This is to practice the precept of protecting your body. When you want to watch TV or go to the movies, first look deeply in order to determine what should be viewed and what should not be viewed by you and your children. Think about the books and magazines you read, and decide what should be read and what should not be read by you and your children. Practicing together as a community, we don't need to take refuge in entertaining ourselves with any more poisons. Based on our own insight, we can decide what to ingest and what not to ingest into our bodies and our souls.

Please discuss with your family and friends a diet for your body, a diet for your consciousness, and also a diet for the collective consciousness of our society. This is a meditation practice, and it is true peace work. Peace begins with each of us taking care of our bodies and our minds every day.

I hope you will practice according to the letter and spirit of these five precepts, reciting them regularly, and discussing them with friends. If you prefer to use the equivalent from your own tradition, that is wonderful. At Plum Village, we recite these precepts every week. One person reads each precept slowly and then breathes three times before saying, "This is the (first) of the five precepts. Have you made an effort to study and to practice it during the last week?" We do not answer yes or no. We just breathe three times and let the question enter us. That is good enough. "Yes" would not be entirely correct, but "No" would not be correct either. No one can practice these precepts perfectly. If you are a vegetarian, for example, the food you eat still contains living beings. But we have to do something, and practicing the precepts is a direction we can follow to produce the dramatic changes that are needed in ourselves and in society.

Sangha Building

*E*very time I see someone without roots, I see him as a hungry ghost. In Buddhist mythology, the term "hungry ghost" is used to describe a wandering soul who is extremely hungry and thirsty but whose throat is too narrow for food or drink to pass through. On the full moon day of the seventh lunar month in Vietnam, we offer food and drink to the hungry ghosts. We know that it is difficult for them to receive our offerings, so we chant a *Mantra to Expand Hungry Ghosts' Throats*. There are so many hungry ghosts, and our houses are small, so we make these offerings in the front yard.

Hungry ghosts long to be loved, but no matter how much we love and care for them, they may not have the capacity to receive it. They may understand in principle that there is beauty in life, but they are not capable of touching it. Something seems to be standing in their way preventing them from touching these refreshing and healing elements of life. They want only to forget life, and so they turn to alcohol, drugs, or sex to help them forget. If we say, "Do not do that," they will not respond. They have heard enough admonitions. What they need is something to believe in, something that proves to them that life is meaningful. We all need something to believe in. To help a hungry ghost, we have to listen to him or her in mindfulness, provide him with an atmosphere of family and brotherhood, and then help him experience something good, beautiful, and true to believe in.

One afternoon in Plum Village, I saw a woman who looked exactly like a hungry ghost. Plum Village was beautiful at that time of year—the flowers were blooming and everyone was smiling—but she could not touch anything. I could feel her pain and suffering. She walked alone, and she seemed to be dying of loneliness with each step. She had come to Plum Village to be with others, but when she arrived, she was not able to be with anyone.

Our society produces millions of hungry ghosts, people of all ages—I have seen some not yet ten years old—who have no roots at all. They have never experienced happiness at home, and they have nothing to believe in or belong to. This is the main sickness of our time. With nothing to believe in, how can you survive? How can you find the energy to smile or to touch the linden tree or the beautiful sky? You are lost, and you live without any sense of responsibility. Alcohol and drugs are destroying your body.

Our government believes that the way to deal with the problem of drugs is to try to prevent drugs from being smuggled into the country and to arrest those who sell or use them. But the availability of drugs is only a secondary cause of the problem. The main cause is the lack of meaning in the lives of so many people, the lack of something to believe in. If you abuse drugs or alcohol, it is because you are not happy—you do not accept yourself, your family, your society, or your tradition, and you want to renounce them all.

We have to find ways to rebuild the foundations of our communities and to offer people something to believe in. The things you were offered in the past may have been too abstract and presented too coercively. Perhaps you thought that science would bring ease to society or Marxism would bring social justice, and your beliefs have been shattered. Even the God you prayed to—the one President Bush invoked to help the United States defeat Iraq—was too small. Many of the people who represented your traditions had not themselves experienced the deepest values of the tradition; they only spoke in its name and tried to force you to believe, and you felt turned off.

Mindfulness is something we can believe in. It is our capacity of being aware of what is going on in the present moment. To believe in mindfulness is safe, and not at all abstract. When we drink a glass of water and know that we are drinking a glass of water, mindfulness is there. When we sit, walk, stand, or breathe and know that we are sitting, walking, standing, or breathing, we touch the seed of mindfulness in us, and after a few days, our mindfulness will grow quite strong. Mindfulness is the kind of light that shows us the way. It is the living buddha inside of each of us. Mindfulness gives birth to insight, awakening, compassion, and love.

Not only Buddhists, but also Christians, Jews, Muslims, and Marxists can accept that each of us has the capacity of being mindful, everyone has the seed of mindfulness in himself or herself. If we know how to water this seed, it will grow, and we will become alive again, capable of enjoying all the wonders of life. I know many families that were about to break, but whose harmony has been restored thanks to the practice of mindfulness. That is why if you ask me what I believe, I would say that I believe in mindfulness. Faith is the first of the five powers taught by the Buddha. The second is energy, the third mindfulness, the fourth concentration, and the fifth understanding. If you do not have faith, if you do not believe in anything, you are without energy. That is why faith brings about energy. A good friend is someone who can inspire faith.

When we touch the ground, we can feel the stability of the Earth. We can also feel stability in the sunshine, the air, and the trees—we can count on the sun to rise tomorrow and the trees to be there for us. We have to put our trust in what is stable. When we build a house, we build it on solid ground. When we say, "I take refuge in the sangha," it means we put our trust in a community of fellow practitioners who are solid. A teacher can be important and also the teachings, but friends are the most essential element of the practice. It is difficult or even impossible to practice without a sangha.

As we look deeply in order to discover our true self, we find that what we have been calling a "self" is made entirely of non-self elements. Our body and mind have their roots in society, in nature, and in those we love. Some of us may not like to talk or think about our roots because we have suffered so much from the violence of our family or our culture. We want to leave these things behind and search for something new. It is easy to understand why we feel this way, but when we practice looking deeply, we discover that our ancestors and our traditions are still in us. We may be angry at them, but they are still there, urging us to come back and connect with their joys and their pains. We have no choice but to get in touch with the roots that are in us. The moment we connect with them, a transformation takes place in us and our pain begins to melt away. We see that we are an element in a continuation of our ancestors, and we are also the way for future generations.

It is not possible for us to throw away one thing and run after another. Whether our tradition is Christianity, Judaism, Islam, or something else, we have to study the ways of our ancestors and find the best elements in the tradition for ourselves and our children. We have to live in a way that allows the ancestors in us to be liberated. The moment we can offer joy, peace, freedom, and harmony to our ancestors, we offer joy, peace, freedom, and harmony to ourselves, our children, and their children at the same time.

Many people were abused or beaten by their parents, and many more were severely criticized or rejected by them. Now in their store consciousness, these people have so many seeds of unhappiness they don't even want to hear their father's or their mother's name. When I meet someone like this, I always offer the meditation on the five-year-old child, which is a mindfulness massage. "Breathing in, I see myself as a five-year-old child. Breathing out, I smile to the five-year-old child in me." During the meditation, you try to see yourself as a five-year-old child. If you can look deeply at that child, you can see that you are vulnerable and can be easily hurt. A stern look or a shout can cause internal formations in your store consciousness. When your parents fight and scream at each other, your five-year-old receives many seeds of suffering. I have heard young people say, "The most precious gift my parents can give is their own happiness." By living unhappily, your father made you suffer a lot. Now you are visualizing yourself as a five-year-old child. When you smile at that child in yourself, you smile with compassion. "I was so young and tender, and I received so much pain."

The next day, I would advise you to practice, "Breathing in, I see my father as a five-year-old child. Breathing out, I smile to that child with compassion." We are not used to seeing our father as a five-year-old child. We think of him as having always been an adult—stern and with great authority. We have not taken the time to see our father as a tender, young

boy who can also be easily wounded by others. So
the practice is to visualize your father as a five-year-
old boy—fragile, vulnerable, and easily hurt. If it
helps, you can look in the family album to study the
image of your father as a boy. When you are able to
visualize him as vulnerable, you will realize that he
may have been the victim of his father. If he received
too many seeds of suffering from his father, of course
he will not know how to treat his son well. So he
made you suffer, and the circle of samsara continues.
If you don't practice mindfulness, you will do exactly
the same to your children. The moment you see your
father as a victim, compassion will be born in your
heart. When you smile to him with compassion, you
will begin to bring mindfulness and insight into your
pain. If you practice like that for several hours or several days, your anger toward him will dissolve. One
day, you will smile to your father in person and hug
him, saying, "I understand you, Dad. You suffered
very much during your childhood."

Through meditation, we rediscover the value of
our families and our roots, including those values
that have been buried under years of suffering. Every
tradition has some gems, the fruits of thousands of
years of practice. Now they have come down to us,
and we cannot ignore or deny them. Even the food
we eat has our ancestors and our cultural values in it.
How can we say that we have nothing to do with our
culture? We can find ways to honor our own tradition, and other traditions as well. Meditation teaches
us the way to remove barriers, limits, and discrimina-

tion in order to see the non-self elements within the
self. Through the practice, we can remove the dangers of separation and create a world in which our
children can have peace. Divisions between people,
nations, and religious beliefs have contributed much
to our suffering for many centuries. We have to practice in a way that releases these tensions in ourselves
and between peoples so we can open up and enjoy
one another as brothers and sisters. In whatever tradition you practice, if you obtain insight into the nature of interbeing, it is true meditation.

Some people, some hungry ghosts, have become
so uprooted that we really cannot ask them to go
back to their own roots, at least not yet. We have to
help them by providing an alternative, a second
chance. People like this live on the margin of society,
and, like trees without roots, they cannot absorb
nourishment. I have met meditators who have been
practicing for twenty years who are still unable to
transform themselves because they are so rootless.
The practice is to help them get some roots, to find an
environment where they can take root.

In Asia we have made an effort to model practice
communities after families. We call one another
dharma brothers, dharma sisters, dharma uncles, or
dharma aunts, and we call our teacher a dharma father or mother. The children in Plum Village call me
"Grandpa Teacher." I always approach them as a
grandfather, not as someone outside the family. A
practice center should possess that kind of warmth,
that kind of familial brotherhood and sisterhood that

will continue to nourish us. In the context of a spiritual family, we have a real opportunity, a second chance, to get rooted. The members of the sangha are aware that we are seeking love, and they treat us in a way that we will have the best chance to be rooted in this second family. They do their best to take care of us, acting like a sister or a brother to us. After three or six months, a smile is born on our lips when some real relationship between us and another member of the sangha is seen and acknowledged, and they know we are beginning to make progress and that transformation will be possible. New roots are beginning to spring out.

Interpersonal relationships are the key for success in the practice. Without an intimate, deep relationship with at least one person, transformation is unlikely. With the support of one person, you have stability and support, and later you can reach out to a third person, and eventually be a brother or sister to everyone in the sangha. You demonstrate your willingness and capacity to live in peace and harmony with everyone in the sangha.

It is my deep desire that communities of practice in the West be organized this way, as families in a friendly, warm atmosphere, so that people can succeed in their practice. A sangha in which each person is an island, not communicating with each other, is not helpful. It is just a collection of trees without roots. Transformation and healing cannot be obtained in such an atmosphere. We must be rooted if we want to have a chance to learn and practice meditation.

The nuclear family is a rather recent invention. Besides mother and father, there are just one or two children. Sometimes in such a small family, there is not enough air to breathe. When there is trouble between father and mother, the whole family feels the effects. The atmosphere in the house is heavy, and there is nowhere to escape. Sometimes the child may go to the bathroom and lock the door just to be alone, but there is still no escape; the heavy atmosphere permeates the bathroom, too. So the child grows up with many seeds of suffering and then transmits these seeds to his or her children.

In the old times, uncles, aunts, grandparents, and cousins all lived together. Houses were surrounded by trees where they could hang hammocks and organize picnics, and people did not have many of the problems we have now. When mother and father were having a problem, the children could always escape by going to an aunt or an uncle. They still had someone to look up to, and the atmosphere was not so threatening. I think that communities that practice mindful living can replace our former big families, because when we go to these communities, we see many aunts, uncles, and cousins who can help us.

Having a community where people gather as brothers and sisters in the dharma and where children have a number of uncles and aunts is a very wonderful thing. We have to learn to create that kind of family. We have to see the other members of the community as our brothers and sisters. This is al-

ready a tradition in the East, and it can be learned in
the West. We can take the best from both cultures.

Here in the West, I have seen many single parents.
A single parent can also benefit from a practice community. He or she may think that it is necessary to
remarry to have more stability, but I do not agree.
You may have more stability now by yourself than
you did when you were with a partner. Another person coming into your life could destroy the stability
you now have. It is most important to take refuge in
yourself, recognizing the stability you already have.
By doing so, you become even more solid, and you
develop yourself into a refuge for your child and
your friends. So first you have to make yourself into
someone stable and give up the idea that you cannot
be yourself unless "that someone" is with you. You
yourself are sufficient. When you transform yourself
into a comfortable hermitage, with air, light, and order inside, you begin to feel peace, joy, and happiness, and you begin to be someone others can rely
on. Your child and your dharma brothers and sisters
can all rely on you.

So first return to your hermitage and arrange
things from within. You can benefit from the sunshine, the trees, and the Earth. You can open your
windows for these healthy, stable elements to enter,
and you become one with your environment. When
unstable elements try to enter your hermitage, close
the windows and do not let them in. When thunder,
high winds, or great heat want to intrude, prevent
them from entering. Being a refuge unto yourself is a

basic practice. Do not rely on someone you do not know much about, someone who may be unstable. Go back to yourself and take refuge in your own hermitage.

If you are a mother raising your child alone, you must learn how to do it. You have to be a father also; otherwise you will continue to need someone else to play the role of a father for your child, and you will lose your sovereignty, you will lose your hermitage. If you can say, "I can learn how to be both a father and mother to my child. I can succeed by myself, with the support of my friends and my community," it is a good sign.

The love of a father is different from that of a mother. A mother's love is somehow unconditional. You are the child of your mother, that is why you are loved by her. There is no other reason. A mother tries to use her body and mind to protect that very soft, vulnerable part of herself. She has a tendency to consider her child as an extension of herself, as herself. This is good, but it may create problems in the future. She has to learn gradually that her son or daughter is a separate person.

A father's love is a little different. The father seems to say, "If you do this, you will receive my love. If you don't, you will not." It's a kind of deal. I have that in myself, too. I am capable of disciplining my students, and I also have the capacity of loving my students as a mother. I know it is not easy for a mother to be a father, but if you have a good sangha and good relationships with those in the sangha, other members of your sangha can be an uncle or an aunt for your child. With a community of practice, a single parent can be self-sufficient. She is capable of playing the roles of both mother and father, and she can also benefit from the help of some of the other adults.

Single parenting is widespread in the West. We need retreats and seminars to discuss the best ways to raise our children. We do not accept the ancient way of parenting. At the same time, we have not fully developed modern ways of parenting. We need to draw from our own experiences and practice and bring another dimension to the life of the nuclear family. When nuclear family life is combined with the life of a practice community, a sangha, it can be very successful. You can bring your child to the practice center very often, and both you and your child will benefit from the atmosphere there. The practice center will benefit from your presence also. Children are jewels who can help the practice. If the children are happy, all the parents and non-parents will enjoy the practice.

It is a joy to find ourselves in the midst of a sangha where people are practicing well together. Each person's way of walking, eating, and smiling can be a real help to us. She is walking for me, I am smiling for her, and we do it together, as a sangha. By practicing together like this, we can expect a real transformation within us. We don't have to practice intensively or force ourselves. We just have to allow ourselves to be in a good sangha where people are hap-

py, living deeply each moment, and transformation
will come naturally, without much effort.

I think that sangha building is the most important
art for us to learn. Even if we are a skilled meditator
and well versed in the sutras, if we don't know how
to build a sangha, we cannot help others. We have to
build a sangha that is happy, where communication
is open. We have to take care of each person, staying
aware of his pain, her difficulties, his aspirations, her
fears and hopes in order to make him or her comfortable and happy. This requires time, energy, and concentration.

Each of us needs a sangha. If we don't have a
good sangha yet, we should spend our time and energy building one. If you are a psychotherapist, a
doctor, a social worker, a peace worker, or if you are
working for the environment, you need a sangha.
Without a sangha, you will not have enough support,
and you will burn out very soon. A psychotherapist
can choose among his or her clients who have overcome their difficulties, who recognize you as a friend,
a brother, or a sister in order to form a group of
people to practice as a sangha, to practice being together in peace and joy in a familial atmosphere. You
need brothers and sisters in the practice in order to
be nourished and supported. A sangha can help you
in difficult moments. Your capacity of helping people
can be seen by looking at those around you.

I have met psychotherapists who are not happy
with their families, and I doubt very much that these
therapists can help us if we need them. I proposed

that they form a sangha. Among the members of this sangha are people who have profited and recovered from their illness and have become friends with the therapist. The sangha is to meet and practice together—breathing, living mindfully and in peace, joy, and loving kindness. That would be a source of support and comfort for the therapist. Not only do meditators and therapists have to learn the art of sangha building, every one of us needs to. I do not believe that you can go very far without a sangha. I am nourished by my sangha. Any achievement that can be seen in the sangha supports me and gives me more strength.

To build a sangha, begin by finding one friend who would like to join you in sitting or walking meditation, precept recitation, tea meditation, or a discussion. Eventually others will ask to join, and your small group can meet weekly or monthly at someone's home. Some sanghas even find land and move to the countryside to start a retreat center. Of course, your sangha also includes the trees, the birds, the meditation cushion, the bell, and even the air you breathe—all the things that support you in the practice. It is a rare opportunity to be with people who practice deeply together. The sangha is a gem.

The principle is to organize in the way that is most enjoyable for everyone. You will never find a perfect sangha. An imperfect sangha is good enough. Rather than complain too much about your sangha, do your best to transform yourself into a good element of the sangha. Accept the sangha and build on it. When you and your family practice doing things mindfully, you are a sangha. If you have a park near your home where you can take the children for walking meditation, the park is part of your sangha.

A sangha is also a community of resistance, resisting the speed, violence, and unwholesome ways of living that are prevalent in our society. Mindfulness is to protect ourselves and others. A good sangha can lead us in the direction of harmony and awareness.

The substance of the practice is most important. The forms can be adapted. During one retreat at Plum Village, a Catholic priest asked me, "Thây, I see the value of mindfulness practice. I have tasted the joy, peace, and happiness of it. I enjoy the bells, the tea meditations, the silent meals, and the walking. My question is, how shall I continue to practice when I get back to my church?"

I asked him, "Is there a bell in your church?"

He said, "Yes."

"Do you ring the bell?"

"Yes."

"Then please ring the bell the way we ring the bell here. In your church do you share a meal? Do you have tea or cookies?"

"Yes."

"Please do it the way we do here, in mindfulness. There is no problem at all."

When you go back to your own tradition, when you go back to your sangha or start a new sangha, you can enjoy doing everything you do in mindfulness. It is not necessary to throw away your tradition or your family. Keep everything and introduce mindfulness, peace, and joy into it. Your friends will see the value of the practice through you—not through what you say, but through your being.

Realizing Ultimate Reality

We come to the practice of meditation seeking relief from our suffering, and meditation can teach us how to transform our suffering and obtain basic relief. But the deepest kind of relief is the realization of *nirvana*. There are two dimensions to life, and we should be able to touch both. One is like a wave, and we call it the historical dimension. The other is like the water, and we call it the ultimate dimension, or nirvana. We usually touch just the wave, but when we discover how to touch the water, we receive the highest fruit that meditation can offer.

In the historical dimension, we have birth certificates and death certificates. The day your mother passes away, you suffer. If someone sits close to you and shows her concern, you feel some relief. You have her friendship, her support, her warm hand to hold. This is the world of waves. It is characterized by birth and death, ups and downs, being and nonbeing. A wave has a beginning and an end, but we cannot ascribe these characteristics to water. In the world of water, there is no birth or death, no being or non-being, no beginning or end. When we touch the water, we touch reality in its ultimate dimension and are liberated from all of these concepts.

The second century philosopher Nagarjuna asked, "Before something was born, did it exist or not?" Before the egg was born from a chicken, was it existent or nonexistent? If it were already there, how could it have been born? Since a baby is also already present in the womb of her mother, how can we say she is not yet born? Nagarjuna says that something already present cannot be born. To be born means from nothing you become something; from no one you become someone. But nothing can be born from nothing. A flower is born from soil, minerals, seeds, sunshine, rain, and many other things. Meditation reveals to us the no-birth of all things. Life is a continuation. Instead of singing "Happy Birthday," we can sing "Happy Continuation." Even the day of our mother's death is a day of continuation; she continues in many other forms.

A friend of mine has been taking care of her 93-year-old mother. The doctors say that her mother will die any day. For more than a year, my friend has been teaching her mother meditation exercises that have been very helpful. She began by watering the seeds of happiness in her mother, and now her mother becomes very alive every time my friend comes around. Recently she told her mother, "This body is not exactly yours. Your body is much larger. You have nine children, dozens of grandchildren, and also great-grandchildren. We are all continuations of you, and we are very happy and healthy. You are quite alive in us."

Her mother was able to see that, and she smiled. My friend continued, "When you were young, you were able to teach many people how to cook and do many other things. You made people happy. Now we are doing the same thing; we are continuing the work you have begun. When you were young, you wrote poetry and sang, and now many of us write poems and sing beautifully. You are continuing in us. You are many beings at the same time." This is a meditation on non-self. It helps her mother see that her body is just a small part of her true self. She understands that when her body departs, she will continue in many other forms.

Who can say that your mother has passed away? You cannot describe her as being or non-being, alive or dead, because these notions belong to the historical dimension. When you touch your mother in the ultimate dimension, you see that she is still with you. The same is true of a flower. A flower may pretend to be born, but it has always been there in other forms. Later it may pretend to die, but we should not be fooled. She is just playing a game of hide-and-seek. She reveals herself to us and then hides herself away. If we are attentive, we can touch her anytime we want. Your mother is also playing a game. She pretended to be born as your mother, she played the role of a mother so well, and then she pretended not to be there in order to help you grow up.

One day as I was about to step on a dry leaf, I saw the leaf in the ultimate dimension. I saw that it was not really dead, but it was merging with the moist soil and preparing to appear on the tree the following spring in another form. I smiled at the leaf and said, "You are pretending."

In the *Lotus Sutra*, the Buddha tells us about a physician who had many children. One time while the physician was away, his children ate something toxic and got food poisoning. When he returned home and saw them all sick, he gave them the proper medicine right away. Some of the children took it and got well, but others did not because they relied solely on the presence of their father. Finally the physician had to hide and pretend that he had died in order to get his children to take their medicine. Maybe your mother is playing that kind of game with you to encourage you to practice peace and happiness.

Everything is pretending to be born and pretending to die, including the leaf I almost stepped on. The Buddha said, "When conditions are sufficient, the body reveals itself, and we say the body is. When conditions are not sufficient, the body cannot be perceived by us, and we say the body is not." The day of our so-called death is a day of our continuation in many other forms. If you know how to touch your mother in the ultimate dimension, she will always be there with you. If you touch your hand, your face, or your hair, and look very deeply, you can see that she is there in you, smiling. This is a deep practice, and it is also the deepest kind of relief.

Nirvana means extinction, the extinction of all notions and concepts, including the concepts of birth, death, being, non-being, coming, and going. Nirvana is the ultimate dimension of life, a state of coolness, peace, and joy. It is not a state to be attained after you die. You can touch nirvana right now by breathing, walking, and drinking your tea in mindfulness. You have been "nirvanized" since the very non-beginning. Everything and everyone is dwelling in nirvana.

Nikos Kazantzakis tells the story of St. Francis of Assisi standing in front of an almond tree in midwinter. St. Francis asked the tree to tell him about God, and suddenly the tree began to blossom. In just a few seconds, the almond tree was covered with beautiful flowers. When I read this story, I was very impressed. I saw that St. Francis stood on the side of the ultimate dimension. It was winter; there were no leaves, flowers, or fruits, but he saw the flowers.

We may feel that we are incapable of touching the ultimate dimension, but that is not correct. We have done so already. The problem is how to do it more deeply and more frequently. The phrase, "Think globally," for example, is in the direction of touching the ultimate dimension. When we see things globally, we have more wisdom and we feel much better. We are not caught by small situations. When we see globally, we avoid many mistakes, and we have a more profound view of happiness and life.

There are times when we feel angry at someone, and we think that if we do not confront him, our dignity will be lost. Perhaps that person challenged our authority, and we feel frustrated that we did not respond right away. We may go to bed unhappy and barely manage to get a good night's sleep, but the next day, we feel completely different. We laugh and smile, and see the situation entirely differently. Suddenly, what happened yesterday is not important. Only one night separates us from the event, and already things are quite different. This is to think globally, in terms of time.

When we dwell in the historical dimension, we are tossed about by many waves. Perhaps we have a difficult time at work. Or we have to wait too long in line at the supermarket. Or we have a bad telephone connection with our friend. We feel tired, a little depressed, or angry. This is because we are caught in the present situation. But if we close our eyes and visualize the world one hundred years from now, we will see that these problems are not important. Embracing just one hundred years, we see things very differently. Imagine how drastic a change is brought about by touching the ultimate dimension!

We are entirely capable of touching the ultimate dimension. As I write this page, I am aware that my feet are on the ground in Plum Village, standing on French soil. I am also aware that France is linked to Germany, Spain, Czechoslovakia, and Russia, and even to India, China, and Vietnam. Thinking globally, I see that I am standing on more than just a spot, because when I touch Plum Village, I touch all of Europe and Asia. China is just an extension of the small piece of land under my feet. Standing on one part of the Eurasian continent, I am standing on the whole continent.

This kind of awareness transforms the spot you are standing on to include the whole Earth. When you practice walking meditation and realize that you are making steps on the beautiful planet Earth, you will see yourself and your walking quite differently, and you will be liberated from narrow views or boundaries. Each step you take, you see that you are touching the whole Earth. When you touch with that awareness, you liberate yourself from many afflictions and wrong views.

When you touch one thing with deep awareness, you touch everything. The same is true of time. When you touch one moment with deep awareness, you touch all moments. According to the *Avatamsaka Sutra*, if you live one moment deeply, that moment contains all the past and all the future in it. "The one contains the all." Touching the present moment does not mean getting rid of the past or the future. As you touch the present moment, you realize that the present is made of the past and is creating the future. Touching the present, you touch the past and the future at the same time. You touch globally the infinity of time, the ultimate dimension of reality. When you drink a cup of tea very deeply, you touch the present moment and you touch the whole of time. It is what St. Francis did when he touched the almond tree so profoundly that he could see it flowering even in the middle of winter. He transcended time.

Meditation is to live each moment of life deeply. Through meditation, we see that waves are made only of water, that the historical and the ultimate dimensions are one. Even while living in the world of waves, we touch the water, knowing that a wave is nothing but water. We suffer if we touch only the waves. But if we learn how to stay in touch with the water, we feel a great relief. Touching nirvana frees us from many worries. Things that upset us in the past are not that important, even one day later—imagine when we are able to touch infinite time and space.

We come to the practice seeking relief in the historical dimension. We calm our body and mind, and establish our stillness, our freshness, and our solidity. We practice loving kindness, concentration, and transforming our anger, and we feel some relief. But when we touch the ultimate dimension of reality, we get the deepest kind of relief. Each of us has the capacity to touch nirvana and be free from birth and death, one and many, coming and going.

Last autumn while in England, I had a dream that seemed epic in nature. My brother, An, and I were in an open marketplace when a man invited us to come look at a stand in the corner of the market. When we arrived there, I immediately recognized that every item on display represented an event that I had directly lived and experienced with my brother and those close to me. Almost all of the items, the experiences, were of suffering—poverty, fire, floods, storms, hunger, racial discrimination, ignorance, hatred, fear, despair, political oppression, injustice, war, death, and misery. As I touched each item, a feeling of sorrow arose in me, and also a feeling of compassion.

Then we walked into the center of the stand and stood beside a long table, on which were displayed many elementary school notebooks. At the left end of the table, I recognized one notebook as mine and one as my brother's. I approached my notebook and looked through its pages, and I recognized in it many happy and meaningful experiences I had had during my childhood, and also many experiences of suffering. Then I looked through my brother's notebook and recognized our experiences together as little boys. I have been writing the memoirs of my childhood, but I had not included any of the materials that were in those notebooks. Perhaps these were experiences I lived only in dreams and had forgotten when I woke up. Perhaps they were experiences from previous lives. I was not sure which, but I was certain that these experiences were authentically mine, and I had the idea to bring these materials home so I could include them in my memoirs. I was very pleased with this idea, as I didn't want to forget again.

At the very moment I had this thought, I heard the man who had invited us to come look at the stand pronounce a terrible sentence. Standing on my right, he said, "You will have to go through all of this again!" The way he spoke, it sounded like a verdict or a condemnation, and his voice conveyed that he had the authority to decide such a thing. He sounded like God, or Destiny. I was shocked! Do I really have to go through all that suffering again, all that fire, flood, storm, hunger, racial discrimination, ignorance, hatred, despair, fear, sorrow, political oppression, misery, war, and death? I had the feeling I had gone through these things for countless lifetimes, together with my brother and all my companions from the past. We had been through so many dark tunnels, and now we were finally in a place with space and freedom. Did we really have to go through these experiences again?

I felt a kind of revulsion, and I said to myself, "Oh no!" But in less than a second, my reaction changed. I pointed two fingers of my right hand into the man's face and told him with all my determination and might, "You cannot frighten me. Even if I have to go through all of this again, I will do it! Not just once, but thousands more times if that is necessary. And all of us will do it together!"

At that moment, I woke up and could not remember the contents of the dream. I only knew I had just had a powerful and important dream. So I stayed in bed and practiced conscious breathing, and slowly the details came back. I understood that the man represented something I had to find out, and my first thought was that I was going to die very soon in order to begin anew the journey that had been appointed to me. I felt calm. Dying was no problem for me at that time. I was not afraid. I told myself that the

only thing to do was tell Sister True Emptiness, one
of my closest companions over the past thirty years,
so that she and others would be prepared. But right
away, I could see that it was not true that I had to die
at that moment. The dream had to have a deeper
meaning.

Looking more deeply, I discovered that the man
represented the seed of fear, or laziness, in me, the
equivalent of Buddha's Mara, and it arose from the
depth of my soul, my store consciousness. In my
first reaction to him, I had been standing in the historical dimension, the dimension of the wave. But in
my second reaction, I was acting from the ultimate
dimension, the dimension of water. When I touched
the world of no birth and no death, I was no longer
afraid, and I demonstrated that by pointing my two
fingers in his face. I saw that the strength that had
helped me challenge the man was the energy of faith
born from insight and freedom. I had told him in a
lucid way that since insight and freedom were present, I had the strength and courage to go through
any kind of hardship countless times.

I looked at my clock. It was 3:30 in the morning.
I thought of the children in Vietnam, Cambodia, So-
malia, Yugoslavia, and South America, and I felt a
strong solidarity with all of them. I felt ready to go
through these hardships with them, again and again.
And then I saw you, my dear friends who have been
practicing the Way of Emancipation. I saw that you
are also ready to join us, so that together we can
bring our collective wisdom and freedom to the chil-

dren of the world and help them bear these hardships.

When we studied the *Lotus Sutra* last year at Plum
Village, we discussed the ultimate dimension and the
historical dimension; and then we added the action
dimension, represented by bodhisattvas practicing
engaged Buddhism. Having touched the ultimate dimension, these bodhisattvas return to the historical
dimension to help however they can to transform the
suffering and offer relief. They live the life of a wave,
but they also live the life of water, and in doing so,
they offer us non-fear.

You, my brothers and sisters, my companions on
the Way, are those very bodhisattvas riding on the
waves of birth and death without drowning in birth
and death. We have gone though interminable suffering, an endless tunnel of sorrow and darkness. But
we have practiced, and through the practice we have
obtained some insight and freedom. Now it is time
for us to join with the children—the children of all
colors—and bring our strength to bear on the chal-
lenges that are before us. I am sure we will do better
this time.